P9-CJD-162

★ THE WEST POINT ATLAS OF WAR ★

WORLD WAR II: THE PACIFIC

Compiled by The Department of Military Art and Engineering
The United States Military Academy

Chief Editor
Brigadier General Vincent J. Esposito, USA

Photo credits: page 120 APImages; page 121 left APImages; page 121 top NARA/U.S. Army;
page 121 bottom APImages; page 122 left U.S. Navy; page 122 center U.S. Navy; page 122 right APImages;
page 123 left APImages; page 123 center NARA; page 123 right APImages; page 124 left NARA/U.S. Army;
page 124 top APImages; page 124 bottom U.S. Signal Corps; page 125 left APImages; page 125 top U.S. Air Force;
page 125 bottom APImages; page 126 APImages; page 127 APImages; page 128 APImages

Published by Tess Press, an imprint of
Black Dog & Leventhal Publishers, Inc.
151 West 19th Street
New York, NY 10011

Cover and interior design: Lindsay Wolff

The content of this book was originally published in 1959 under the title *The West Point Atlas of American Wars, Volume I (1689-1900)* and *Volume II (1900-1953)*. Since then, generations of West Point cadets have used the atlases as an important part of their study of military history in preparation for their service as officers in the United States Army. While the maps and corresponding text represented the finest military scholarship available at that time, subsequent scholarship has in some cases altered historical interpretations. Readers of this book—like West Point cadets—therefore should complement their study with more current works to develop a complete picture of the history presented.

ISBN-10: 1-60376-022-9
ISBN-13: 978-1-60376-022-5

h g f e d c b a

Printed in Hong Kong

CONTENTS

THE WAR WITH JAPAN

★

Japan exhibited the aggressive and expansionist traits which had generally characterized its growth as a nation by attacking China in 1894–95 and seizing Formosa (*lower right*) and the Kwantung Peninsula (*upper right*). International pressure nullified the Kwantung seizure, but after the Russo-Japanese War (1904–05)—her first war with a European power—Japan reclaimed that peninsula, which Russia had meanwhile leased from China. In 1910, Korea was annexed, and Japanese nationals promptly occupied all the responsible governmental and professional positions in the country. Token participation in World War I gave Japan the opportunity to claim former German rights in the Shantung Peninsula (*right center*) and in the Caroline, Marshall, and Marianas (except Guam) Islands (*see map 113, center*). The League of Nations gave Japan a mandate over these islands, but the wary United States and Great Britain pressed the Japanese at the Washington Nine-Power Conference (1922) to recognize China's territorial integrity, thereby forcing her to withdraw from Shantung.

Japanese acquiescence in this territorial setback, as well as her earlier acceptance of inferior naval status (the five-five-three ratio at the Washington Naval Conference in 1921), was due to the emergence of a liberal government which clamped a restraining hand on the militaristic clique. However, the militarists (led by the Army), aided by social unrest and economic depression, plotted their way to power in 1931 on the heels of the "Mukden Incident" (the alleged bombing of a section of the Japanese-controlled Mukden-Harbin railroad [*this map, upper right*]). Here was Japan's excuse for overrunning Manchuria (renamed Manchukuo) on the pretense that the Chinese could not control their "bandits." When the League of Nations protested this occupation, Japan resigned from the League, and promptly incorporated Jehol into Manchukuo (1933). Meanwhile, China had retaliated with an anti-Japanese boycott—particularly in Shanghai. Attendant riots in that city led to bloodshed, and the Japanese landed 50,000 troops to enforce demands for reparations. They withdrew in May 1932, after driving the Chinese Army inland.

During the next four years, Japan plagued China with ever-increasing demands, all intended to extend Japanese domination over the hapless Chinese. The Chinese Central Government of Generalissimo Chiang Kai-Shek, striving desperately to unite a nation previously torn by civil war, at first acceded to the demands; but, as Chiang built an army, resistance stiffened. Finally, the Japanese decided to use force. War came with the manufactured "China Incident" (a clash between Japanese and Chinese troops at the Marco Polo Bridge near Peiping) on 7 July, 1937.

Japan—with an industrial base geared for a minor war—had a well-trained, recently modernized 300,000-man regular army backed up by 2,000,000 reserves. An efficient navy and surprisingly effective army and navy air forces supported them. China's Army numbered 2,000,000, but only 100,000 were reasonably well equipped. Chiang—dependent upon outside sources for supplies—had no navy, very little artillery, and only a few obsolete aircraft; his subordinates lacked real military ability.

Japan decided to make a main attack from Manchukuo and a secondary effort at Shanghai. This plan took advantage of the existing base in Manchukuo and might lead to Chiang's encirclement between the two attacks before he could withdraw into mountainous western China.

In the north, the Japanese secured their right flank by the capture of Paotow (*upper center*) in August and then regrouped. The three-pronged drive south down the railroads in September stalled by November as the Chinese defended stubbornly and used guerrillas to harass Japanese communications at night. More telling, however, had been the reduction in Japanese strength occasioned by the need for troops at Shanghai. There, the fighting—beginning in August—had been bitter; Chiang's German-trained 88th Division contained the attack until reinforcements enabled the Japanese to pinch out the city by landing on either side of it. Then they crossed Lake Tai easily (using armored motorboats) and captured Nanking on 13 December; the infamous rape of that city continued for days. By the end of the year, the Japanese had made gains as shown (*solid red lines*). Meanwhile, their aircraft had rained destruction on China's cities in a campaign of terror.

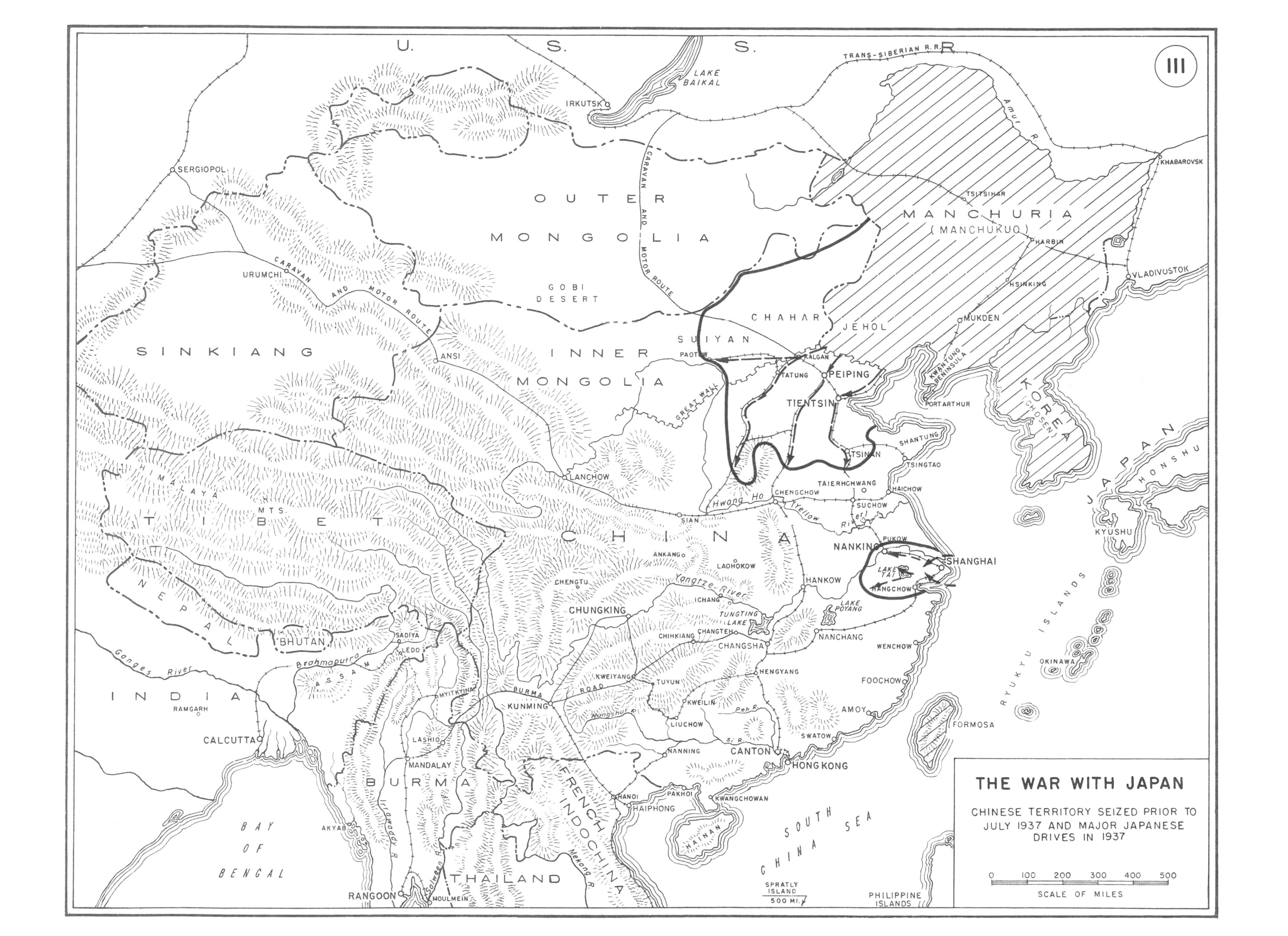

III
THE WAR WITH JAPAN
CHINESE TERRITORY SEIZED PRIOR TO JULY 1937 AND MAJOR JAPANESE DRIVES IN 1937
0 100 200 300 400 500
SCALE OF MILES
U. S. S. R.
TRANS-SIBERIAN R.R.
LAKE BAIKAL
IRKUTSK
SERGIOPOL
OUTER MONGOLIA
CARAVAN AND MOTOR ROUTE
GOBI DESERT
MANCHURIA (MANCHUKUO)
Amur R.
KHABAROVSK
TSITSIHAR
HARBIN
HSINKING
VLADIVOSTOK
MUKDEN
KWANTUNG PENINSULA
PORT ARTHUR
KOREA (CHOSEN)
JAPAN
HONSHU
KYUSHU
RYUKYU ISLANDS
OKINAWA
FORMOSA
URUMCHI
SINKIANG
ANSI
INNER MONGOLIA
CHAHAR
JEHOL
SUIYAN
PAOTOW
KALGAN
TATUNG
PEIPING
TIENTSIN
GREAT WALL
SHANTUNG
TSINAN
TSINGTAO
TAIERHCHWANG
HAICHOW
CHENGCHOW
SUCHOW
Hwang Ho
Yellow River
LANCHOW
SIAN
HIMALAYA MTS.
TIBET
CHINA
NANKING
PUKOW
SHANGHAI
LAKE TAI
HANGCHOW
ANKANG
LAOHOKOW
HANKOW
CHENGTU
Yangtze River
ICHANG
CHUNGKING
TUNGTING LAKE
LAKE POYANG
CHIHKIANG
CHANGTEH
CHANGSHA
NANCHANG
WENCHOW
FOOCHOW
AMOY
SWATOW
HENGYANG
KWEIYANG
TUYUN
KWEILIN
LIUCHOW
Peh R.
Si R.
CANTON
HONG KONG
NANNING
KWANGCHOWAN
PAKHOI
HAINAN
HANOI
HAIPHONG
FRENCH INDOCHINA
BURMA ROAD
KUNMING
NEPAL
BHUTAN
SADIYA
LEDO
ASSAM
Brahmaputra R.
Ganges River
INDIA
RAMGARH
CALCUTTA
MYITKYINA
LASHIO
MANDALAY
BURMA
Irrawaddy R.
Salween R.
Mekong R.
THAILAND
RANGOON
MOULMEIN
AKYAB
BAY OF BENGAL
SOUTH CHINA SEA
SPRATLY ISLAND 500 MI.
PHILIPPINE ISLANDS

JAPANESE ADVANCES 1938 AND 1939

★

Japan's strategists were disappointed with the gains made in the first year of the war. They had hoped to defeat Chiang's organized forces quickly before he could unite the several factions in China, and before the war imposed an excessive drain on the Japanese economy. But they had been frustrated by the Chinese, who desperately traded space for time and avoided decisive battle. Nor had Chiang's ability to import desperately needed supplies been materially limited. Though the loss of Shanghai was a blow, he still controlled most of the seaports and the four remaining overland routes out of China: the Haiphong-Kunming (*bottom center*) railroad; the Rangoon-Lashio-Kunming railroad and road; and the two caravan and motor routes to Russia (*upper left and top center*).

Japan's initial operations in 1938 were designed to close the Lunghai Corridor (*center, right*)—the area still under Chinese control between the two fronts. Süchow, an important rail center, was the first objective. Chinese resistance was stubborn, but the twin drives from north and south ultimately captured the city in May. The northern prong had met serious resistance at Taierhchwang, where 60,000 Japanese troops were cut off in April; two-thirds cut their way out of the trap but were forced to leave large quantities of equipment and supplies behind. This success stimulated the morale of the Chinese and stiffened their determination to resist the invader. In June, the Japanese began a drive on Chengchow (*center, right*) to sever the railroad to Hankow. This advance bogged down when the Chinese demolished the Yellow River dikes, allowing the swollen river to inundate the countryside. The drive on the Chinese capital (Hankow) was now reinforced while, in October, a 40,000-man force landed twenty miles above the British crown colony of Hong Kong (*lower right*), and easily occupied Canton, thus cutting off Hankow from its major source of supply. Consequently, in November—after five months of bloody fighting—Chiang abandoned Hankow, moved its industrial machinery inland, adopted a scorched-earth policy, and reestablished his capital at Chungking (*lower center*).

By the end of 1938, the Japanese occupied an important segment of China (*solid red lines*). But within this area, they continued to meet smoldering resentment; armed bands—professing to be guerrillas—increased Japanese administrative problems. Meanwhile, relations with the Western powers had deteriorated, and the Japanese militarists lobbied for an alliance with Germany. The United States began to provide more supplies for Chiang, moving them primarily via Lashio and the Burma Road. Japan countered by expressing her intention of creating a "Co-Prosperity Sphere" in east Asia.

In 1939, Japan, having been unable to obtain a quick victory in China in two years, adopted a policy of strangulation, employing minimum forces at strategic places. This met with the wholehearted approval of Japan's naval leaders, who had been urging the government to move southward in preparation for the domination of the Netherlands East Indies (*off map, bottom*). Consequently, only limited offensives were conducted in 1939. In the interior, these were unsuccessfully aimed at securing control of the Canton-Hankow railroad. But along the coast, Chiang's remaining ports were seized, and the capture of Nanning (*lower center*) placed the Haiphong-Kunming railroad within range of Japanese bombers. French Indochina was threatened and Hong Kong isolated by the seizure of Hainan Island in February.

In 1939, stern treatment of foreign nationals in occupied China indicated a stiffening Japanese attitude toward the Western powers. In July, the United States, exasperated with Japan's aggressions in China, declared its intention to abrogate the 1911 Trade Treaty, thereby threatening to cut off United States exports to Japan after 1 January, 1940. Then, without warning, Hitler concluded a neutrality pact with Russia in September. Coming after months of fruitless German efforts to get the Japanese to commit themselves to war against the Anglo-French bloc, it seemed to repudiate the 1936 Anti-Comintern Pact, and caused grave concern in Japan about Russia's future actions in Asia. The Army went into temporary political eclipse, and a more liberal group of politicians sought better relations with the West.

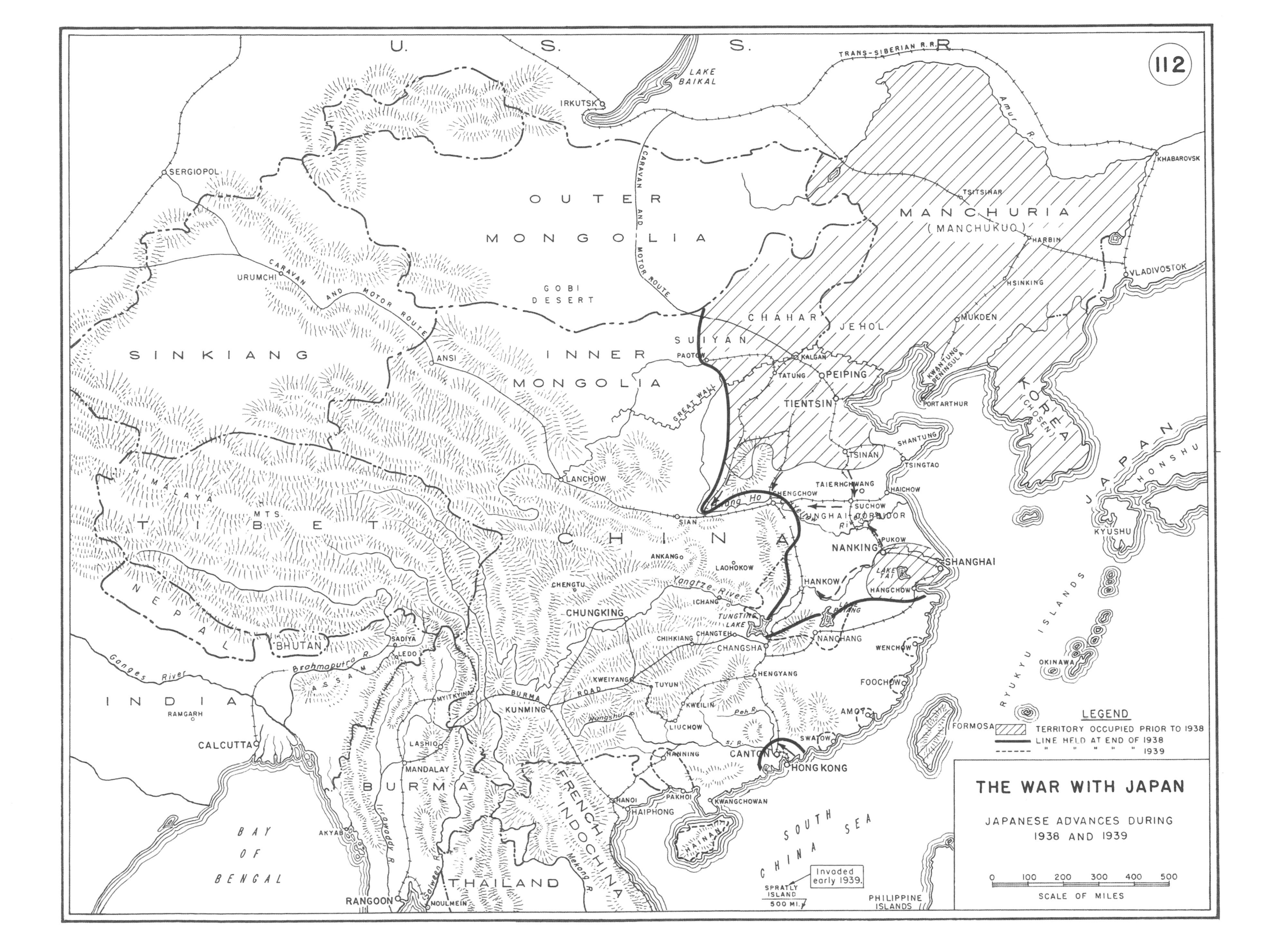
112
THE WAR WITH JAPAN
JAPANESE ADVANCES DURING
1938 AND 1939
LEGEND
TERRITORY OCCUPIED PRIOR TO 1938
LINE HELD AT END OF 1938
" " " " 1939
0 100 200 300 400 500
SCALE OF MILES
U. S. S. R.
TRANS-SIBERIAN R.R.
LAKE BAIKAL
IRKUTSK
SERGIOPOL
OUTER MONGOLIA
CARAVAN AND MOTOR ROUTE
GOBI DESERT
URUMCHI
SINKIANG
ANSI
INNER MONGOLIA
MANCHURIA
(MANCHUKUO)
Amur R.
KHABAROVSK
TSITSIHAR
HARBIN
HSINKING
VLADIVOSTOK
MUKDEN
KWANTUNG PENINSULA
PORT ARTHUR
KOREA
(CHOSEN)
JAPAN
HONSHU
KYUSHU
RYUKYU ISLANDS
OKINAWA
FORMOSA
CHAHAR
JEHOL
SUIYAN
PAOTOW
KALGAN
TATUNG
PEIPING
TIENTSIN
GREAT WALL
SHANTUNG
TSINAN
TSINGTAO
TAIERHCHWANG
HAICHOW
CHENGCHOW
SUCHOW
LANCHOW
SIAN
TIBET
HIMALAYA MTS.
NEPAL
BHUTAN
CHINA
NANKING
PUKOW
SHANGHAI
LAKE TAI
HANGCHOW
ANKANG
LAOHOKOW
HANKOW
Yangtze River
CHENGTU
ICHANG
TUNGTING LAKE
CHUNGKING
CHIHKIANG
CHANGTEH
CHANGSHA
NANCHANG
WENCHOW
FOOCHOW
AMOY
SWATOW
HENGYANG
KWEIYANG
TUYUN
BURMA ROAD
KWEILIN
Peh R.
LIUCHOW
Si R.
KUNMING
NANNING
CANTON
HONG KONG
KWANGCHOWAN
PAKHOI
HAINAN
HANOI
HAIPHONG
FRENCH INDOCHINA
Mekong R.
THAILAND
SADIYA
LEDO
Brahmaputra R.
ASSAM
Ganges River
INDIA
RAMGARH
CALCUTTA
MYITKYINA
LASHIO
MANDALAY
BURMA
Irrawaddy R.
Salween R.
AKYAB
RANGOON
MOULMEIN
BAY OF BENGAL
SOUTH CHINA SEA
SPRATLY ISLAND
500 MI.
Invaded early 1939.
PHILIPPINE ISLANDS

CONTEMPLATED EXPANSION OF THE JAPANESE EMPIRE

★

Throughout 1940–41, Japan continued her policy of economic strangulation of China and conducted her campaigns there with a minimum of men and materials. All the while, the armed forces, though in the background, were preparing for ultimate domination of the rich Southern Resources Area (*left center*)—by peaceful penetration if possible, but by force if necessary.

The Japanese were not deterred even when an awakening United States applied a minor embargo on exports to Japan in January 1940. That spring, Hitler overran Western Europe, completely changing the Pacific balance of power. With France and Holland defeated, the Southern Resources Area lay helpless—if the United States could be deterred from interfering. Accordingly, in July, a new cabinet, dominated by the Army, set as its goal the establishment of the Greater East Asia Co-Prosperity Sphere (generally intended to include the Southern Resources Area, plus the Philippines and New Guinea). Preliminary measures were to be a successful conclusion of the war in China, closer alliance with the Axis, and negotiation of a nonaggression pact with Russia. That same month, the United States tightened the embargo.

After the fall of France, Japan coerced the weak Vichy government into granting her the right to move troops into northern Indochina (*left center*). Japanese troops entered in late September, and secured bases from which the Burma Road into China could be bombed. The United States retaliated by increasing the amount of aid to Chiang. Also, in September, Congress enacted the first peacetime Selective Service Act and authorized a strength of 1,400,000 for the burgeoning American Army. Meanwhile, Japanese attempts to press the Netherlands East Indies into allocating practically their entire oil output to Nippon failed. On 27 September, Japan signed the Tripartite Pact with Germany and Italy, effecting a diplomatic coup which—unrealistically and erroneously—was expected to deter the United States from taking positive action.

About this time, President Roosevelt, vitally concerned over developments in Europe, leased fifty destroyers to England, and a reappraisal was made of existing American war plans. It was concluded that, in the event of a global war, operations against Germany would be given first priority. In a January, 1941, combined planning conference (*ABC-1*), this "Germany-first" policy was heartily accepted by the British. Thus, one of the major Allied strategic decisions of World War II had, in effect, been made before the United States entered the war.

In February 1941, Japan sent Admiral Kichisaburo Nomura to Washington to settle disagreements between the two countries. The next month, Congress passed the Lend-Lease Act, thereby providing more aid for China as well as Britain. The Japanese theoretically secured their north flank in April by signing a non-aggression pact with Russia. In July, when the Japanese occupied the rest of Indochina, President Roosevelt reacted by freezing Japanese assets in the United States—thereby making the embargo complete. Some Japanese now panicked and urged reaching agreement with the United States, but the Army leaders maintained that oil reserves were sufficient to wage war and that Japan must not turn back. The die was cast; though negotiations would continue in Washington in an attempt to reach agreement, the Army and Navy leaders—for the first time—sat down to evolve a comprehensive strategy for the coming war.

Japan's war plan—based upon limited objectives—consisted of three phases. The first phase (expected to take five months) would consist of a surprise attack to neutralize the United States Pacific Fleet so that it could not interfere with Japanese operations; seizure of the Southern Resources Area; and the capture of strategic areas required to establish a defensive perimeter (*dashed red line*) around the proposed Co-Prosperity Sphere. Phase two would be the consolidation and strengthening of the perimeter. Phase three would be defensive—the destruction of any forces attempting to penetrate the perimeter. The ultimate expectation was that long and costly operations in the far reaches of the Pacific would destroy the will of the United States to fight and would lead to acceptance of the Japanese conquests.

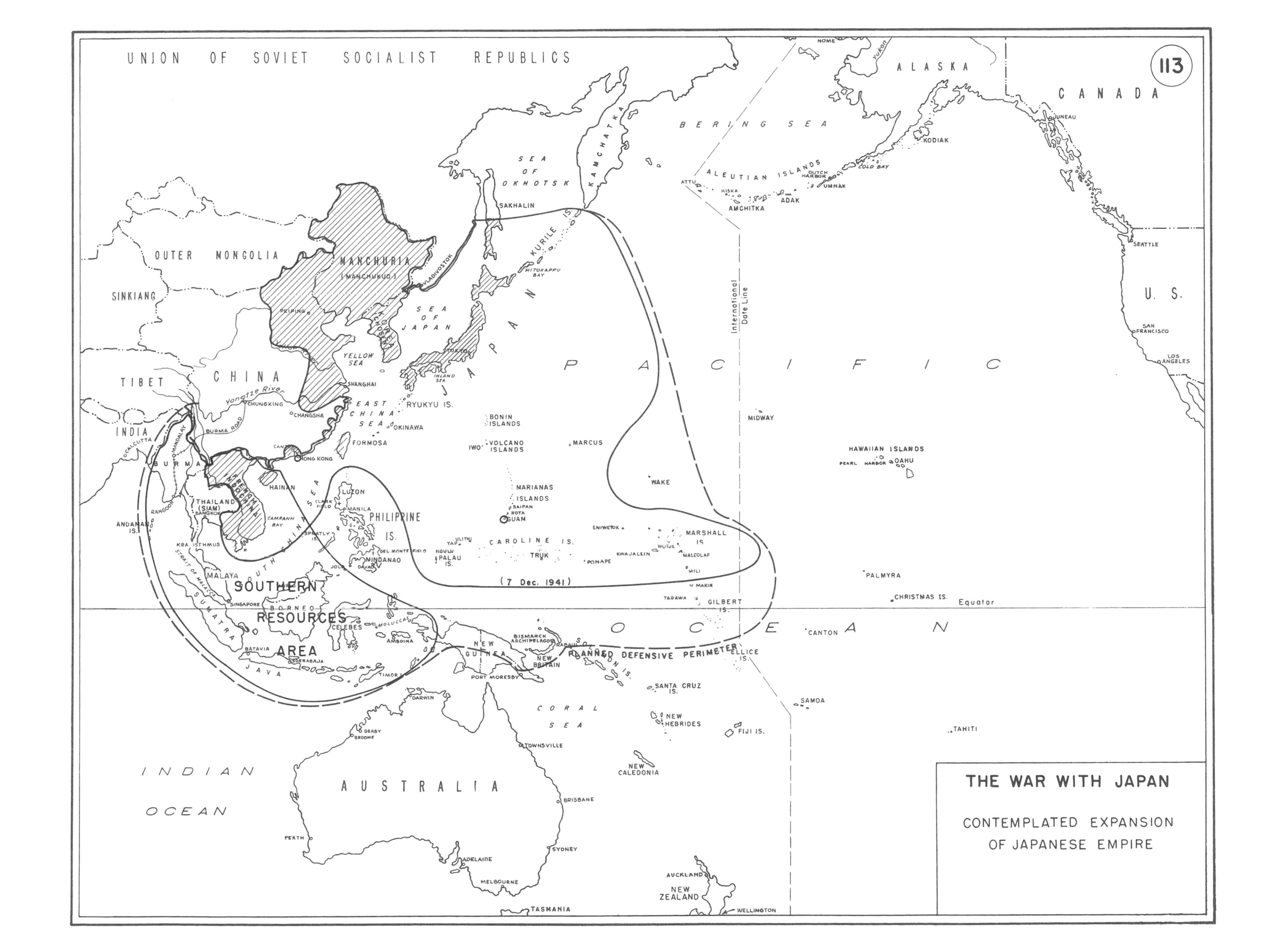
113
THE WAR WITH JAPAN
CONTEMPLATED EXPANSION
OF JAPANESE EMPIRE
UNION OF SOVIET SOCIALIST REPUBLICS
OUTER MONGOLIA
SINKIANG
TIBET
CHINA
INDIA
BURMA
MANCHURIA
(MANCHUKUO)
KOREA
(CHOSEN)
SEA OF OKHOTSK
SAKHALIN
KAMCHATKA
KURILE IS.
HITOKAPPU BAY
VLADIVOSTOK
SEA OF JAPAN
JAPAN
TOKYO
INLAND SEA
YELLOW SEA
PEIPING
SHANGHAI
CHUNGKING
CHANGSHA
Yangtze River
BURMA ROAD
MANDALAY
CALCUTTA
RANGOON
ANDAMAN IS.
EAST CHINA SEA
RYUKYU IS.
OKINAWA
FORMOSA
HONG KONG
HAINAN
FRENCH INDOCHINA
THAILAND (SIAM)
BANGKOK
CAMRANH BAY
KRA ISTHMUS
STRAIT OF MALACCA
MALAYA
SINGAPORE
SUMATRA
BATAVIA
SOERABAJA
JAVA
BORNEO
SOUTH CHINA SEA
SPRATLY IS.
SOUTHERN RESOURCES AREA
CELEBES
MOLUCCAS
AMBOINA
TIMOR
LUZON
CLARK FIELD
MANILA
PHILIPPINE IS.
DEL MONTE FIELD
MINDANAO
DAVAO
JOLO
BONIN ISLANDS
IWO
VOLCANO ISLANDS
MARCUS
MARIANAS ISLANDS
SAIPAN
ROTA
GUAM
ULITHI
YAP
PALAU IS.
CAROLINE IS.
TRUK
PONAPE
(7 Dec. 1941)
ENIWETOK
KWAJALEIN
WOTJE
MALOELAP
MARSHALL IS.
MILI
MAKIN
TARAWA
GILBERT IS.
WAKE
MIDWAY
International Date Line
P A C I F I C
O C E A N
NEW GUINEA
PORT MORESBY
BISMARCK ARCHIPELAGO
RABAUL
NEW BRITAIN
SOLOMON IS.
PLANNED DEFENSIVE PERIMETER
ELLICE IS.
SANTA CRUZ IS.
NEW HEBRIDES
FIJI IS.
NEW CALEDONIA
CORAL SEA
SAMOA
TAHITI
CANTON
PALMYRA
CHRISTMAS IS.
Equator
HAWAIIAN ISLANDS
PEARL HARBOR
OAHU
BERING SEA
ALEUTIAN ISLANDS
ATTU
KISKA
AMCHITKA
ADAK
DUTCH HARBOR
UMNAK
COLD BAY
KODIAK
NOME
Yukon
ALASKA
CANADA
JUNEAU
SEATTLE
U. S.
SAN FRANCISCO
LOS ANGELES
AUSTRALIA
DARWIN
DERBY
BROOME
TOWNSVILLE
BRISBANE
SYDNEY
MELBOURNE
ADELAIDE
PERTH
TASMANIA
NEW ZEALAND
AUCKLAND
WELLINGTON
INDIAN OCEAN

OPENING OPERATIONS OF THE JAPANESE OFFENSIVE

★

Negotiations continued in Washington during the late summer and early fall of 1941 in an atmosphere of frustration, for neither side would compromise. In Japan, the Army and Navy leaders stressed the growing shortage of resources and the need for a decision as to Japan's future course of action. The premier, Prince Konoye, argued for an extension of the secret 15 October deadline Japan had set for negotiations with the United States, and even suggested acceding to United States demands to withdraw from China; but the war minister, General Hideki Tojo, refused. The cabinet resigned, and, on 18 October, Tojo became premier. On 5 November, he authorized continuation of negotiations until 25 November (later extended to the 29th). But Japan's new proposals, though they contained conditional agreement to a Japanese withdrawal from China, could not be accepted by America without condoning Japan's policy of aggression. Consequently, the proposals were rejected, and the United States submitted a counterproposal to Nomura on the 26th. The Japanese, considering both their own proposals and the American counterproposals as ultimatums, now made final preparations for war. As early as 6 November, field commanders had been alerted to prepare detailed plans to implement the war strategy, and, on the 25th, the Pearl Harbor Striking Force had departed the Kurile Islands (*upper left*). On 1 December, the date for initiation of hostilities was selected—8 December, a Sunday (7 December) at Pearl Harbor. (Dates given in the text recognize the International Date Line.)

Japan's operation plan for the execution of phase one of the war plan was based upon a finely calculated distribution of forces. Of the fifty-one divisions and fifty-nine brigades comprising the Army ground forces in December, only ten and four, respectively, were allocated to the four offensive armies; the remaining units were held in Japan and China in the event that alternative courses of action had to be adopted. The primary objective of the offensive was the rich Southern Resources Area, whose seizure—the Japanese believed—would not be possible without also capturing the Philippines and neutralizing the United States Pacific Fleet. Operations would begin with a surprise air attack on Pearl Harbor (*center, right*), to be followed immediately by similar strikes against the Philippines and Malaya (*center, left*). Then landings would be made in the Philippines and Malaya to initiate a two-pronged drive on Java (*lower left*). Concurrently, Thailand would be occupied; Guam, Wake (*both center*), and Hong Kong seized; and Borneo (*lower left*) invaded. These comprised the initial operations planned for the first phase. (The concluding operations in this phase—subjugation of the Philippines, Burma, and the Netherlands East Indies—are covered on subsequent maps.) The almost simultaneous execution of operations against the widely separated objectives attests to the thoroughness of Japanese planning. Surprisingly, in none of the joint operations was there unity of command—army and navy elements merely "cooperated."

The idea of attacking Pearl Harbor had been conceived in January 1941 by Admiral Isoruku Yamamoto, commander of the Combined Fleet; but its very boldness scared his navy superiors who did not finally incorporate it into the overall plan until October. Meanwhile, Yamamoto selected elite personnel, thoroughly trained them, and gathered intelligence on Pearl Harbor. His task force was ready when it was alerted for the operation in mid-November. The nucleus of this Pearl Harbor Striking Force consisted of six aircraft carriers bearing 414 aircraft, of which 360 made the attack. A northerly route (*upper center*) was selected in spite of the refueling difficulties created by prevailing poor weather, since a more southerly route would expose the force to discovery by American planes or ships. By 0600, 7 December, the force had arrived—exactly as scheduled—at the launching point 200 miles north of Oahu. To the west, two of its destroyers were nearing Midway to carry out a scheduled naval bombardment. United States forces in the Hawaiian Islands were completely unaware of the location of this potent carrier task force and had no premonition of the destruction it would soon loose upon them.

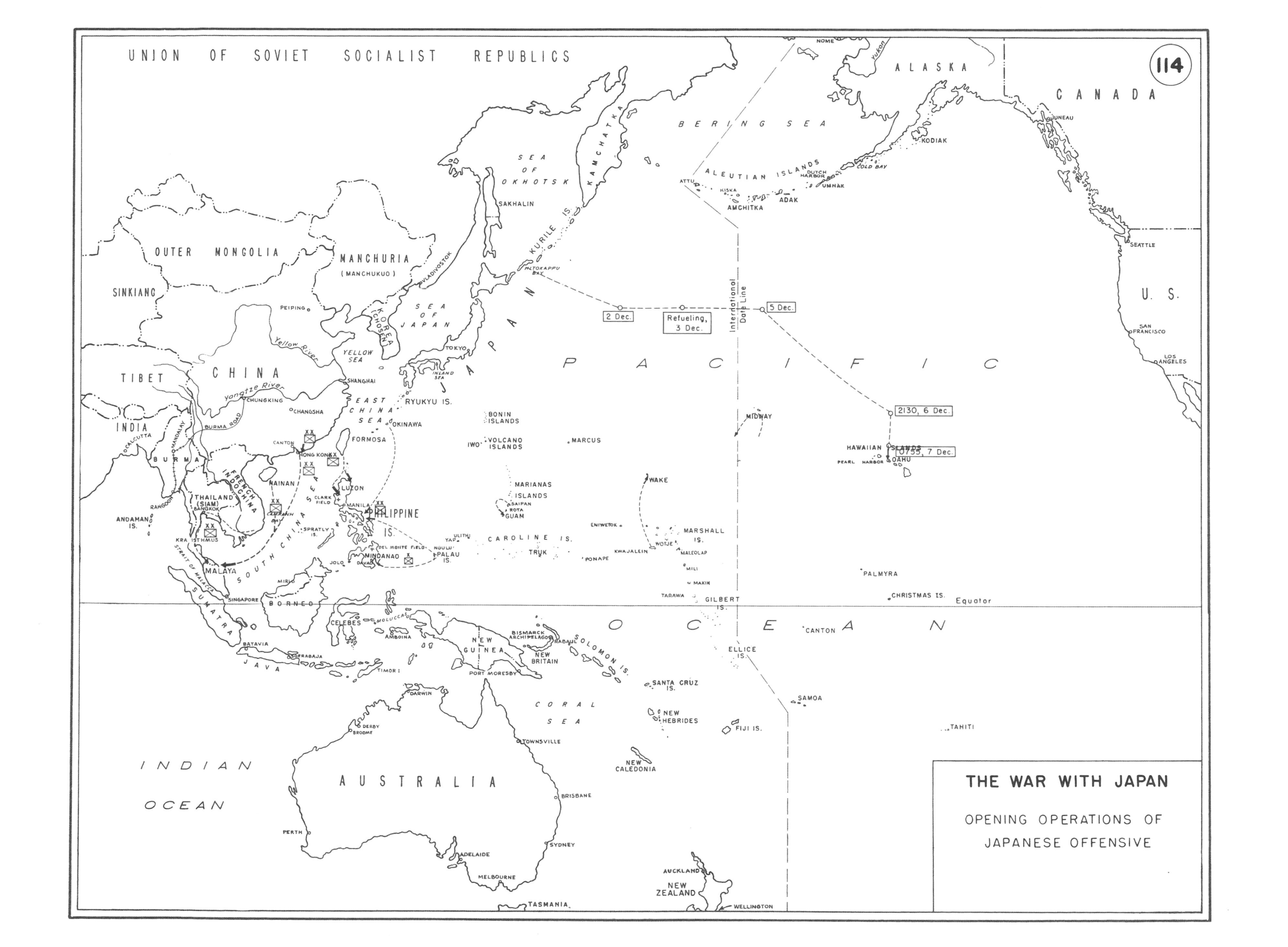
114
THE WAR WITH JAPAN
OPENING OPERATIONS OF JAPANESE OFFENSIVE
UNION OF SOVIET SOCIALIST REPUBLICS
ALASKA
CANADA
U. S.
PACIFIC OCEAN
INDIAN OCEAN
AUSTRALIA
CHINA
TIBET
INDIA
OUTER MONGOLIA
SINKIANG
MANCHURIA (MANCHUKUO)
KOREA (CHOSEN)
JAPAN
BERING SEA
SEA OF OKHOTSK
SEA OF JAPAN
YELLOW SEA
EAST CHINA SEA
SOUTH CHINA SEA
CORAL SEA
ALEUTIAN ISLANDS
KURILE IS.
KAMCHATKA
SAKHALIN
HITOKAPPU BAY
2 Dec.
Refueling, 3 Dec.
5 Dec.
International Date Line
2130, 6 Dec.
0755, 7 Dec.
HAWAIIAN ISLANDS
PEARL HARBOR
OAHU
MIDWAY
WAKE
MARCUS
BONIN ISLANDS
IWO
VOLCANO ISLANDS
MARIANAS ISLANDS
SAIPAN
ROTA
GUAM
CAROLINE IS.
TRUK
PONAPE
ULITHI
YAP
NGULU
PALAU IS.
ENIWETOK
KWAJALEIN
WOTJE
MALEOLAP
MARSHALL IS.
MILI
MAKIN
TARAWA
GILBERT IS.
ELLICE IS.
CANTON
PALMYRA
CHRISTMAS IS.
Equator
SAMOA
TAHITI
FIJI IS.
NEW HEBRIDES
SANTA CRUZ IS.
NEW CALEDONIA
SOLOMON IS.
BISMARCK ARCHIPELAGO
RABAUL
NEW BRITAIN
NEW GUINEA
PORT MORESBY
NEW ZEALAND
AUCKLAND
WELLINGTON
TASMANIA
BRISBANE
SYDNEY
MELBOURNE
ADELAIDE
PERTH
TOWNSVILLE
DARWIN
DERBY
BROOME
TIMOR
JAVA
BATAVIA
SOERABAJA
SUMATRA
STRAIT OF MALACCA
SINGAPORE
BORNEO
MIRI
CELEBES
AMBOINA
MOLUCCAS
MALAYA
KRA ISTHMUS
THAILAND (SIAM)
BANGKOK
FRENCH INDOCHINA
CAMRANH BAY
HAINAN
BURMA
BURMA ROAD
MANDALAY
RANGOON
ANDAMAN IS.
CALCUTTA
CHUNGKING
Yangtze River
Yellow River
PEIPING
CHANGSHA
CANTON
HONG KONG
SHANGHAI
FORMOSA
OKINAWA
RYUKYU IS.
TOKYO
INLAND SEA
VLADIVOSTOK
LUZON
MANILA
CLARK FIELD
PHILIPPINE IS.
MINDANAO
DEL MONTE FIELD
DAVAO
JOLO
SPRATLY IS.
NOME
Yukon
KODIAK
COLD BAY
DUTCH HARBOR
UMNAK
ADAK
AMCHITKA
KISKA
ATTU
JUNEAU
SEATTLE
SAN FRANCISCO
LOS ANGELES

THE ATTACK ON PEARL HARBOR

★

The early 1930's were years of isolation and economic depression in America. The armed forces, in drastic need of modernization, struggled along with military appropriations which were naturally meager. Not until Germany's threatening actions alarmed the administration was attention directed toward enlarging the nation's armed forces. Thus, by December 1941, the Army had a strength of 1,500,000, but the great majority of the troops lacked training and equipment. (Lend-Lease to Britain and Russia took priority in some cases.) The Hawaiian Islands were probably garrisoned by as well-equipped and trained army ground and air forces as were available; the Navy, of course, had its imposing Pacific Fleet based there.

With the adoption of the "Germany-first" strategy in January 1941, initial operations in the Pacific Ocean areas were relegated to purely defensive roles. The Philippines would be defended, but no reinforcements would be sent there; the Navy would capture positions in the Marshall Islands, but only prepare for further advances to the west. Under this plan (Rainbow-5), a powerful base in the Hawaiian Islands was essential.

The defenses of Hawaii were the joint responsibility of the local army and navy commanders; unity of command did not exist. A defense plan—periodically tested—was in being, but its implementation depended upon close cooperation between services, which, in December, was not completely effective. Nor was the army aircraft warning system in the islands fully developed by 7 December, because of shortages of trained personnel and radar equipment. Offshore air patrols were maintained, but they, too, were inadequate on the critical day.

After the United States rejected Japan's final proposal in Washington, the two commanders in Hawaii (Lt. Gen. Walter C. Short and Admiral Husband E. Kimmel) were notified on 27 November that war was imminent. Neither commander put his forces on a full war alert. Additional information—some of it rather nebulous—was received from Washington prior to 7 December which could have indicated an attack, but still the defenses were not fully alerted. On the morning of the attack, ominous signs appeared. Unidentified submarines were spotted, and one radar indicated the approach of a large unidentified group of planes. In the holiday atmosphere of that Sunday morning, these signs aroused little reaction. The Pacific Fleet—minus the carriers which, fortunately, were at sea—rode at anchor exactly as the Japanese expected. Aircraft were likewise neatly lined up on runways throughout Oahu. At the time, the critical threat in the Hawaiian Islands, in General Short's opinion, was sabotage.

The Japanese had planned well; their execution of the attack was equally efficient. The attack was made in two waves following the general routes shown. The fighters were expected to attain air superiority and then attack grounded aircraft, but when no American aircraft appeared aloft, they turned to those on the ground. The first wave of fighters struck at all the airfields (*blue circles*) except Haleiwa (*upper left*), while the bombers attacked Pearl Harbor. The highly skilled torpedo-bomber pilots inflicted the heaviest damage on the fleet. By 0825, most of the first wave had departed. A few American planes rose from the stricken fields, only to be smothered by the incoming second wave. Its bombers—armed with light bombs destined for the missing carriers—did less damage to the fleet than the first wave. By 0945, all Japanese planes had left Oahu, and the Pearl Harbor Striking Force—never detected—quickly withdrew to the west.

The United States Pacific Fleet and the air forces in Hawaii had been dealt a shattering blow. Eighteen ships were sunk or so seriously damaged that they would be out of action for months; included were seven of the eight battleships. Of some 394 aircraft, 188 were destroyed and an additional 159 damaged. American casualties, predominantly naval, totaled 3,581 (2,403 were killed). The Japanese lost only twenty-nine aircraft and six submarines (five of them midget types). The Japanese made one error: they failed to destroy the oil-storage and harbor facilities, so that Pearl Harbor soon resumed its function as a base.

Far to the west, the isolated garrison of Guam (*see map 114*) was soon overcome. United States Marines at Wake Island repelled one landing, but succumbed to a second on 23 December.

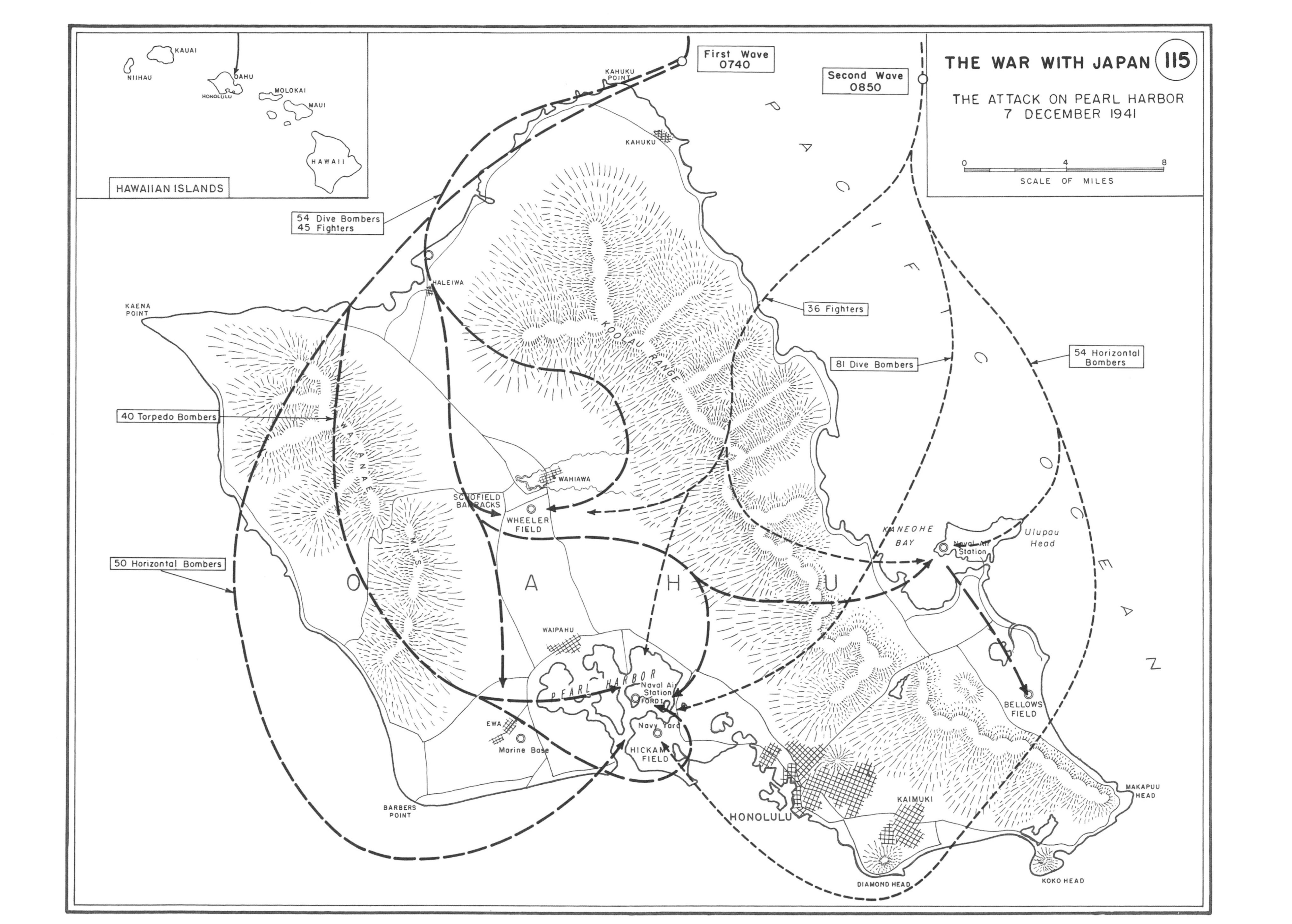
THE WAR WITH JAPAN
115
THE ATTACK ON PEARL HARBOR
7 DECEMBER 1941
0
4
8
SCALE OF MILES
HAWAIIAN ISLANDS
KAUAI
NIIHAU
OAHU
HONOLULU
MOLOKAI
MAUI
HAWAII
First Wave
0740
Second Wave
0850
54 Dive Bombers
45 Fighters
36 Fighters
81 Dive Bombers
54 Horizontal
Bombers
40 Torpedo Bombers
50 Horizontal Bombers
P A C I F I C
O C E A N
O A H U
KAHUKU POINT
KAHUKU
HALEIWA
KAENA POINT
KOOLAU RANGE
WAIANAE
MTS.
WAHIAWA
SCHOFIELD BARRACKS
WHEELER FIELD
KANEOHE BAY
Naval Air Station
Ulupau Head
WAIPAHU
PEARL HARBOR
Naval Air Station
FORD I.
Navy Yard
HICKAM FIELD
EWA
Marine Base
BARBERS POINT
HONOLULU
KAIMUKI
BELLOWS FIELD
MAKAPUU HEAD
DIAMOND HEAD
KOKO HEAD

HONG KONG CAMPAIGN

★

Hong Kong—consisting of the island of that name, Kowloon Peninsula, and leased territory on the Chinese mainland—was acquired by Great Britain in 1841. It gradually became an international shipping center and a symbol of British influence in the Far East. In 1941, Hong Kong was not so important militarily to Japan as it was politically: should the British be forcibly ejected from the colony, it would mean a serious loss of face for them in the Orient. This was well understood by the British who, though regarding the colony as an untenable outpost, recognized that the harbor should be denied to the Japanese as long as possible. Two Canadian infantry battalions were sent to the colony in November 1941, as a calculated show of force, making a total of six battalions available for defense.

The British plan of defense envisioned occupation of the Gin Drinker's Line (*center*) by three battalions, while the other three occupied beach defense positions on Hong Kong Island. It was recognized that the mainland line was too long to be manned in sufficient strength to repel a strong attack; but the three battalions were expected to hold for about a week before withdrawing to the island, where the main battle would be fought. The island had twenty-nine coastal guns, some of which could fire on mainland targets, but only token naval forces (one destroyer, eight torpedo boats, and four gunboats) remained in Hong Kong waters after war broke out. The army troops, only partially trained, were short of transport and lacked adequate mortar ammunition. But the greatest armament weakness was in aircraft—the garrison had only six obsolete planes. The Japanese were undoubtedly familiar with British military defense measures, for in the prewar months the members of the Japanese Consulate moved about freely, and unhindered traffic to and from the mainland facilitated the activities of Japanese agents.

In November 1941, the British commander moved the three mainland defense battalions from training camps into the Gin Drinker's Line, where they set to work improving the defenses. By this time, a false sense of confidence existed among the troops and many of the civilians. The island was impregnable, it was said, and the Japanese equipment, troops, and tactics were decidedly inferior; they were inept at night operations, and their aircraft were obsolete. Nor was British intelligence on 7 December very reliable: reports of 20,000 Japanese concentrating near Sham Chun Hu (*top center*) were discounted. Actually, this was the Japanese 38th Division, preparing to attack across the border. Fortunately, the British commander, Maj. Gen. C. M. Maltby, took no risks and manned all his defenses.

About 0800, 8 December, the Japanese struck without warning. Air raids destroyed the British aircraft, and concurrently the Japanese 38th Division moved across the border toward the Gin Drinker's Line. By dusk, 9 December, they were probing the British position. That night, their strength massed in the west, they ripped a hole in the defenses by seizing and holding the key strong point, Shing Mun Redoubt. The British failed to make any counterattack to recapture the redoubt, and, on the 10th, the Japanese exploited their success by widening the gap and forcing a British withdrawal. On 11 December, with his troops being driven southward, Maltby ordered a withdrawal to the island. By the 13th, it had been successfully executed. That day, and again on the 15th, the Japanese summoned Maltby to surrender and, upon being refused, unleashed intensive artillery and aerial bombardments. On the night of 18 December, the 38th Division crossed to the island as shown. By nightfall of the 19th, they had split the defenders in two groups—Maltby had erred in failing to hold the key Wong Nai Chong Gap (*lower right*) in strength, and his belated counterattacks were unavailing. By the 24th, their water supply almost exhausted, the disorganized British were beaten. On Christmas Day, Maltby surrendered.

In just eighteen days, an efficient, well-trained, and adequately led Japanese division, supported by an equally effective air force and navy, had overrun the stately British crown colony. Its total casualties were 2,754; the British lost 11,848.

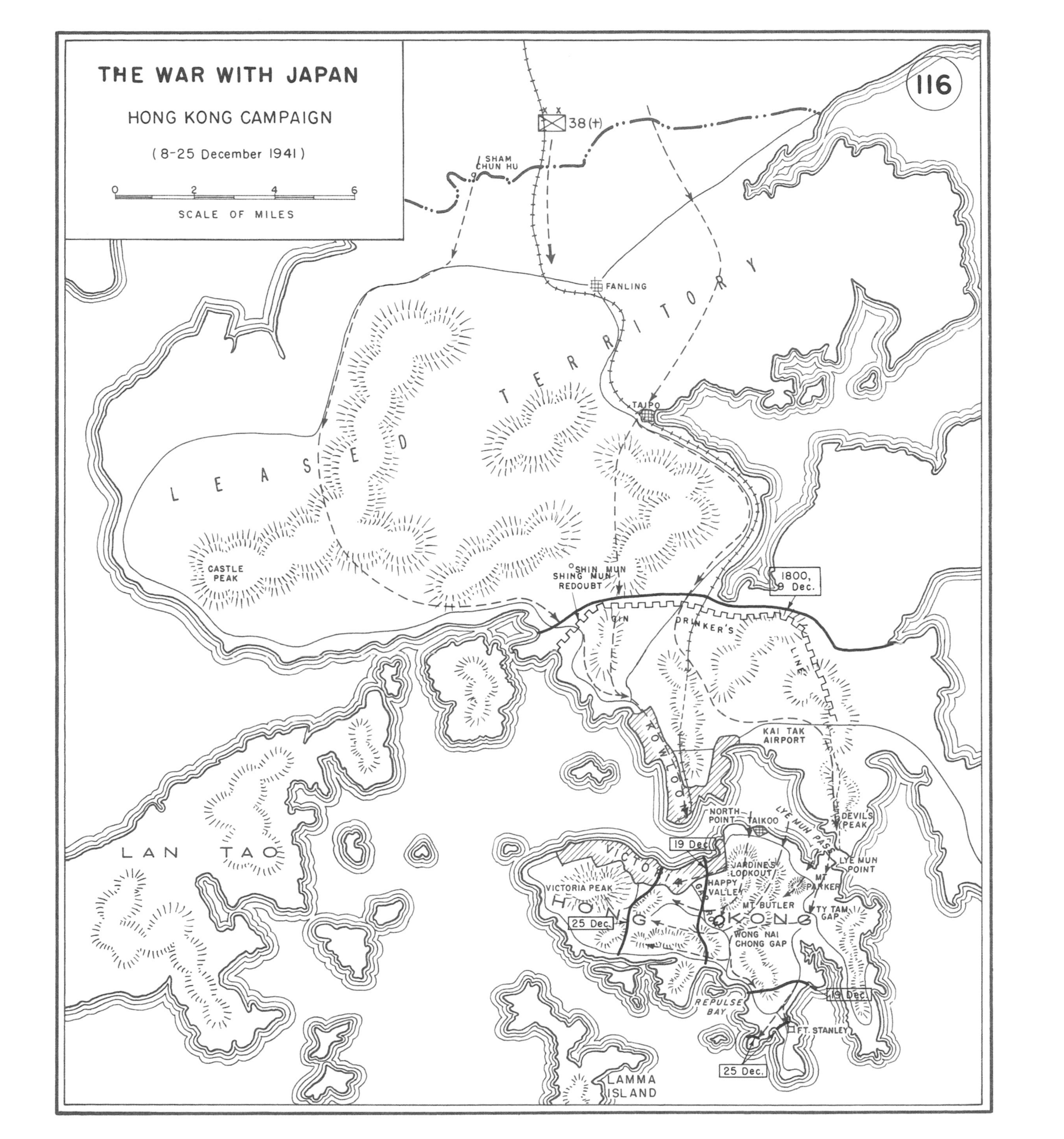
THE WAR WITH JAPAN
HONG KONG CAMPAIGN
(8-25 December 1941)
0 2 4 6
SCALE OF MILES
116
38(+)
SHAM CHUN HU
FANLING
LEASED TERRITORY
TAIPO
CASTLE PEAK
SHIN MUN
SHING MUN REDOUBT
1800, 9 Dec.
GIN
DRINKER'S LINE
KOWLOON
KAI TAK AIRPORT
NORTH POINT
TAIKOO
LYE MUN PASS
DEVILS PEAK
LYE MUN POINT
LAN TAO
19 Dec.
VICTORIA
JARDINE'S LOOKOUT
HAPPY VALLEY
MT PARKER
VICTORIA PEAK
MT BUTLER
TY TAM GAP
HONG KONG
25 Dec.
WONG NAI CHONG GAP
19 Dec.
REPULSE BAY
FT. STANLEY
25 Dec.
LAMMA ISLAND

MALAYAN CAMPAIGN

★

One of Japan's earliest targets for conquest in 1941 was Malaya, the rich British possession lying between the Strait of Malacca and the South China Sea (*right sketch*). It is bordered on the north by Thailand, and in 1941 extended southward to include the island of Singapore. A mountain range, crossed by very few east-west roads, runs down the center of the peninsula and occasionally reaches 7,000 feet in height. The many streams, choked by tropical vegetation and belabored by the heavy rainfall, overflow and create sizable jungle swamps. The equatorial climate is extremely humid; until troops are acclimatized—requiring at least two months—physical exertion in the steaming jungle will quickly sap their energy. In 1941, more than half of Malaya was covered by dense, luxuriant jungle, broken by occasional areas under cultivation. Extensive tin deposits, rubber plantations, and rice paddies abound along the western plain.

At the southern extremity of the peninsula lies the island of Singapore, site of a naval base large enough to service a sizable fleet and so strongly fortified as to be considered impregnable by many Britishers. Upon the completion of this base in the 1920's, the mission of the army garrison became that of defending the base until a fleet arrived from European waters; this fleet was expected to isolate any hostile forces invading Malaya. As air power developed, however, the mission was broadened in 1933 to include the protection of air bases. By 1940, the British had concluded that air power was to be the primary weapon of defense, but—under tremendous pressure in Europe and North Africa—they were never able to station sufficient modern aircraft in Malaya to implement this policy. Consequently, the army, dispersed by its mission to defend the scattered air bases, bore the brunt of defense against the Japanese attack.

The ground forces commander (Lt. Gen. A. E. Percival) assigned the defense of air bases in the north to the Indian 9th and 11th Divisions (forming the III Corps), while the Australian 8th Division defended Johore. Fortress troops garrisoned Singapore, and the Reserve Brigade (*not shown*) was near Port Swettenham (*lower center*). Percival did not overlook the possibility of a Japanese attack on Singapore from the north, but he expected the jungle to seriously impede such a move. To defend Malaya, he had about 80,000 troops (seventeen infantry battalions and two tank regiments short of his estimated requirements). The air force had only 158 first-line aircraft of the 336 considered a minimum requirement. Ground troops were short of artillery and tank support, but their greatest deficiency was lack of realistic training in jungle warfare. On 2 December, the battleship *Prince of Wales* and the battle cruiser *Repulse* arrived in Singapore to join the Far Eastern Fleet; this intended show of force no more impressed Japan than had the earlier reinforcement of Hong Kong.

Japan's occupation of Indochina in 1941 was an important strategic step toward the conquest of Southeast Asia. It provided her with air and naval bases near Malaya which—coupled with Thailand's complacent attitude—thoroughly compromised the British plans for the defense of Malaya. The Japanese Twenty-Fifth Army (Lt. Gen. Tomoyuki Yamashita) was selected to seize Malaya. It consisted of four divisions, two of which had seen combat in China and had recently received thorough training in jungle warfare. This army was well supported by the Japanese Second Fleet and the Third Air Army. Yamashita's plan envisioned initial air strikes, followed by landings at Singora and Patani in Thailand and at Kota Bharu in Malaya (*all top*). These forces, seizing air bases for early Japanese use, would then drive down the east and west coasts toward Singapore. Later, they would be joined by a third force which initially would move through Bangkok (*left sketch, top;* this sketch is an extension northward of the right sketch) to overawe the Siamese, and then down the peninsula into Malaya.

(It should be noted that a Japanese [or Chinese] "army" corresponded roughly to a corps of the Western powers.)

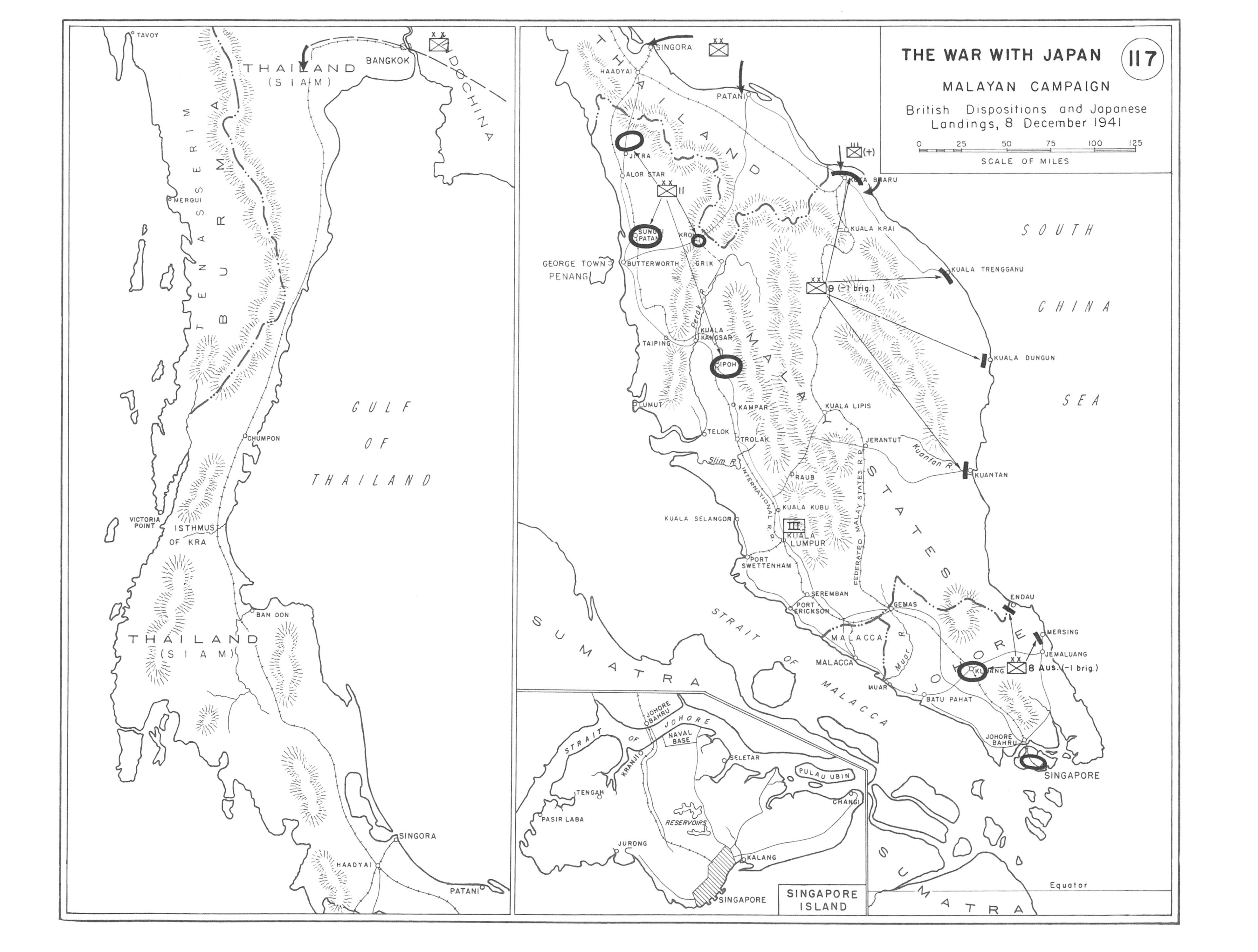

THE WAR WITH JAPAN
117
MALAYAN CAMPAIGN
British Dispositions and Japanese Landings, 8 December 1941
0
25
50
75
100
125
SCALE OF MILES
TAVOY
THAILAND (SIAM)
BANGKOK
INDOCHINA
MERGUI
TENASSERIM
BURMA
GULF OF THAILAND
CHUMPON
VICTORIA POINT
ISTHMUS OF KRA
BAN DON
THAILAND (SIAM)
SINGORA
HAADYAI
PATANI
THAILAND
JITRA
ALOR STAR
SUNGEI PATANI
KROH
GEORGE TOWN
PENANG
BUTTERWORTH
GRIK
Perak R.
KUALA KANGSAR
TAIPING
IPOH
LUMUT
KAMPAR
TELOK
TROLAK
Slim R.
INTERNATIONAL R.R.
KUALA SELANGOR
KUALA KUBU
RAUB
KUALA LUMPUR
PORT SWETTENHAM
SEREMBAN
PORT ERICKSON
KOTA BHARU
KUALA KRAI
KUALA TRENGGANU
9 (-1 brig.)
KUALA DUNGUN
KUALA LIPIS
JERANTUT
Kuantan R.
KUANTAN
FEDERATED MALAY STATES R.R.
MALAY STATES
SOUTH CHINA SEA
GEMAS
MALACCA
Muar R.
MALACCA
MUAR
STRAIT OF MALACCA
SUMATRA
ENDAU
MERSING
JEMALUANG
8 Aus. (-1 brig.)
KLUANG
JOHORE
BATU PAHAT
JOHORE BAHRU
SINGAPORE
Equator
JOHORE BAHRU
STRAIT OF JOHORE
NAVAL BASE
KRANJI
SELETAR
PULAU UBIN
CHANGI
TENGAH
PASIR LABA
RESERVOIRS
JURONG
KALANG
SINGAPORE
SINGAPORE ISLAND

MALAYAN CAMPAIGN

The Japanese attack on Malaya came with startling swiftness early on 8 December. Airfields in Singapore and northern Malaya were bombed, beginning at 0430. Within three days, the British were forced to evacuate the northern fields. Meanwhile, the Japanese had landed unopposed at Singora and Patani (*right sketch, top*) in Thailand and established air bases. A landing at Kota Bharu had to overcome considerable opposition. Supported by aircraft operating from Singora and Patani, two ground columns quickly struck out for the Malayan border.

On 6 December, a British reconnaissance plane had sighted part of the Japanese landing force at sea, but it then lost contact. The convoy's destination was not discovered until it began disgorging troops at Singora two days later. During this two-day interlude, the British high command pondered whether or not to adopt MATADOR (a plan for movement into Thailand if Japan violated that country's neutrality)—hampered by restraining notes from London, uncertainty concerning the Japanese convoy, and the delicate political situation concerning Thailand. As a result, MATADOR was never attempted; instead, an alternate plan, involving a short advance across the frontier (*top left*) to commanding defensive terrain, was undertaken. The Siamese vigorously resisted this move, until reinforced by the Japanese who soon drove the British back to Jitra. The 11th Division was forced out of the Jitra position on 10 December; nor could it hold at Sungei Patani, for the Japanese column coming down from Patani to Kroh threatened its rear.

Meanwhile, a Japanese regiment landed at the Isthmus of Kra (*left sketch*) and seized the airfield at Victoria Point, thereby cutting the British aerial reinforcement route to Malaya. And off Kuantan (*right sketch, center*), the *Prince of Wales* and *Repulse* were sunk on 10 December by Japanese torpedo bombers based in Indochina. Despite their lack of air cover—either carrier or land-based—the ships had sallied forth in the true tradition of the British Navy to assist the ground forces by striking at the Japanese landing force at Singora.

By the 23d, the 11th Division was in position behind the Perak River, and most of the 9th was at Kuala Lipis. Already the Japanese had clearly demonstrated their superior training and skill in jungle warfare. Their soldiers were lightly clad and equipped, and moved phantomlike in the dense jungle to infiltrate or envelop British positions; tanks were boldly used in surprise moves down the roads; aircraft played the role of direct-support artillery; and liberal use was made of night attacks. Under persistent pressure, the British were forced back from position to position as shown. In efforts to cut off the British, the Japanese attempted several amphibious envelopments along the west coast, using small, captured fishing craft. Percival wanted to continue fighting a delaying action to gain time for reinforcements to reach Singapore, but Wavell (en route to Java to assume command of all Allied forces in the western Pacific) ordered a withdrawal to the province of Johore on 8 January. When he was unable to hold Yamashita at the Johore position, Percival was forced to retire to Singapore Island (*inset sketch*) on 31 January.

The Japanese brought up heavy artillery, intensified their air attacks against the island, and prepared an assault. The British had ample supplies and a sizable defending force, but they had not utilized the previous two months diligently enough to prepare against landings. Yamashita crossed three divisions as shown, outflanked the British, and—in spite of fierce resistance—forced Percival to capitulate on 15 February.

Malaya's loss opened the Indian Ocean to the Japanese and imperiled Sumatra, Java, and Borneo (*see map 126*). The British sustained 138,708 casualties; Yamasbita's totaled 9,824.

During the latter part of December 1941, the first Allied heads-of-state conference took place in Washington (ARCADIA). From this meeting stemmed the Combined Chiefs of Staff (CCS) organization, headed by the British and American Joint Chiefs of Staff (JCS). Members of the respective JCS planning committees met as CCS committees on matters of mutual concern. The British Chiefs actually sat in London, but had permanent representatives at CCS Headquarters in Washington. The principal functions of the CCS were to advise the heads of state on military matters and to implement the broad strategic decisions made at the periodic international conferences. This implementation generally concerned the assignment of spheres of activity, the allocation of resources, and the coordination of effort.

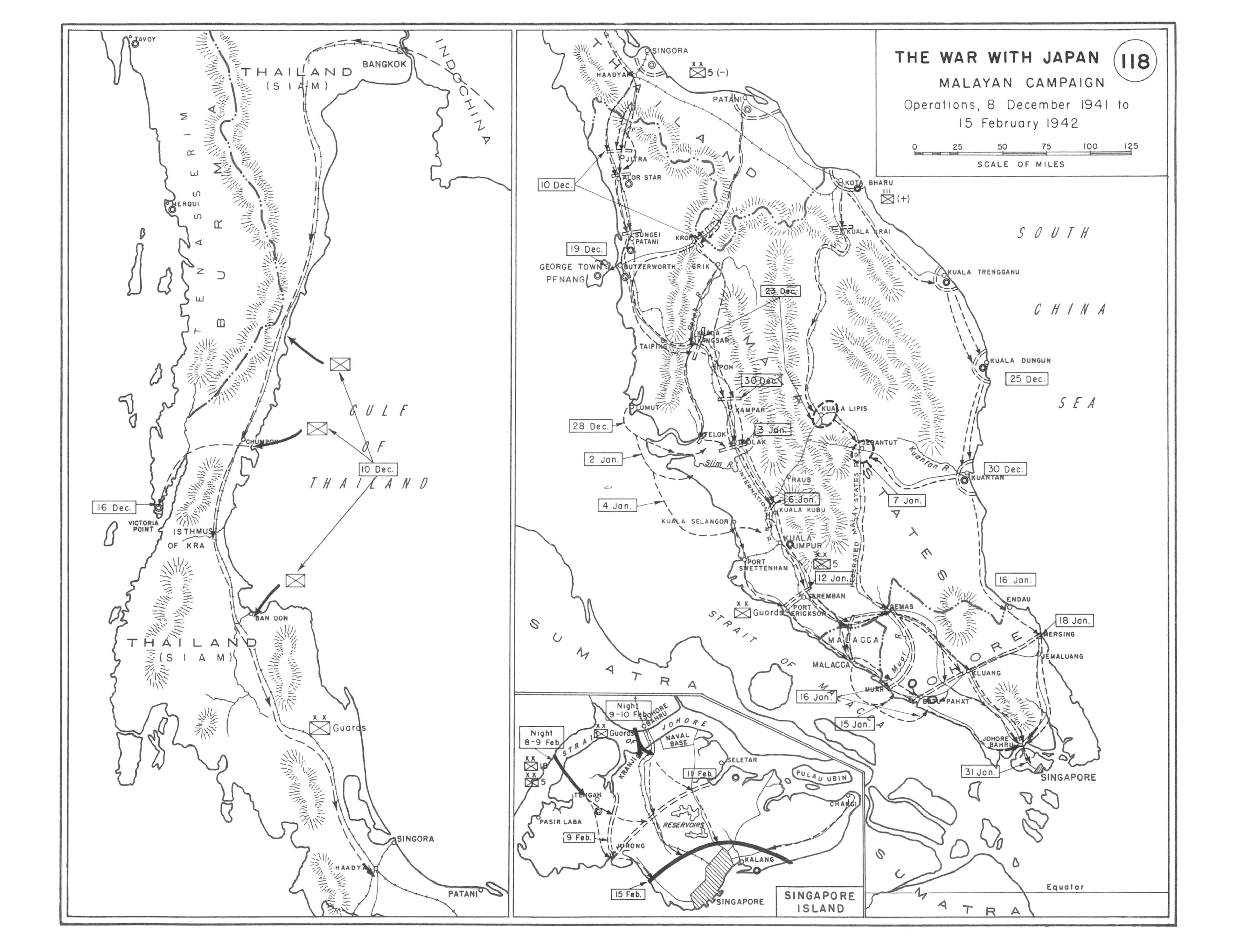
THE WAR WITH JAPAN
118
MALAYAN CAMPAIGN
Operations, 8 December 1941 to 15 February 1942
0 25 50 75 100 125
SCALE OF MILES
TAVOY
BANGKOK
THAILAND (SIAM)
INDOCHINA
TENASSERIM
BURMA
MERGUI
GULF OF THAILAND
10 Dec.
CHUMPON
16 Dec.
VICTORIA POINT
ISTHMUS OF KRA
BAN DON
Guards
SINGORA
HAADYAI
PATANI
5 (-)
JITRA
ALOR STAR
SUNGEI PATANI
KROH
BUTTERWORTH
GRIK
19 Dec.
GEORGE TOWN
PENANG
KOTA BHARU
KUALA KRAI
KUALA TRENGGANU
SOUTH CHINA SEA
23 Dec.
KUALA KANGSAR
TAIPING
IPOH
30 Dec.
KAMPAR
KUALA DUNGUN
25 Dec.
KUALA LIPIS
UMUT
28 Dec.
TELOK ANSON
SLIM
3 Jan.
2 Jan.
Slim R.
JERANTUT
Kuantan R.
30 Dec.
KUANTAN
RAUB
6 Jan.
KUALA KUBU
7 Jan.
4 Jan.
KUALA SELANGOR
KUALA LUMPUR
FEDERATED MALAY STATES
PORT SWETTENHAM
12 Jan.
SEREMBAN
16 Jan.
ENDAU
PORT DICKSON
GEMAS
18 Jan.
MERSING
JEMALUANG
STRAIT OF MALACCA
MALACCA
Muar R.
JOHORE
KLUANG
SUMATRA
16 Jan.
MUAR
BATU PAHAT
15 Jan.
JOHORE BAHRU
31 Jan.
SINGAPORE
Night 9-10 Feb.
Night 8-9 Feb.
18
STRAIT OF JOHORE
NAVAL BASE
KRANJI
SELETAR
11 Feb.
PULAU UBIN
TENGAH
CHANGI
PASIR LABA
RESERVOIRS
9 Feb.
JURONG
KALANG
15 Feb.
SINGAPORE ISLAND
Equator

PHILIPPINE CAMPAIGN

★

The Philippine Archipelago, comprising some 7,000 islands, lies only 500 miles from the China coast and dominates the eastern approaches to the South China Sea (*see map 114*). Luzon is the largest island and, in 1941, was the most important militarily. Under foreign influence since the third century, the Philippines harbored a conglomeration of oriental and occidental institutions when the United States seized them from Spain in 1898 (*see text, map 158, Volume I*). In the ensuing years, a benevolent policy—including a promise of full independence in 1946—won the loyalty of the Filipinos to an unusual degree.

In 1935, General Douglas MacArthur was designated military advisor to the Philippine Commonwealth. Ably assisted by a small group of military men—including Major Dwight D. Eisenhower—MacArthur prepared plans for a Philippine defense establishment, designed for maturity in 1946. But implementation was slow and costly, and by 1941 the Philippine Army was neither prepared nor equipped to repel the Japanese onslaught. Nor were the American armed forces' contingents in the Philippines sufficient for the task.

Under the "Germany-first" strategy conceived in January 1941, Japan would be contained with a minimum defensive effort. In effect, the over-all war plan (Rainbow-5) accepted likely defeat in the far-away Philippines and held out no hope for major reinforcements.

When relations with Japan worsened, American and Filipino ground and air forces were consolidated into the United States Army Forces Far East (USAFFE) under MacArthur (recalled to active duty on 26 July). As shown (*this map, lower left*), USAFFE contained only a few American troops—primarily the Philippine Division (USAFFE's only adequately trained and equipped division) and artillery, tank, and service units. Now, primarily because of MacArthur's stature and overly optimistic claims for the offensive capabilities of the new B-17 bomber, the defensive policy suddenly changed. MacArthur injected optimism and the spirit of the offensive into the plan for the defense of the Philippines (Orange-3): defeat was no longer conceded, the enemy would be met at the beaches, the entire archipelago would be defended. Reinforcements began moving to Luzon, and it was expected that by April 1942, USAFFE would be strong enough to hold the islands. But the Japanese had other ideas.

The Fourteenth Army planned to use only two reinforced divisions to conquer Luzon, and expected to complete the task in fifty days; thereafter, most of the troops would be used in operations elsewhere. Concurrent with the initial air strikes against American aircraft and installations, landings would be made at Aparri, Vigan (*both top*), and Legaspi (*bottom right*) to seize airfields. Operating from these fields, army planes would complete the destruction of American air and naval forces. Then the main landing would be made at Lingayen Gulf (*left center*), and a secondary attack at Lamon Bay (*lower center*); these forces would advance to seize Manila, and thereafter the rest of Luzon. (Coincident with the early landings, a reinforced battalion would seize Davao in Mindanao [*see map 114*] as a springboard for future operations in Borneo.)

The Philippine garrison went on full war alert on 27 November. By 10 December, its forces were disposed as shown. Shortly after noon on 8 December, Japanese navy bombers from Formosa struck MacArthur's air force a devastating blow. In spite of being alerted by the Pearl Harbor attack, most of the planes were caught on the runways. By the end of the day, half of the B-17's and modern fighters had been destroyed, and the striking force of the small American Asiatic Fleet was steaming southward from Luzon and Cebu. During the next week, Japanese air power hammered at Luzon air bases and the Cavite naval base near Manila. On the 11th, the remaining bombers were withdrawn to Mindanao and, six days later, to Australia—without ever having been able to mount one effective strike. By 15 December, the fighters had been reduced to a handful.

Meanwhile, the preliminary Japanese landings on 10 and 12 December had been successful. The Japanese moved inland against very light resistance as MacArthur, still awaiting the main landing, refused to commit forces in strength to stop these small detachments. However, the 11th Division, Philippine Army (PA), sector was extended along Lingayen Gulf to San Fernando, the 26th Cavalry Regiment (Philippine Scouts) was moved north to that area, one regiment of the 71st Division (PA) was sent northward to intercept the Kanno and Tanaka Detachments, and two companies were committed to delay the Kimura Detachment.

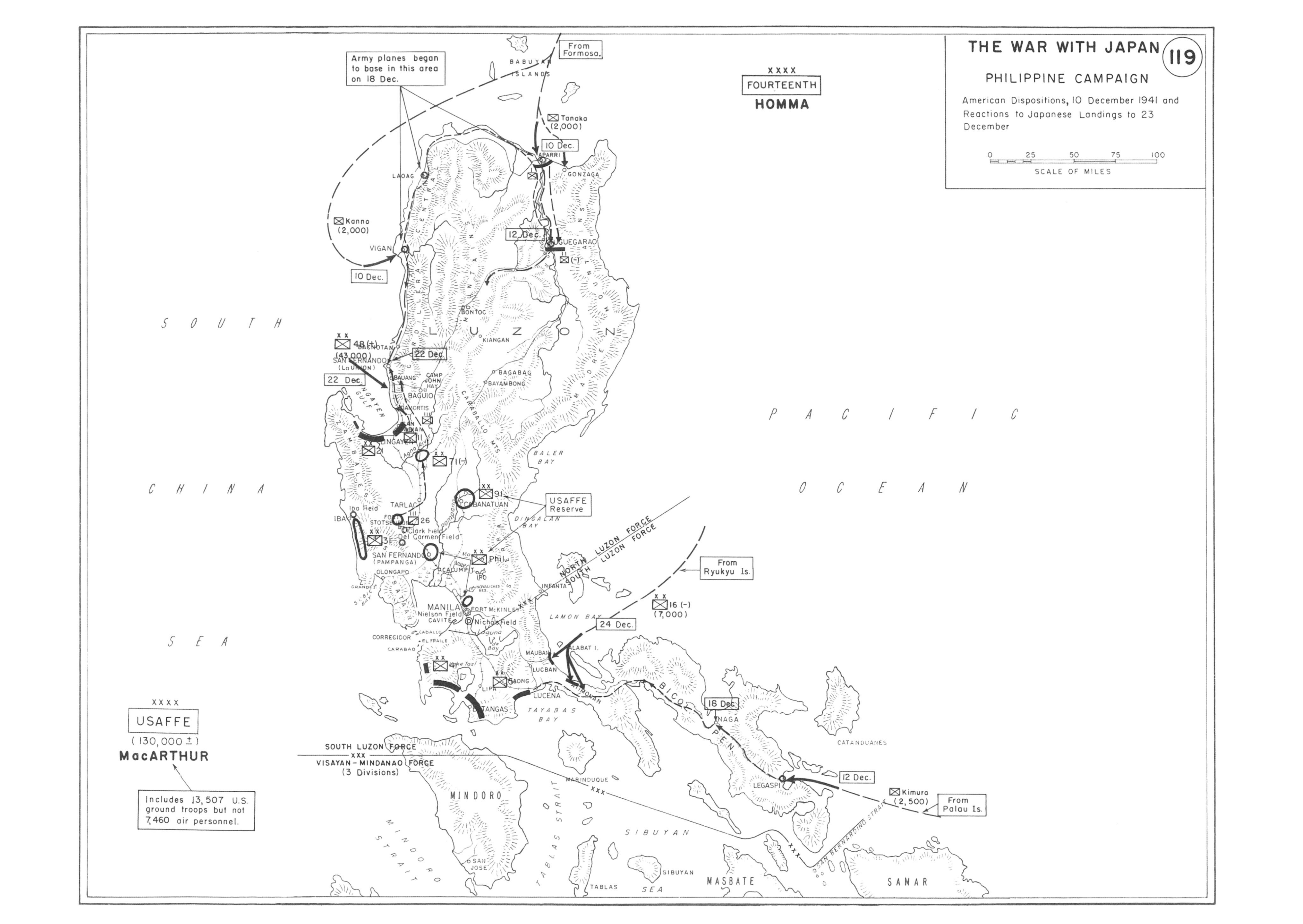

THE WAR WITH JAPAN
119
PHILIPPINE CAMPAIGN
American Dispositions, 10 December 1941 and Reactions to Japanese Landings to 23 December
0 25 50 75 100
SCALE OF MILES
XXXX
FOURTEENTH
HOMMA
XXXX
USAFFE
(130,000 ±)
MacARTHUR
Includes 13,507 U.S. ground troops but not 7,460 air personnel.
Army planes began to base in this area on 18 Dec.
From Formosa.
From Ryukyu Is.
From Palau Is.
Tanaka (2,000)
Kanno (2,000)
Kimura (2,500)
16 (-) (7,000)
48 (-) (43,000)
10 Dec.
10 Dec.
12 Dec.
12 Dec.
18 Dec.
22 Dec.
22 Dec.
24 Dec.
USAFFE Reserve
NORTH LUZON FORCE
SOUTH LUZON FORCE
VISAYAN-MINDANAO FORCE
(3 Divisions)
SOUTH CHINA SEA
PACIFIC OCEAN
BABUYAN ISLANDS
APARRI
GONZAGA
LAOAG
VIGAN
TUGUEGARAO
BONTOC
KIANGAN
BAGABAG
BAYAMBONG
SAN FERNANDO (La UNION)
BAUANG
CAMP JOHN HAY
BAGUIO
DAMORTIS
LINGAYEN GULF
LUZON
CARABALLO MTS.
BALER BAY
DINGALAN BAY
CABANATUAN
TARLAC
Iba Field
IBA
Clark Field
Del Carmen Field
SAN FERNANDO (PAMPANGA)
OLONGAPO
CALUMPIT
IPO
MANILA
Nielson Field
FORT McKINLEY
Nichols Field
CAVITE
CORREGIDOR
CARABAO
EL FRAILE
INFANTA
LAMON BAY
ALABAT I.
MAUBAN
LUCBAN
LUCENA
LIPA
BATANGAS
TAYABAS BAY
BICOL PEN.
NAGA
LEGASPI
CATANDUANES
MINDORO
MINDORO STRAIT
SAN JOSE
MARINDUQUE
TABLAS STRAIT
SIBUYAN SEA
SIBUYAN
TABLAS
MASBATE
SAN BERNARDINO STRAIT
SAMAR

PHILIPPINE CAMPAIGN

★

Shortly after midnight, 22 December, eighty-five heavily escorted Japanese troop transports dropped anchor in Lingayen Gulf. Seas were heavy and there was a slight drizzle, but, by 0800, assault elements were ashore at the four points shown. This area, recently occupied by elements of the 11th Division (PA), was not held in strength. Only at Bauang did the Japanese meet any resistance, for though the landing did not surprise USAFFE—the convoy had been detected as early as 18 December, and Maj. Gen. Jonathan Wainwright had been alerted—it had been expected at the head of the gulf.

The regiment of the 71st Division (PA), moving north to intercept the Tanaka-Kanno Detachments, was struck in flank by the Japanese 9th Regiment, and (along with 11th Division [PA] elements) part of it was forced into the mountains toward Baguio. (Wainwright ordered this composite force to rejoin the North Luzon Force [NLF] at Rosario, but it delayed overnight at Baguio and was forced to withdraw eastward when the Japanese cut Route 11 near Rosario.) By 1700, the 9th Regiment had secured Bauang and started a column up the twisting road to Baguio.

Farther south, the Japanese 48th Division assault elements aggressively expanded the beachhead. One regimental column struck out for Rosario, while the other two columns moved along Route 3 toward Damortis. (Meanwhile, rough weather had forced the transports farther south into the gulf, thus temporarily exposing them to fire from emplaced 155-mm. guns at San Fabian and Dagupan. American submarines and three B-17's also attacked Japanese shipping, but with disappointing results.) When the 11th Division (PA) troops opposing the landing of the Japanese 48th Division fled in rout southward beyond Damortis, Wainwright ordered the 26th Cavalry Regiment (horse-mounted, with some light scout cars) forward from Rosario and instructed it to hold Damortis. At 1300, this regiment came under heavy attack; three hours later, it was forced to withdraw toward Rosario. Fighting a skillful delaying action, the regiment—by now reinforced with a company of USAFFE's precious tanks—held off the superior Japanese force until the enemy column coming from Agoo made its position untenable. The American tankers, operating much too independently, had not been of much assistance; nor had the 71st Division (PA) (sent forward by Wainwright) arrived in time to aid the gallant cavalrymen.

Homma's troops continued their relentless drive south on the 23d. That afternoon, the 71st Division (PA) fled when attacked near Sison, and that night the 91st Division (PA) regimental combat team that had reached Pozorrubio also broke under attack. Earlier that day, the hard-hit 26th Cavalry had gone into reserve at Binalonan, where it had established an outpost line. Here, on 24 December, while the demoralized 71st Division (PA) was withdrawn for reorganization and the 91st Division (PA) moved into the D-2 line, the heroic cavalrymen held off the Japanese; late that afternoon, they withdrew to the east to Tayug.

Meanwhile, on the afternoon of the 23d, Wainwright had asked permission to withdraw to the Agno River; from here—if given the Philippine Division—he wanted to launch a counterattack. But the demonstrated inability of the green Philippine Army divisions to hold the Japanese, and the sighting of an enemy convoy moving toward Lamon Bay, caused MacArthur to adhere to an older plan for the last-ditch defense of Luzon: withdrawal to Bataan (*see map 119, lower left*). This plan hinged upon the NLF delaying at the previously selected positions marked D-1 to D-5 (*this map*), while the South Luzon Force withdrew into Bataan. The first four lines were to be held lightly, and only to force the Japanese to deploy for attack; the D-5 line was to be organized in strength.

On the 24th, Wainwright's troops were on the D-1 line. That night, he ordered a withdrawal to the D-2 line. By Christmas night, the NLF was along that line, but on the right—where the 26th Cavalry had fought all day—it had been touch and go holding the Japanese. The next night, the troops withdrew to the D-3 line, but the 11th Division (PA) and USAFFE's two tank battalions took heavy losses in disengaging near Rosales. While Homma paused to regroup, Wainwright withdrew to the D-4 line and—contrary to his original plan—decided to hold there as long as possible. The Japanese moved most of their strength toward Cabanatuan on the 28th; only the 9th Regiment moved on Tarlac, on the direct road to Bataan. Outflanked by a Japanese tank column, the 91st Division (PA) withdrew from Cabanatuan on the night of 29 December, just as Japanese infantry began to cross the Pampanga River.

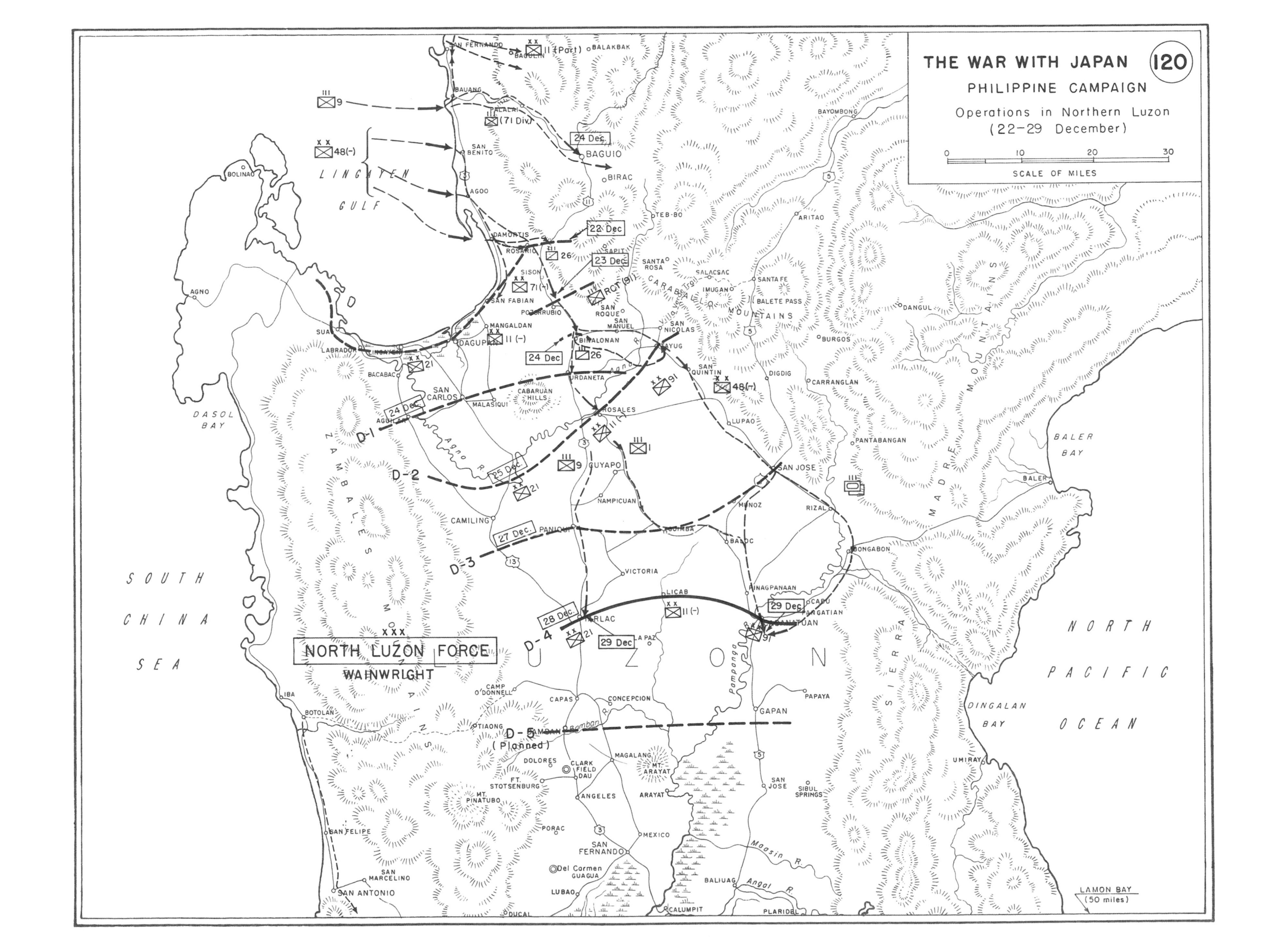
THE WAR WITH JAPAN
120
PHILIPPINE CAMPAIGN
Operations in Northern Luzon
(22-29 December)
0 10 20 30
SCALE OF MILES
LINGAYEN GULF
SOUTH CHINA SEA
NORTH PACIFIC OCEAN
DASOL BAY
BALER BAY
DINGALAN BAY
LAMON BAY (50 miles)
NORTH LUZON FORCE
WAINWRIGHT
LUZON
ZAMBALES MOUNTAINS
CARABALLO MOUNTAINS
MADRE MOUNTAINS
SIERRA
D
D-1
D-2
D-3
D-4
D-5 (Planned)
22 Dec
23 Dec
24 Dec
24 Dec.
25 Dec.
27 Dec.
28 Dec.
29 Dec
11 (Part)
71 Div
48(-)
9
26
71(-)
RCT(91)
11 (-)
21
91
48(-)
1
SAN FERNANDO
BAGUIO
BALAKBAK
BAUANG
SAN BENITO
AGOO
BIRAC
BAYOMBONG
ARITAO
TEB-BO
DAMORTIS
ROSARIO
SAPIT
SISON
SAN FABIAN
POZORRUBIO
SAN ROQUE
SAN MANUEL
SANTA ROSA
SALACSAC
IMUGAN
SANTA FE
BALETE PASS
DANGUL
BURGOS
MANGALDAN
DAGUPAN
BINALONAN
SAN NICOLAS
AGNO
BOLINAO
SUAL
LABRADOR
LINGAYEN
BACABAC
SAN CARLOS
AGUILAR
MALASIQUI
CABARUAN HILLS
URDANETA
ROSALES
SAN QUINTIN
DIGDIG
CARRANGLAN
LUPAO
PANTABANGAN
BALER
Agno R.
GUYAPO
SAN JOSE
NAMPICUAN
MUNOZ
RIZAL
CAMILING
PANIQUI
BALOC
BONGABON
VICTORIA
LICAB
RINAGPANAAN
CABU
PANGATIAN
TARLAC
LA PAZ
PAPAYA
IBA
BOTOLAN
CAMP O'DONNELL
CAPAS
CONCEPCION
Pampanga
GAPAN
TIAONG
BAMBAN
Bamban R.
DOLORES
CLARK FIELD
DAU
MAGALANG
MT. ARAYAT
FT. STOTSENBURG
MT. PINATUBO
ANGELES
ARAYAT
SAN JOSE
SIBUL SPRINGS
UMIRAY
PORAC
SAN FELIPE
SAN FERNANDO
MEXICO
Maasin R.
Del Carmen
GUAGUA
SAN MARCELINO
SAN ANTONIO
LUBAO
BALIUAG
Angat R.
CALUMPIT
PLARIDEL
DUCAL

PHILIPPINE CAMPAIGN

★

At 0200, 24 December, the Japanese began to land at Lamon Bay (*lower right*). Resistance to the landing by two battalions of the 1st Infantry Regiment (1st Regular Division [PA]) at Mauban was fierce, and Japanese gains for the day were slight. But farther south, the main Japanese force caught the 51st Division (PA) in the process of shifting units and had little difficulty taking Atimonan and advancing toward Lucena. One of its units (*not shown*) moved southeast and cut off a battalion on the Bicol Peninsula—located there to oppose the earlier Japanese landing at Legaspi (*see map 119*).

On the 24th, Maj. Gen. George M. Parker relinquished command of the Southern Luzon Force (SLF) to Maj. Gen. Albert M. Jones and was given the mission of preparing defensive positions on Bataan (*this map; center, left*), utilizing forces already there (elements of the Philippine Division and a few supporting troops) and other units as they arrived. The 31st Division (PA) and most of the 41st began moving to Bataan at once. Jones, now under orders to block the Japanese advance but to withdraw to Bataan when forced to do so, had no previously selected delaying positions, though he was favored by excellent defensive terrain. Utilizing accepted retrograde techniques—no easy task, considering his green and poorly armed troops—he withdrew as the Japanese aggressively pushed two major columns eastward beyond Lucena and Lucban. The 1st Infantry squandered a good tank platoon west of Lucban in an ill-advised counterattack and had to be stiffened with a 300-man force of retired Philippine Scouts, but it slowed the northern enemy column. In the south, Jones leapfrogged battalions back to Taiong, where he established a strong position on the 28th. But that night, alarmed by the Japanese advance against Wainwright, USAFFE ordered Jones to clear the Calumpit bridges (*center*) by 0600, 1 January. (The previous date set had been 8 January.) Reluctantly, Jones withdrew his forces to the edge of Laguna de Bay (*lower center; dashed blue line, dated 29 December*) and started elements toward Bataan. Then USAFFE equivocated—probably because there were still supplies in Manila to be evacuated—and told Jones early on 30 December to hold his position until driven back.

A glance at the map (*center*) indicates the importance of Plaridel, Calumpit, and San Fernando. If either of the first two were to fall into the hands of the Japanese advancing down Route 5, Jones' force would be cut off from Bataan (strangely enough, Japanese air power made no attempt to destroy the Calumpit bridges); if Homma were to capture San Fernando, Wainwright would have difficulty moving into Bataan. On the 30th, the Japanese captured Gapan, the 91st Division disintegrated, and an unexpected thrust to La Paz (*upper center*) threatened to turn the D-4 line, forcing Wainwright to withdraw to the line Bamban–Mt. Arayat. That night, MacArthur ordered the SLF to start north at once.

The night of the 30th; the SLF moved around Manila (declared an open city on the 26th) and toward Plaridel. By dawn, much of it had crossed the Calumpit bridges. About the same time, the demoralized 91st Division (PA) reached Baliuag, two battalions of the 51st Division (PA) took up a position at Plaridel, and 71st Division (PA) elements arrived to reinforce the 91st. At 1000, Jones was given command of all troops east of the Pampanga River, but, apparently unaware of this change, Wainwright told the troops at Baliuag to withdraw in time to clear Calumpit by 0600, 1 January. At 1200, 31 December, the 91st Division (PA) began its withdrawal; shortly thereafter, the 71st did likewise. Jones, when apprised, futilely tried to halt the withdrawal. Desperate because the Japanese—now in Baliuag—were massing for an attack, he ordered two tank platoons to make a spoiling attack at 1700. The tankers surprised the Japanese, wreaked havoc in the town, and gained the precious time needed. By 0500, 1 January, all USAFFE troops—except a few small detachments—had crossed the Pampanga; at 0615, the bridges were destroyed.

On 1 January, Wainwright withdrew the 11th and 21st Divisions (PA) to the Borac-Guagua line, where these decimated units held off the two attacking Japanese regiments until 4 January, and then pulled back into Bataan. The reinforced 71st Division (PA) held one last delaying position, but the Japanese, supported by overwhelming air and artillery, cracked this line in one day. By 7 January, USAFFE—now on Bataan and organized as shown—was improving its defenses to resist the inevitable attack.

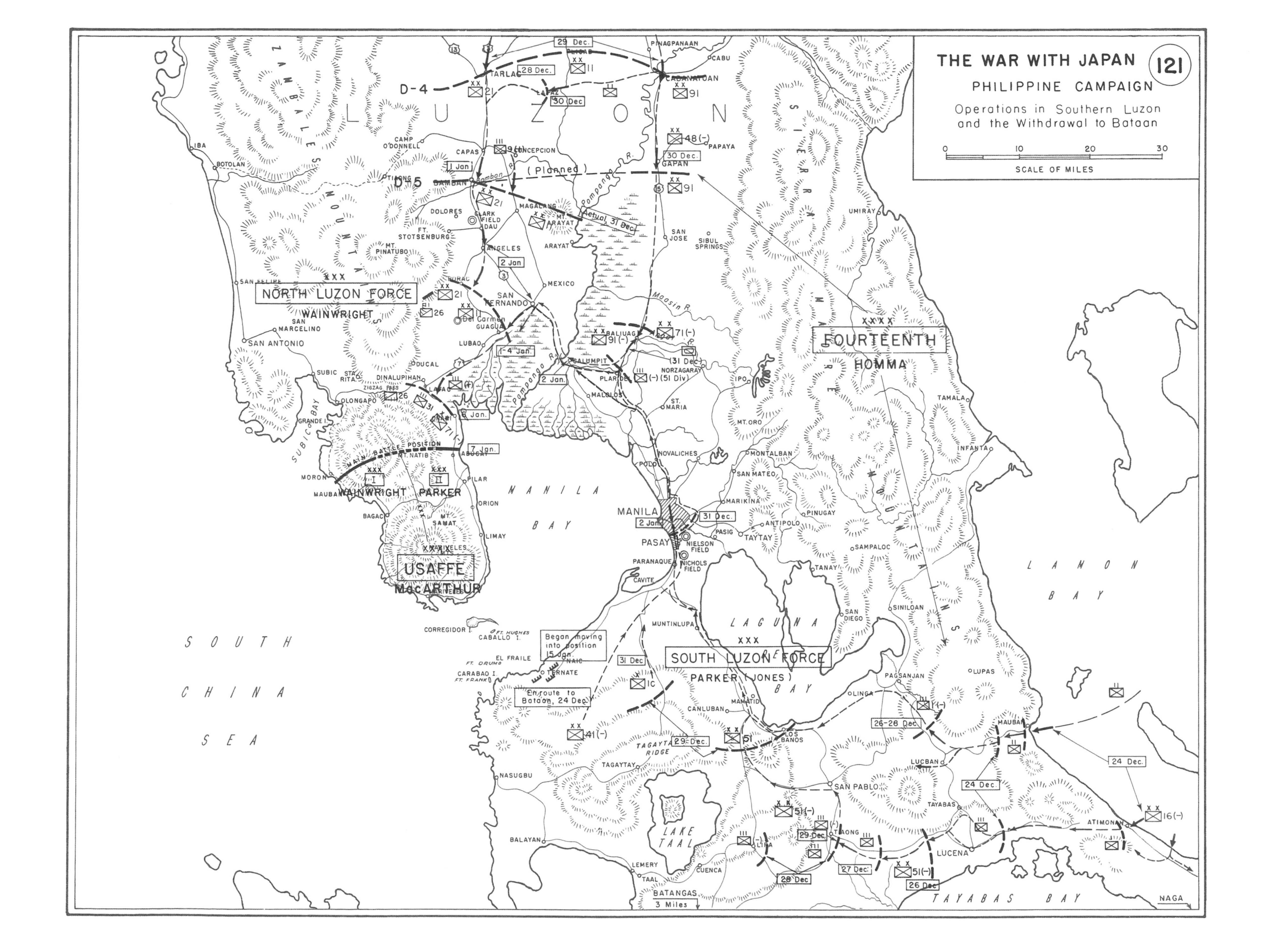
THE WAR WITH JAPAN
121
PHILIPPINE CAMPAIGN
Operations in Southern Luzon and the Withdrawal to Bataan
0 10 20 30
SCALE OF MILES
LUZON
NORTH LUZON FORCE
WAINWRIGHT
FOURTEENTH
HOMMA
SOUTH LUZON FORCE
PARKER (JONES)
USAFFE
MacARTHUR
WAINWRIGHT
PARKER
MAIN BATTLE POSITION
D-4
D-5
(Planned)
Actual 31 Dec.
29 Dec.
28 Dec.
30 Dec.
1 Jan.
2 Jan.
1-4 Jan.
6 Jan.
7 Jan.
31 Dec.
24 Dec.
26-28 Dec.
27 Dec.
26 Dec.
Began moving into position 15 Jan.
Enroute to Bataan, 24 Dec.
MANILA BAY
LAGUNA BAY
LAMON BAY
TAYABAS BAY
SOUTH CHINA SEA
LAKE TAAL
SUBIC BAY
ZAMBALES MOUNTAINS
SIERRA MADRE MOUNTAINS
TAGAYTAY RIDGE
MANILA
PASAY
CAVITE
CORREGIDOR I.
BATANGAS 3 Miles
NAGA

★

The Bataan peninsula is mountainous and covered—particularly on its west—with dense jungle. The mountains run generally down the middle of the peninsula, the dominant heights being Mt. Natib (in the north) and the rugged Mariveles Mountains (in the south). Emanating from these towering terrain masses, many small streams have cut steep gullies as they wind their way to the coast. In the west, the mountains drop off abruptly at the coast, forming high cliffs which dominate the narrow coastal corridor; on the opposite coast, between Abucay and Orion, the terrain is flat and water-logged, but farther south it resumes the mountainous pattern. The only good beaches are along the Manila Bay shore. At the peninsula's tip, a cove provides a natural harbor for the small port of Mariveles. In 1941, though many small trails existed, there were only two roads generally suitable for vehicular use. These were: the perimeter road running down the east coast from Abucay to Mariveles (one lane, all weather) and thence north to Moron (dry weather); and the Pilar-Bagac road, the only lateral communication route for USAFFE forces.

The USAFFE defense plan provided for defense in depth, utilizing main and reserve battle positions. Provision was also made for defending the beaches. Though the prewar plans had selected the Orion-Bagac line as the main battle position, MacArthur had chosen the Mauban-Abucay line as the initial position in order to gain more time to prepare the rearward line, and to protect the best means of lateral communication—the Pilar-Bagac road.

Fortifications along Parker's front were much stronger than in Wainwright's sector because the relatively open terrain in the east had dictated first priority when preparations began in late December. Parker held the vital coastal sector with the fresh and well-trained 57th Regiment (Philippine Scouts) of the Philippine Division. Wainwright, likewise, concentrated on the coastal corridor in his sector, stationing most of the 1st Regular Division (PA) near Mauban. (Elements of the 26th Cavalry and 1st Infantry Regiments [*not shown*] occupied the likely enemy concentration area between Moron and Mauban.) His reserve was not as strong as it appears; the 71st and 91st Divisions (PA) had taken a severe beating in the withdrawal from Lingayen, and the 26th Cavalry was similarly greatly reduced in strength. Both corps enjoyed substantial artillery support. In addition to divisional artillery, Wainwright had about thirty-five corps artillery pieces (mostly 75-mm.) and Parker had about sixty (half of 155-mm. caliber). The greatest defect in the main battle position was the inability of the corps to establish firm contact in the fantastically rugged Mt. Natib area, which was held primarily with patrols.

Of critical influence in the defense of Bataan was the supply situation. It was unsatisfactory in the beginning and—growing steadily worse—probably had as much effect on the ultimate capitulation as any other single factor. Some supplies were stored on Bataan when war came, and every attempt was made to transfer more there beginning 23 December. But the number of troops—and civilians—eventually moved to the peninsula far exceeded the prewar planning figures. Further, the scarcity of ships (the prime means of movement) and vehicles, coupled with Japanese air superiority, severely handicapped movement.

Some efforts were made in December to provide relief for MacArthur's harried forces. When war came, a supply convoy was en route to Manila. After considerable debate in Washington, it was diverted to Australia, but General Marshall ordered that every effort be made to move its vitally needed artillery, airplanes, and ammunition northward. Naval planners, shocked by the Pearl Harbor disaster, conceded the loss of the Philippines and were unwilling to risk the small Asiatic Fleet in an attempt to escort ships through the tightening Japanese naval blockade. Attempts at supply by submarine were generally fruitless. A disappointed MacArthur, grasping better than anyone else how thinly spread the Japanese were, continued to urge attempts at reinforcement and even limited offensive strikes at the Japanese home islands. But the Pacific theater had second call on Allied resources. By 7 January, it was clear that USAFFE would have to fight with what it had.

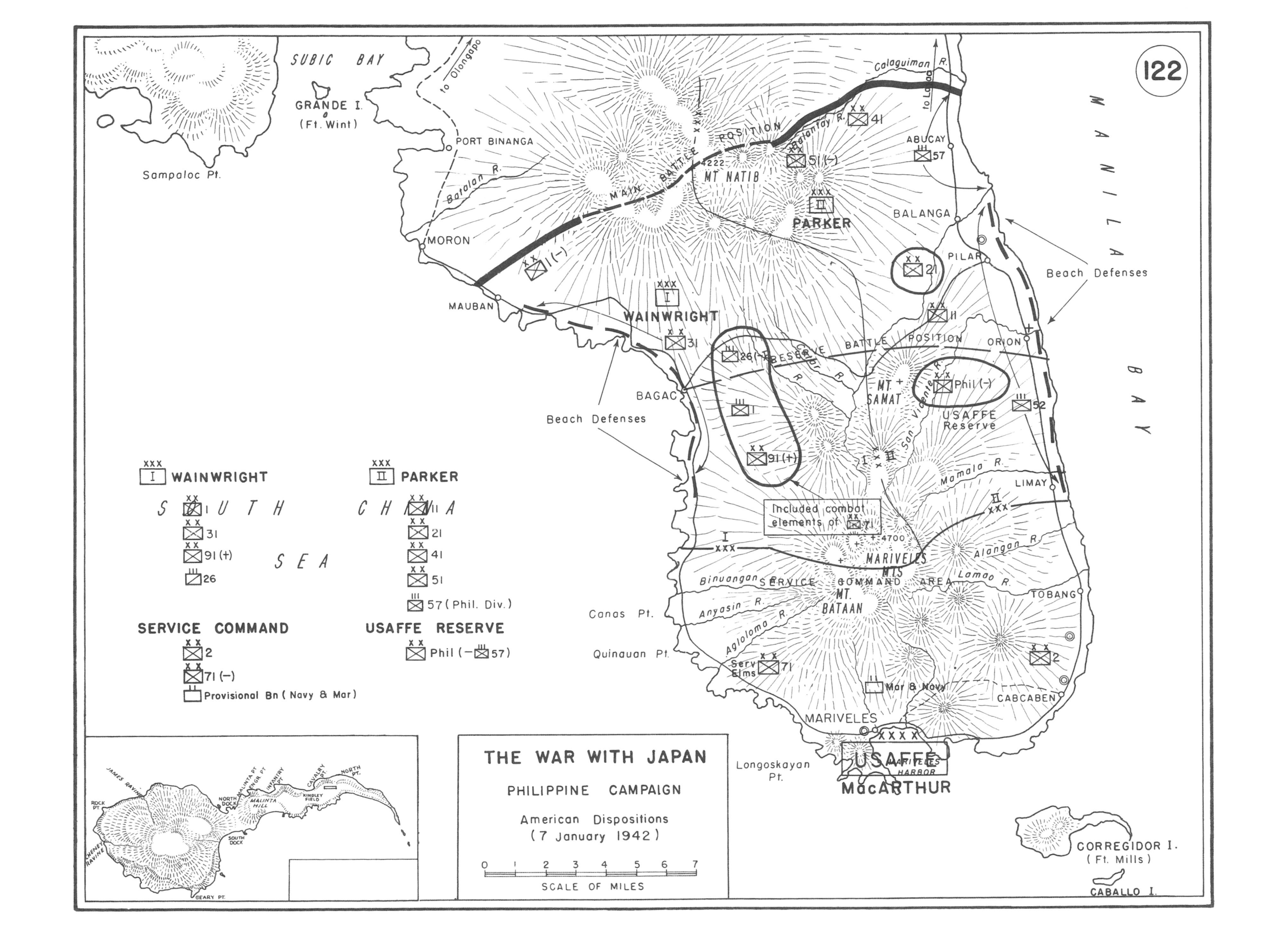
122
THE WAR WITH JAPAN
PHILIPPINE CAMPAIGN
American Dispositions
(7 January 1942)
0 1 2 3 4 5 6 7
SCALE OF MILES
MANILA BAY
SUBIC BAY
SOUTH CHINA SEA
GRANDE I.
(Ft. Wint)
Sampaloc Pt.
to Olongapo
PORT BINANGA
Batalan R.
MORON
MAUBAN
MAIN BATTLE POSITION
MT NATIB
4222
Calaguiman R.
to Layac
Balantay R.
ABUCAY
BALANGA
PILAR
ORION
LIMAY
TOBANG
CABCABEN
MARIVELES
MARIVELES HARBOR
Longoskayan Pt.
Quinauan Pt.
Canas Pt.
BAGAC
Beach Defenses
Beach Defenses
WAINWRIGHT
PARKER
USAFFE Reserve
RESERVE BATTLE POSITION
MT. SAMAT
San Vicente R.
Mamala R.
Alangan R.
Lamao R.
Binuangan R.
Anyasin R.
Aglaloma R.
MARIVELES MTS
4700
MT. BATAAN
SERVICE COMMAND AREA
Included combat elements of 71
Serv Elms 71
Mar & Navy
USAFFE
MacARTHUR
CORREGIDOR I.
(Ft. Mills)
CABALLO I.
XXX I WAINWRIGHT
XX 1
XX 31
XX 91 (+)
26
XXX II PARKER
XX 11
XX 21
XX 41
XX 51
57 (Phil. Div.)
SERVICE COMMAND
XX 2
XX 71 (-)
Provisional Bn (Navy & Mar)
USAFFE RESERVE
XX Phil (-57)
JAMES RAVINE
ROCK PT
CHENEY RAVINE
NORTH DOCK
MALINTA PT
ENGR. PT
MALINTA HILL
INFANTRY PT
CAVALRY PT
KINDLEY FIELD
NORTH PT
SOUTH DOCK
GEARY PT

PHILIPPINE CAMPAIGN

★

On 5 January—earlier than originally planned—the 48th Division began withdrawing from the Philippines for duty in Java. Homma had some misgivings, but, anticipating slight resistance on Bataan, he gave the mission of reducing that peninsula to Lt. Gen. Akira Nara's recently arrived and poorly trained 65th Brigade (about 6,500 men). Supporting artillery, tanks, and air units, as well as the 9th Infantry Regiment (16th Division), were made available to Nara. He was ordered to make his main effort down the east coast toward Balanga, and a secondary attack from Moron toward Bagac.

Nara advanced against the II Corps on the 9th. He initially employed two regiments—one along the east coast, while the other (the veteran 9th Infantry) moved inland against Parker's left flank, seeking to turn it and drive the defenders against the east coast. A third regiment (the 122d Infantry) moved across the peninsula to attack down the west coast, and the fourth regiment (*not shown*) was positioned in reserve behind the 9th Infantry. North of Abucay, the advance came under heavy artillery fire, whereupon Nara shifted most of the coastal regiment westward into the zone of the 41st Division (PA). On 10 January, the Japanese finally encountered the right of the II Corps' outpost line (*not shown*) and forced it back. For the next four days, savage fighting took place in the zones of the 57th Infantry and 41st Division as Japanese penetrations of the main battle position (*not shown*) were wiped out by counterattacks. During this period, Parker had been forced to commit his corps reserve, the 21st Division (PA). By the 13th, Nara had shifted all except one battalion of his coastal regiment farther inland, where it was exerting pressure against the 51st Division (PA). Meanwhile, his reserve regiment was moving into the sector opposite the 41st Division.

On 15 January, the Japanese attacked vigorously (*top center; red arrow, dated 12–22 January*) along the 41st–51st Division boundary. The 41st held firmly, but Jones' 51st was forced to give ground after committing all its reserve. That night, Parker asked USAFFE for additional troops to bolster the weakened 51st Division. MacArthur had anticipated the request and had already ordered the 31st Division (PA) (from Wainwright's sector) and the Philippine Division to move to Parker's assistance. Pending the arrival of these troops, Parker, over Jones' objections, ordered the 51st Division to counterattack on 16 January. The attack achieved some success initially, but Nara applied overwhelming pressure from three sides—the 9th Infantry was now in line—and suddenly the rightmost regiment of the 51st broke and fled to the rear. The 41st Division refused its left flank and held off the fierce assaults now turned against it. The leftmost regiment of the 51st was ordered to fall back to the southwest into the I Corps' zone. (Some of the men eventually struggled across the mountains to Bagac; others managed to rejoin the division's remnants reforming in the rear.)

In a desperate effort to restore the line, Parker counterattacked piecemeal with the Philippine Division on the 17th, and after five days of vicious fighting had almost recouped his losses; but, on the 22d, heavy artillery and air attacks drove the weary Philippine Division back to its starting point. The 9th Infantry, struggling through the difficult terrain, now threatened the II Corps' left flank, and Parker's position became untenable. On the night of the 22d, he was ordered to withdraw.

Meanwhile, in Wainwright's zone, the 122d Infantry had occupied Grande Island and then moved by water and overland on Moron. It entered this town on 17 January after two days of fighting with elements of the 26th Cavalry and 1st Regular Division (PA). Homma, disconcerted over Nara's slowness, now sent part of the 20th Infantry Regiment from Manila to this sector, attached the 122d Infantry to it, and assigned the command—directly under the Fourteenth Army—to Maj. Gen. Naoki Kimura. On the 19th, Kimura attacked as shown, and two days later had infiltrated the 3d Battalion, 20th Infantry Regiment, through Wainwright's lightly held inner flank to the coastal road. This movement severed the supply line of the 1st Regular Division. When repeated counterattacks failed to dislodge the Japanese, the 1st Regular Division, also under frontal attack, had to withdraw along the narrow coastal flats, abandoning its artillery and vehicles in the process.

By morning, 26 January, both corps were on the Bagac-Orion line, and the Japanese were closing up to continue the attack.

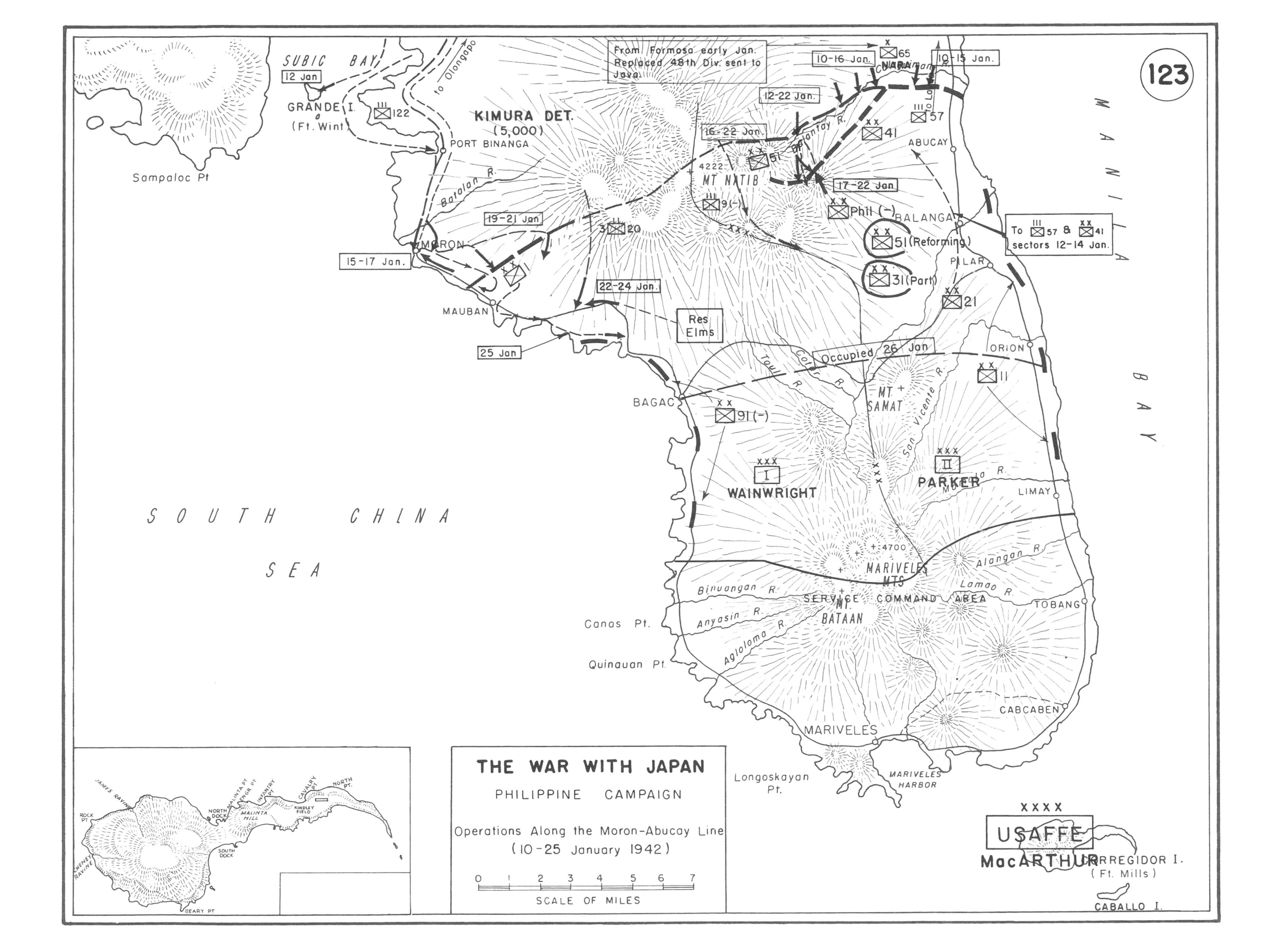
123
THE WAR WITH JAPAN
PHILIPPINE CAMPAIGN
Operations Along the Moron-Abucay Line
(10-25 January 1942)
SCALE OF MILES
0 1 2 3 4 5 6 7
MANILA BAY
SOUTH CHINA SEA
SUBIC BAY
12 Jan
GRANDE I.
(Ft. Wint)
122
to Olongapo
KIMURA DET.
(5,000)
PORT BINANGA
Sampaloc Pt
Batalan R.
MORON
15-17 Jan.
19-21 Jan
MAUBAN
25 Jan
22-24 Jan.
Res Elms
3 20
From Formosa early Jan. Replaced 48th Div. sent to Java.
16-22 Jan.
12-22 Jan.
10-16 Jan.
10-15 Jan.
65
NARA
57
41
51
4222
MT NATIB
9(-)
17-22 Jan
Phil (-)
ABUCAY
BALANGA
51 (Reforming)
31 (Part)
PILAR
21
To 57 & 41 sectors 12-14 Jan.
Occupied 26 Jan
ORION
11
BAGAC
91(-)
MT SAMAT
San Vicente R.
Tiawir R.
Calaguiman R.
Toul R.
Cola R.
I
WAINWRIGHT
II
PARKER
LIMAY
4700
MARIVELES MTS
Alangan R.
Lamao R.
Binuangan R.
SERVICE COMMAND AREA
MT. BATAAN
TOBANG
Canas Pt.
Anyasin R.
Aglaloma R.
Quinauan Pt.
CABCABEN
MARIVELES
Longoskayan Pt.
MARIVELES HARBOR
XXXX
USAFFE
MacARTHUR
CORREGIDOR I.
(Ft. Mills)
CABALLO I.
JAMES RAVINE
ROCK PT
NORTH DOCK
MALINTA PT
ENGR PT
INFANTRY PT
CAVALRY PT
NORTH PT.
MALINTA HILL
KINDLEY FIELD
SOUTH DOCK
CHENEY RAVINE
GEARY PT

PHILIPPINE CAMPAIGN

★

With the arrival of USAFFE troops at the Bagac-Orion line—where MacArthur intended "to fight it out to complete destruction"—the organization of the defense underwent a change. The Service Command was relieved of responsibility for beach defense, each corps absorbing that function in its area. The organization along the main battle position was also modified. Because of the attrition in units and the dearth of qualified officers, defense sectors were established containing a conglomeration of units. Consequently, unit designations became less meaningful as some sectors controlled elements of two divisions. (To avoid confusion, the sectors are not shown; nor are all the units which were disposed along the position.) On 25 January, the Philippine Division was again withdrawn into USAFFE reserve; the division headquarters took over a sector command, and the three regiments were initially positioned as shown—the 31st near Limay, the 45th south of Bagac, and the 57th north of Mariveles.

The new battle position allowed the establishment of a continuous, shorter line across the peninsula. It lacked good lateral communications, but local trails were immediately improved for this purpose. The Mariveles Mountains dominated the position (which ran through dense jungle), and Mt. Samat provided good observation over the entire front. Neither Wainwright nor Parker was able to assemble more than a regiment as a corps reserve. As they desperately shuttled units to fill the gaps created by the withdrawal of the Philippine Division, the Japanese, sensing a quick kill, launched their attack.

Previously (on the night of 22 January), Kimura, hoping to secure his right flank after he took Bagac and turned eastward, had dispatched the 2d Battalion, 20th Infantry, in landing barges to Caibobo Point (*not shown, but five miles below Bagac*). Moving without adequate preparation or suitable maps, the unit suffered losses to a patrolling American PT boat, became dispersed, and landed erroneously at the two points shown. The beach defenses—then manned by Service Command troops, consisting of air corps, naval, marine, and Philippine Constabulary personnel—contained the two forces, but were unable to drive them into the sea. On the 27th, Wainwright secured the release from USAFFE reserve of the 2d Battalion, 57th Infantry (PS), and the 3d Battalion, 45th Infantry (PS). The Longoskayan Point force was quickly eliminated by the former, but at Quinauan Point the latter took heavy casualties and eventually required the support of tanks, Corregidor artillery, and PT boats to complete the task. Meanwhile, Homma had sent the 16th Division commander (Lt. Gen. Susumu Morioka) to western Bataan on the 25th with two additional infantry battalions. Morioka superseded Kimura and at once sent a company to reinforce the Quinauan Point force. Moving out the night of the 26th, it, too, became lost and landed near Canas Point. The air corps unit defending the area was soon reinforced by the 2d Battalion, 45th Infantry (PS), but the Japanese would not be dislodged. Prodded by Homma, Morioka sent the remainder of the 1st Battalion, 20th Infantry, to Quinauan Point on 1 February. Wainwright's troops were waiting and repelled the attempted night landing, but the Japanese turned north and came ashore at Canas Point. The 57th Infantry (PS) now joined the fight, but the tenacious enemy was not eliminated until the 13th, thus concluding the series of engagements known collectively as the "Battle of the Points."

Meanwhile, along the main battle position, the Japanese had attacked in both corps sectors. Nara, continuing to make night assaults, struck Parker's line on 27 January, but he made only slight progress in five days. On 2–3 February, Parker struck back and restored his line. To the west, Japanese attacks were unavailing except along the Toul River. Wainwright eventually blocked this penetration, split it into three pockets (*not shown*), and by 15 February had reduced them.

The last week of this "Battle of the Pockets" was fought with the Japanese withdrawing under orders from Homma, who had ruefully accepted the fact, on 8 February, that he was too weak to crack the USAFFE line. The Japanese moved back to more defensible terrain, and Homma asked Tokyo for reinforcements. Some of Homma's units had literally ceased to exist; by his own estimate, he had only three effective infantry battalions.

The morale of the USAFFE troops was high. But already the effects of short rations and general shortage of all supplies were being felt.

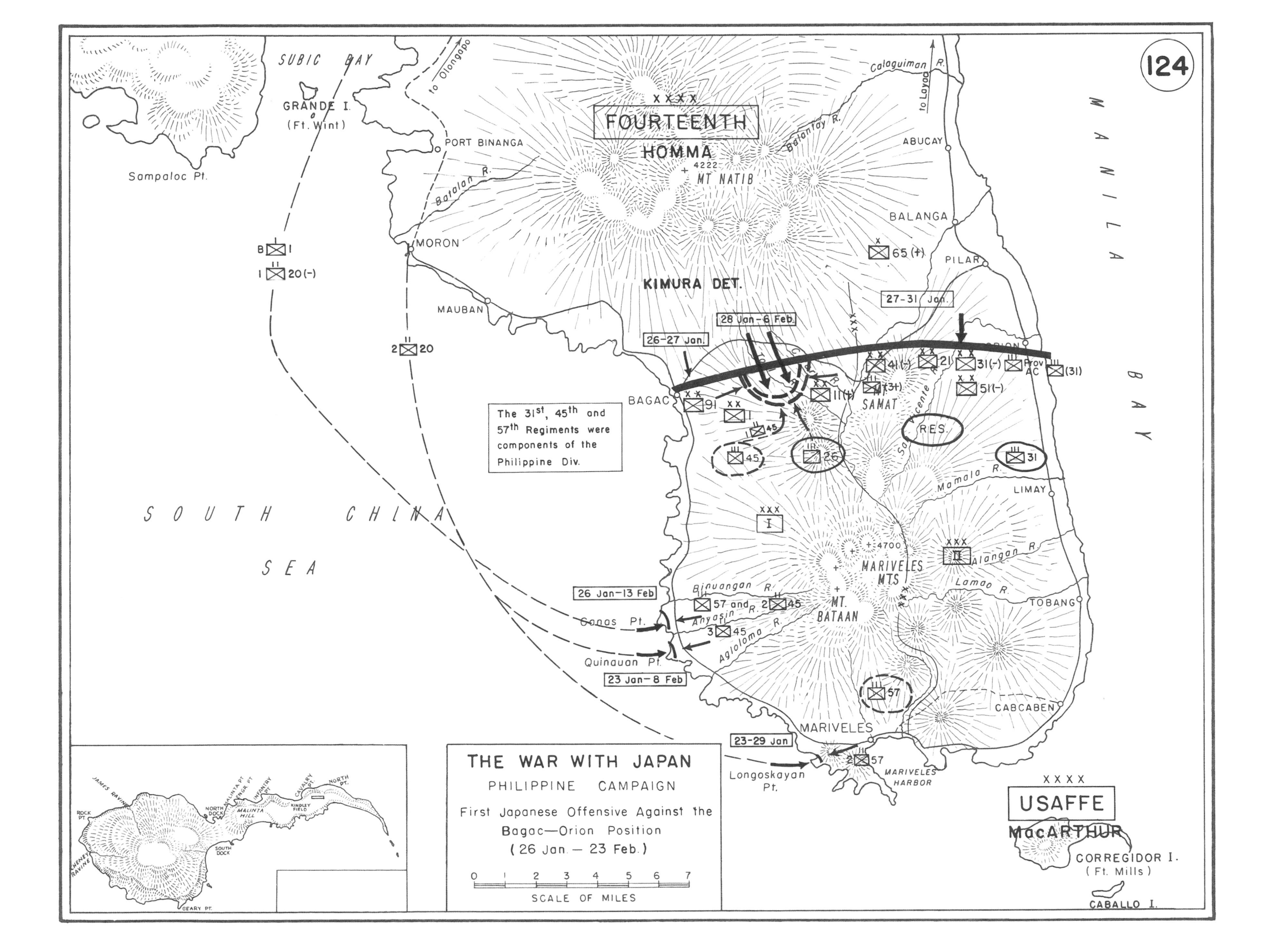
124
FOURTEENTH
HOMMA
KIMURA DET.
MT NATIB
4222
SUBIC BAY
GRANDE I.
(Ft. Wint)
Sampaloc Pt.
PORT BINANGA
MORON
MAUBAN
BAGAC
to Olongapo
Batalan R.
Balantay R.
Calaguiman R.
to Layac
ABUCAY
BALANGA
PILAR
ORION
LIMAY
TOBANG
CABCABEN
MARIVELES
MANILA BAY
SOUTH CHINA SEA
26-27 Jan.
28 Jan-6 Feb.
27-31 Jan.
26 Jan-13 Feb
23 Jan-8 Feb
23-29 Jan
The 31st, 45th and 57th Regiments were components of the Philippine Div.
MT. SAMAT
RES.
MARIVELES MTS.
4700
MT. BATAAN
Mamala R.
Alangan R.
Lamao R.
Binuangan R.
Anyasin R.
Agloloma R.
Canas Pt.
Quinauan Pt.
Longoskayan Pt.
MARIVELES HARBOR
USAFFE
MacARTHUR
CORREGIDOR I.
(Ft. Mills)
CABALLO I.
THE WAR WITH JAPAN
PHILIPPINE CAMPAIGN
First Japanese Offensive Against the Bagac—Orion Position
(26 Jan. — 23 Feb.)
SCALE OF MILES
JAMES RAVINE
ROCK PT.
NORTH DOCK
SOUTH DOCK
MALINTA HILL
KINDLEY FIELD
NORTH PT.
GEARY PT.

PHILIPPINE CAMPAIGN

Upon the suspension of Homma's offensive on 8 February, MacArthur's forces settled down to the dreary existence of a besieged army. Positions were improved, and concerted efforts were made to improve the state of training of the Philippine Army troops. Patrols ranged far to the north, and some of the more optimistic officers even advocated launching a counteroffensive to regain the Abucay-Mauban line. All the while, the fighting efficiency of the troops continued to ebb as malnutrition set in. (On 6 January, the ration had been cut in half—to thirty ounces per man—and by 1 April it had been halved again.) Also, as medical supplies dwindled, dreaded diseases (malaria, dengue, dysentery, and beriberi) made greater inroads; sanitation standards dropped; convalescent periods lengthened; and, significantly, nerve fatigue—in the absence of rest areas—became more serious.

Meanwhile, attempts to supply the beleaguered garrison met with dismal failure. Only three ships pierced the tightening Japanese blockade, and only a fraction of their cargo ever reached Manila Bay. Attempts to use aircraft and submarines were equally disappointing.

As early as February, Washington had concluded that, though every effort to sustain them would be made, the USAFFE garrison was doomed. Accordingly, MacArthur, whose talents the United States could ill afford to sacrifice, was queried concerning his evacuation. He declared his intent to remain to the last, but on 23 February President Roosevelt ordered him to Australia to assume command of Allied forces in the Southwest Pacific. Therefore, on the night of 12 March, MacArthur, accompanied by his family and some of his staff, left Corregidor via PT boats, transferring at Mindanao to B-17's for the last leg of the journey. Just before departing, MacArthur reorganized his forces into four commands (Mindanao, Visayas, Harbor Defenses, and Luzon Force), all to be responsible to him in Australia through an advance headquarters on Corregidor. Wainwright assumed command of the Luzon Force. But Marshall knew nothing of these arrangements and designated Wainwright as commander of United States Forces in the Philippines (USFIP). After considerable embarrassment—and an explanation to MacArthur—Wainwright assumed that command on 20 March, and appointed Maj. Gen. Edward P. King to command the Luzon Force.

In the interim, Homma had refitted his exhausted army, absorbed the reinforcements shown, and prepared for an estimated hard, four-week offensive. In mid-March, Japanese air and artillery bombardments began to increase in intensity. Late on 3 April, after the most devastating air-artillery bombardment of the campaign, Homma savagely struck the 41st Division (PA) in three places. There was little resistance; the bombardment alone had caused the division to break and flee to the rear. The Japanese, overestimating King's strength, halted that night on the line shown. On the 4th and 5th, the attack rolled onward as Parker desperately sought to hold his left flank. On the 6th, King counterattacked with all available reserves, but the Japanese brushed aside the opening thrusts and surged southeastward. By now, many of the II Corps' troops had been overrun and captured; King's only alternative was to withdraw. On the left, the I Corps, under less pressure, began to pull back the night of the 8th, by which time the II Corps' remnants were well to the south. That night, King—under orders to attack—decided that his position was hopeless and that further resistance would mean total annihilation. The next day, he surrendered the Luzon Force, which then began the infamous "Death March" to Camp O'Donnell (*see map 121, upper left*).

Homma, angered that the surrender had not included all troops in the Philippines, turned to Corregidor. The island forts (*lower left*) had been under sporadic air and artillery attack since early February, but now they received the concentrated fire of all the Japanese heavy artillery and aircraft. By early May, Corregidor's defenders were dazed from the continuous bombardment, and their water supply was critically short. On the night of 5 May, the Japanese managed to land one battalion as shown (*this map, inset*) and soon reinforced it with another. Their plan to land a larger force near James Ravine the next night, though implemented, proved unnecessary, for by noon on 6 May, Wainwright had initiated negotiations to surrender the island forts.

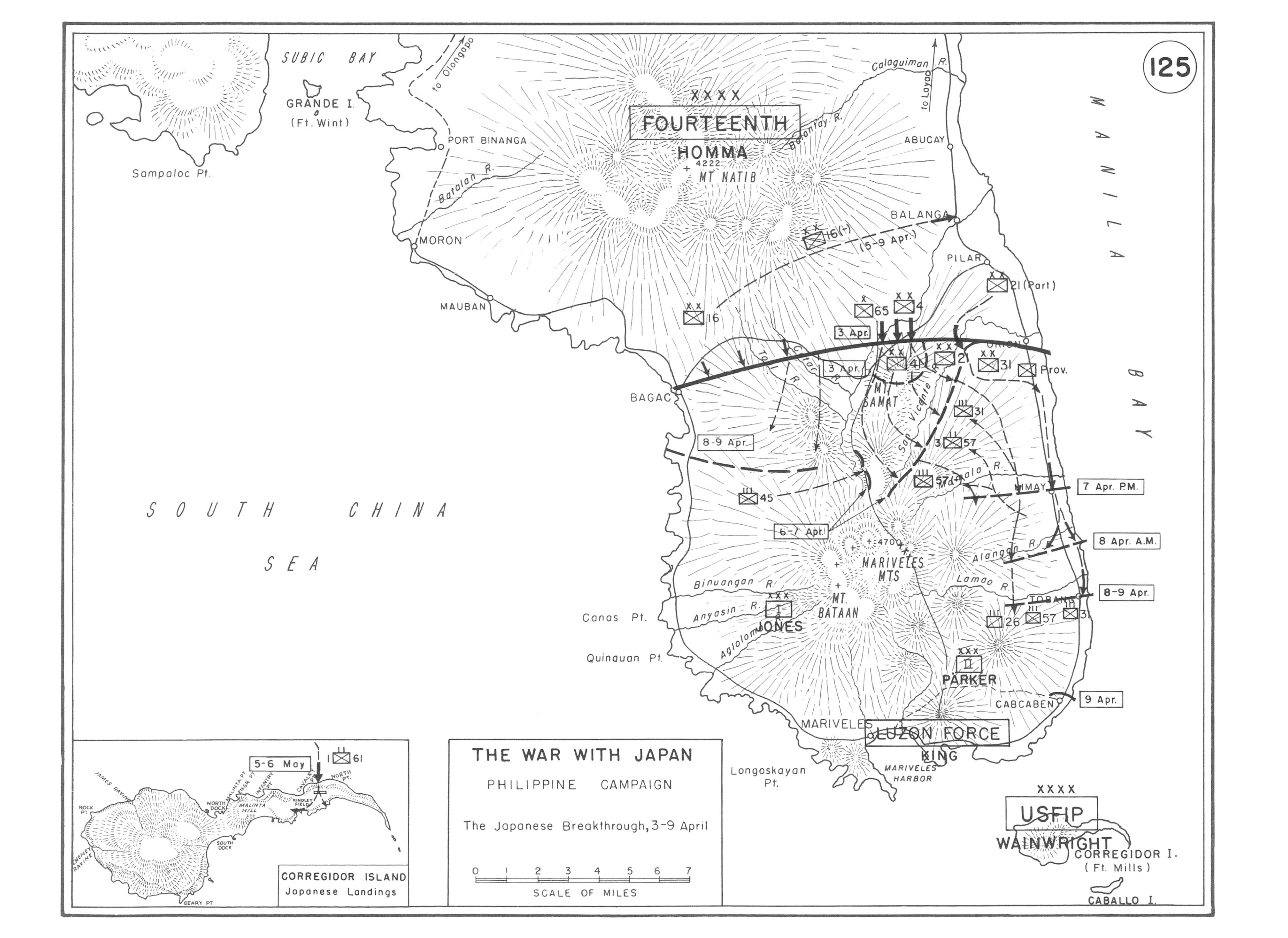
125
THE WAR WITH JAPAN
PHILIPPINE CAMPAIGN
The Japanese Breakthrough, 3-9 April
0 1 2 3 4 5 6 7
SCALE OF MILES
CORREGIDOR ISLAND
Japanese Landings
5-6 May
61
FOURTEENTH
HOMMA
4222
MT NATIB
USFIP
WAINWRIGHT
LUZON FORCE
KING
PARKER
JONES
MANILA BAY
SUBIC BAY
SOUTH CHINA SEA
GRANDE I.
(Ft. Wint)
Sampaloc Pt.
PORT BINANGA
to Olongapo
Batalan R.
MORON
MAUBAN
BAGAC
Calaguiman R.
to Layac
Balantay R.
ABUCAY
BALANGA
PILAR
ORION
LIMAY
CABCABEN
MARIVELES
MARIVELES HARBOR
Longoskayan Pt.
Canas Pt.
Quinauan Pt.
MT. SAMAT
MARIVELES MTS
MT. BATAAN
4700
Binuangan R.
Anyasin R.
Aglaloma R.
Alangan R.
Lamao R.
Mamala R.
San Vicente R.
Tiawir R.
Catmon R.
CORREGIDOR I.
(Ft. Mills)
CABALLO I.
3 Apr.
3 Apr.
5-9 Apr.
6-7 Apr.
7 Apr. P.M.
8 Apr. A.M.
8-9 Apr.
8-9 Apr.
9 Apr.
16
16(-)
65
4
21 (Part)
21
31
Prov.
41
57
45
26
3
JAMES RAVINE
ROCK PT.
CHENEY RAVINE
NORTH DOCK
SOUTH DOCK
MALINTA HILL
MALINTA PT.
INFANTRY PT.
CAVALRY PT.
KINDLEY FIELD
NORTH PT.
GEARY PT.

JAPANESE LANDING OPERATIONS

This map generally sums up Japanese landings in Southeast Asia and the Philippines in implementation of the first phase of the master war plan. In support of operations in Burma (*see text, map 127*), additional troops were landed near Rangoon (*this map, top left*) in April. The landings at Sarawak in British Borneo (*center*) were made by a brigade-size force principally to gain control of oil fields and to facilitate the coming attacks on Java and Sumatra.

It will be recalled (*see text, map 119*) that the Japanese had landed a reinforced battalion at Davao, on Mindanao, on 20 December. Philippine Army troops offered only slight resistance before withdrawing into the hills. This Miura Detachment was reinforced by a regiment, which moved on to seize Job Island on Christmas Eve. Very cheaply, the Japanese had gained air and naval bases from which to support operations against Dutch Borneo.

Brig. Gen. William F. Sharp's Visayan-Mindanao Force was responsible for the defense of all the Philippines except Luzon. (The islands between Luzon and Mindanao are known as the Visayas.) When war broke out, his command (elements of three Philippine Army divisions, a Philippine Scout regiment, and miscellaneous units) was in the same—if not a worse—state of unpreparedness as the troops on Luzon (*this map*). In view of his weakness and dispersion, Sharp's mission was to oppose the Japanese as long as practicable and then retire to the hills and conduct guerrilla operations.

In late December, MacArthur, concerned over the defense of the important Del Monte airfields, ordered Sharp to concentrate the bulk of his troops on Mindanao. Then—just before leaving Corregidor—he made Sharp responsible for Mindanao only, and created the Visayan Force (Brig. Gen. Bradford G. Chynoweth) to control the Cebu, Panay, Negros, Leyte, and Samar garrisons. Sharp, commanding a larger force, made plans to fight vigorously any landings, while Chynoweth's garrisons realistically stocked supplies in mountain hideouts in preparation for guerrilla warfare.

When Homma received reinforcements in March after his Bataan campaign had stalled, he sent two brigade-size forces to subjugate the southern islands, On 10 April, one detachment landed on Cebu and in three days established control over the island; similarly, Panay was invaded on 16 April and subjugated in four days by the other detachment. Both island garrisons, after taking moderate losses, had fallen back to their mountain retreats. Homma then sent the two detachments to Mindanao, where they landed on 29 April and 3 May. Assisted by Miura's detachment, they quickly routed Sharp's forces and forced them into the mountains. (A small Japanese force had occupied Zamboanga on 2 March to establish a seaplane base.) On 10 May, Sharp was given a message carried by one of Wainwright's staff officers (flown by the Japanese from Manila) directing that he surrender his force—or the 11,000 captives on Corregidor would suffer the consequences.

Just before Wainwright surrendered, on 6 May, he had released Sharp from his command, but Homma would not deal with him unless he surrendered all troops in the Philippines. Thus, Wainwright was forced to surrender Corregidor to the local Japanese commander, and then—fearing reprisals against his erstwhile garrison—he reassumed command over Sharp and agreed to surrender the latter's forces as well. Sharp, who had been ordered by MacArthur in the interim to ignore any orders from Wainwright, now had a difficult choice. He elected to surrender and was then compelled to do exactly what Wainwright had done: reassume command over the Visayan garrisons he had released, and order their surrender. Several of Chynoweth's commanders balked, the Japanese having occupied only two of the Visayas, but they all ultimately surrendered; many of their troops simply melted into the hills, some to operate as guerrillas, but most to return to their homes.

For General Homma, victory in the Philippines had been hollow; he was soon relieved of command and ordered to Tokyo. For Wainwright, there would be no victories until 1945, when, gaunt and sickly, he would return to Luzon to witness the surrender of the Japanese at Baguio. But he could take solace in the knowledge that his troops had proved to a Western world awed by Japanese victories that the Japanese were not invincible.

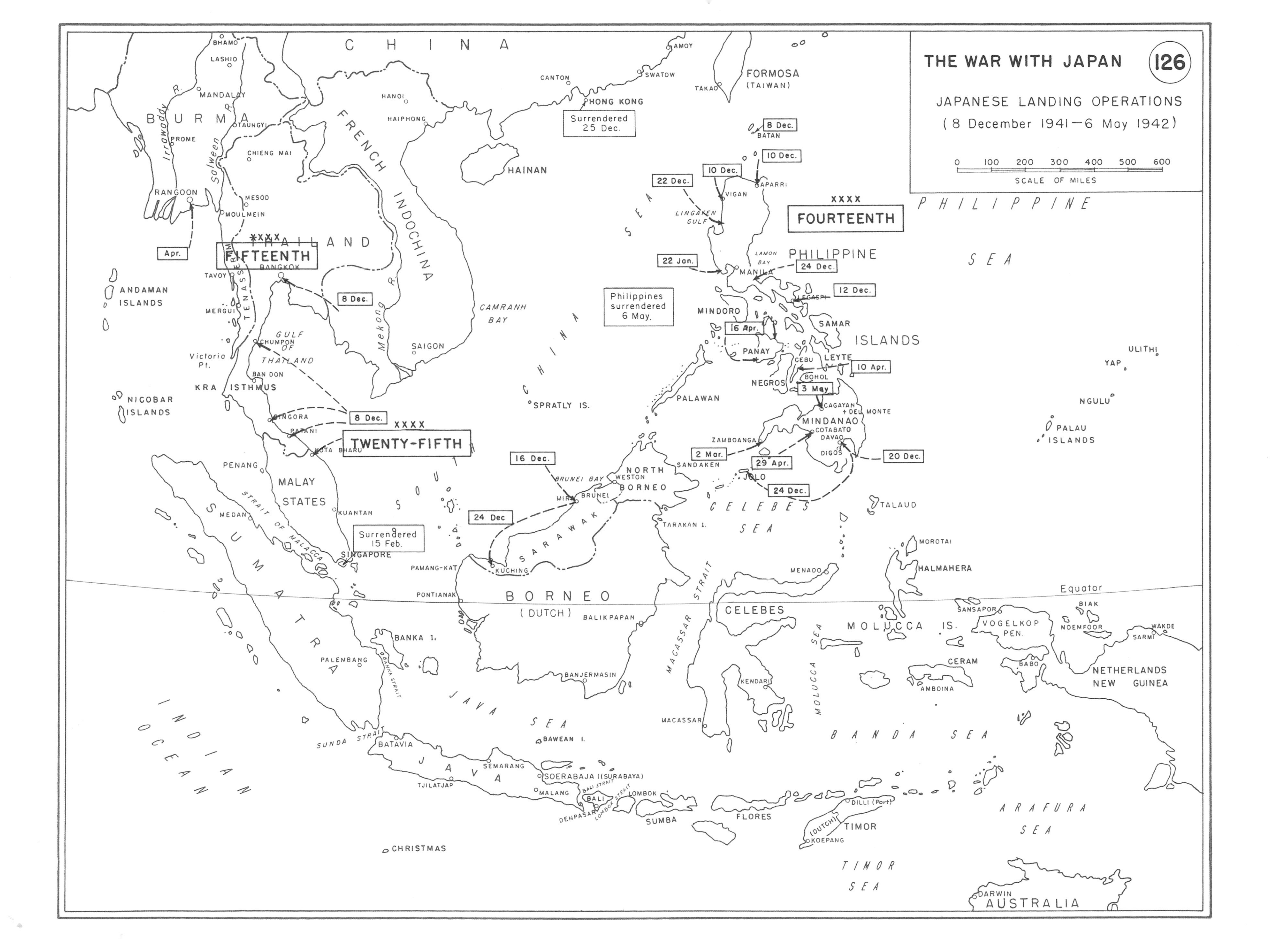
THE WAR WITH JAPAN
126
JAPANESE LANDING OPERATIONS
(8 December 1941—6 May 1942)
0 100 200 300 400 500 600
SCALE OF MILES
CHINA
FORMOSA (TAIWAN)
TAKAO
AMOY
SWATOW
CANTON
HONG KONG
Surrendered 25 Dec.
HAINAN
HANOI
HAIPHONG
FRENCH INDOCHINA
SAIGON
CAMRANH BAY
BURMA
BHAMO
LASHIO
MANDALAY
TAUNGYI
PROME
RANGOON
Irrawaddy R.
Salween R.
Apr.
CHIENG MAI
MESOD
MOULMEIN
THAILAND
XXXX
FIFTEENTH
BANGKOK
8 Dec.
Mekong R.
TAVOY
MERGUI
TENASSERIM
Victoria Pt.
KRA ISTHMUS
GULF OF THAILAND
CHUMPON
BAN DON
ANDAMAN ISLANDS
NICOBAR ISLANDS
8 Dec.
SINGORA
PATANI
KOTA BHARU
XXXX
TWENTY-FIFTH
PENANG
MALAY STATES
KUANTAN
Surrendered 15 Feb.
SINGAPORE
STRAIT OF MALACCA
MEDAN
SUMATRA
PALEMBANG
BANKA I.
BANKA STRAIT
SUNDA STRAIT
BATAVIA
JAVA
TJILATJAP
SEMARANG
SOERABAJA (SURABAYA)
MALANG
BALI STRAIT
BALI
DENPASAR
LOMBOK STRAIT
LOMBOK
SUMBA
FLORES
TIMOR
(DUTCH)
KOEPANG
DILLI (Port)
TIMOR SEA
CHRISTMAS
INDIAN OCEAN
JAVA SEA
BAWEAN I.
SOUTH CHINA SEA
SPRATLY IS.
Philippines surrendered 6 May.
PALAWAN
16 Dec.
BRUNEI BAY
WESTON
BRUNEI
MIRI
NORTH BORNEO
SARAWAK
24 Dec
KUCHING
PAMANG-KAT
PONTIANAK
BORNEO (DUTCH)
BALIKPAPAN
BANJERMASIN
SANDAKEN
TARAKAN I.
MACASSAR STRAIT
MACASSAR
CELEBES
KENDARI
MENADO
CELEBES SEA
MOLUCCA SEA
TALAUD
MOROTAI
HALMAHERA
Equator
MOLUCCA IS.
SANSAPOR
VOGELKOP PEN.
BIAK
NOEMFOOR
SARMI
WAKDE
NETHERLANDS NEW GUINEA
BABO
CERAM
AMBOINA
BANDA SEA
ARAFURA SEA
DARWIN
AUSTRALIA
8 Dec.
BATAN
10 Dec.
APARRI
10 Dec.
VIGAN
22 Dec.
LINGAYEN GULF
22 Jan.
LAMON BAY
MANILA
24 Dec.
XXXX
FOURTEENTH
PHILIPPINE ISLANDS
PHILIPPINE SEA
12 Dec.
LEGASPI
MINDORO
16 Apr.
SAMAR
PANAY
CEBU
LEYTE
10 Apr.
NEGROS
BOHOL
3 May
CAGAYAN
DEL MONTE
MINDANAO
COTABATO
DAVAO
DIGOS
ZAMBOANGA
2 Mar.
29 Apr.
JOLO
24 Dec.
20 Dec.
ULITHI
YAP
NGULU
PALAU ISLANDS

INVASION OF BURMA

★

Burma, as the Japanese saw it, was a natural fortress, ideally situated to guard the western flank of their new empire—and rich in rice and oil.

Burma is a country of alternating north-south mountain ranges and river valleys. In 1942, it was a curiously isolated land; only a few hill trails connected it with India and Thailand, and practically all commerce with the outside world took place through Rangoon (*bottom center*). Beleaguered China also depended on that port for the American Lend-Lease supplies that reached her via the Burma Road (*upper right*). Military operations were almost impossible from mid-May to late September because of the monsoon rains; malaria was endemic; and the jungle which covered much of the country reduced the effectiveness of air power and motor transport.

The forces initially available for the defense of Burma—largely Burmese and Indian troops—were only partially trained and almost without artillery, signal equipment, and antiaircraft weapons. Air support was scant; most of the airfields lay in the exposed Tenasserim area (*bottom center*), but had to be held as long as possible in order to refuel planes bound to Singapore.

The Japanese Fifteenth Army, which had recently occupied Thailand, had the initial missions of seizing the Tenasserim airfields and of protecting the right rear of the Japanese forces invading Malaya. Once the Malayan operations were proceeding satisfactorily, it would advance through Moulmein (*bottom center*) to take Rangoon. Japanese air raids on Rangoon began 23 December, doing little actual damage, but slowing port operations by panicking the longshoremen.

During December, the Japanese occupied the Tenasserim airfields, thereby extending the range of their supporting air units. In January, they advanced on Rangoon. Hoping to gain time for reinforcements to reach Burma, Wavell directed that the British make their first stand as far east as possible. Their forces, however, were too weak and too roadbound. Equipped and trained for jungle fighting, the Japanese would fix the British by frontal attacks while pushing flanking columns across country to get into their rear and organize road blocks across their communications. (The Chinese Communists used the same tactics effectively against American troops eight years later in Korea.) Forced back through Moulmein, across the Salween River, and out of Bilin, the British were almost cut off at the Sittang River bridge, escaping only with heavy losses. Reinforcements, including an armored brigade, hardly made good the wastage. Alexander replaced Lt. Gen. T. J. Hutton as Allied commander in Burma; Rangoon was evacuated on 7 March.

By prior arrangement, Generalissimo Chiang Kai-Shek sent the Chinese Fifth and Sixth Armies into Burma under the nominal command of Maj. Gen. Joseph Stilwell, his American chief of staff, and concentrated the Sixty-Sixth Army on the border as a reserve. Thus reinforced, Alexander hoped to hold the line Prome-Toungoo (*lower center*), but on 21 March the Japanese drove the Chinese 200th Division out of the latter city, seizing the key bridge over the Sittang River there. Also on the 21st, Japanese air raids overwhelmed the few remaining British and American air units, then concentrated at Magwe (*lower center*). In early April, a strong Japanese naval force seized control in the Indian Ocean, and two more Japanese divisions—reinforced by two tank regiments—were put ashore at Rangoon.

Despite the gradual arrival of the Chinese Sixty-Sixth Army, the Allied position grew steadily more desperate. The Burmese civil government began collapsing; Burmese troops began to desert. Then, in late April, the Japanese routed the Chinese Sixth Army near Loikow, chasing it into China and capturing Lashio (*center*) on the 29th. By exhausting marches and hard fighting (and timely help by the Sixty-Sixth Army's leading division), Alexander finally extricated most of the Allied forces through Mandalay, finally evacuating that town on the 30th. He then led the surviving British troops through the Chin Hills to Imphal (*center, left*). Stilwell led a party out farther north through Homalin; most of the Chinese Fifth Army retreated through Ledo (*top center*). The Sixty-Sixth Army retired into China. Burma was lost. Said Stilwell: ". . . we got a hell of a beating."

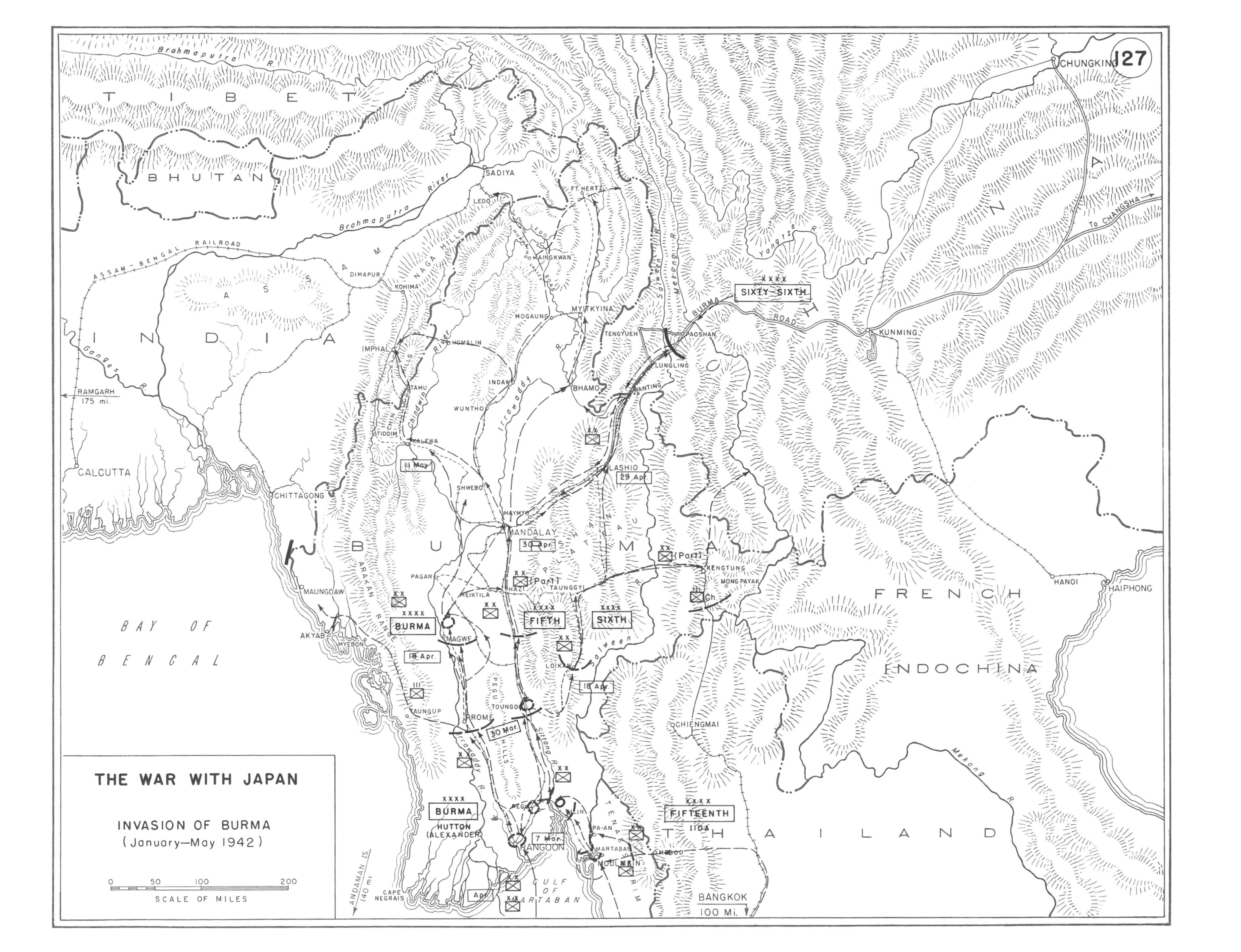
127
THE WAR WITH JAPAN
INVASION OF BURMA
(January—May 1942)
SCALE OF MILES
0
50
100
200
TIBET
BHUTAN
INDIA
ASSAM
BURMA
CHINA
FRENCH INDOCHINA
THAILAND
BAY OF BENGAL
GULF OF MARTABAN
Brahmaputra R.
Brahmaputra River
Ganges R.
Irrawaddy R.
Chindwin River
Salween R.
Mekong R.
Yangtze R.
Sittang R.
ASSAM-BENGAL RAILROAD
BURMA ROAD
LEDO ROAD
HUKAWNG VALLEY ROAD
NAGA HILLS
CHIN HILLS
ARAKAN RANGE
PEGU HILLS
SHAN PLATEAU
TENASSERIM
RAMGARH 175 mi.
CALCUTTA
CHITTAGONG
SADIYA
LEDO
DIMAPUR
KOHIMA
IMPHAL
TAMU
TIDDIM
KALEWA
HOMALIN
MAINGKWAN
FT. HERTZ
MOGAUNG
MYITKYINA
INDAW
WUNTHO
SHWEBO
BHAMO
TENGYUEH
PAOSHAN
LUNGLING
WANTING
LASHIO
29 Apr.
MAYMYO
MANDALAY
30 Apr.
PAGAN
MEIKTILA
THAZI
TAUNGGYI
KENGTUNG
MONG PAYAK
LOIKAW
18 Apr.
MAGWE
18 Apr.
MAUNGDAW
AKYAB
MYEBON
TAUNGUP
PROME
30 Mar.
TOUNGOO
CHIENGMAI
PEGU
RANGOON
7 Mar.
BILIN
PA-AN
MARTABAN
MOULMEIN
MESOD
BANGKOK 100 Mi.
CAPE NEGRAIS
ANDAMAN IS. 140 mi
11 May
Apr.
KUNMING
CHUNGKING
To CHANGSHA
HANOI
HAIPHONG
XXXX SIXTY-SIXTH
XXXX FIFTH
XXXX SIXTH
XXXX BURMA
XXXX BURMA HUTTON (ALEXANDER)
XXXX FIFTEENTH IIDA
XX (Part)
Ch

OPERATIONS IN THE NETHERLANDS EAST INDIES

★

The Netherlands East Indies—rich in oil, rubber, and other strategic materials—were to be the treasure house of Japan's Greater East Asia Co-Prosperity Sphere. Once the Japanese had cleared their flanks by seizing Malaya and the Philippines, and crippling the United States Pacific Fleet at Pearl Harbor, the East Indies were their major objective.

The vast expanse of the East Indies, the great number of their islands, and the lack of good roads on most of the larger islands, made their defense extremely difficult. The Dutch had built an excellent system of airfields throughout the East Indies, but since the Allies had only a handful of planes, mostly obsolete, these airfields could not be exploited, except by the Japanese. In an area where communication was normally by water, the Allies had only a small, hastily assembled fleet of light Dutch, American, and British warships. Available ground forces were chiefly Dutch (most of them native troops, armed and trained for internal security duties); the strongest concentration was on Java (*lower left*), but large numbers of troops were scattered on garrison duty at major ports throughout the East Indies. The Dutch had not endeared themselves to their native subjects; only in the Amboina (*lower right*) area was the population loyal.

The East Indies had been placed under the improvised joint American-British-Dutch-Australian Command (ABDACOM). General Wavell received the unenviable task of commanding it. ABDACOM's creation, however, did not produce a unified Allied strategy, for the British were concerned with Singapore, the Americans with the Philippines, and the Dutch and Australians with self-defense.

The Japanese invasion built up swiftly. In December, with Luzon still unconquered, they had developed bases at Job, Brunei (*both center*), and Davao (*center, right*). At least two naval task forces were formed for the invasion (Central Force may have been a subdivision of Eastern Force); the Sixteenth Army provided the necessary troops. The Carrier Striking Force would assist Eastern Force in cutting ABDACOM's communications with Australia.

Japanese tactics were both aggressive and cautious. Selecting an objective—usually a seaport with an adjoining airfield—the Japanese concentrated their land-based aircraft and wiped out Allied air units stationed there. That accomplished, a naval task force (always including aircraft carriers) landed sufficient marines or troops to overwhelm the local Allied ground forces. The captured airfield was made operational; land-based planes were leapfrogged forward, and the cycle was repeated. Japanese naval task forces seldom moved beyond the combat range of their supporting land-based planes. At Menado (*center, right*) and other critical objectives, small naval paratroop units were employed. Meanwhile, major Allied bases, such as Soerabaja (*bottom center*), were kept under constant air attack. Allied air reconnaissance was smothered; consequently, Allied naval forces operated blindly, and Allied ground forces had little warning of impending attacks. This combination of mass and mobility was more than the isolated Allied garrisons of the outlying islands could withstand; their piecemeal destruction rapidly reduced Allied air and ground strength. Single Allied ships were quickly picked off by the superior Japanese air and naval forces.

Japanese operations proceeded as shown, without a check. At Balikpapan (*lower center*), American destroyers surprised a Japanese convoy, sinking five ships, but did not delay the Japanese a single day. An attack on a convoy in Lombok Strait (*bottom center*) was unsuccessful. The Japanese Carrier Striking Force wrecked the growing Allied base at Darwin (*bottom right*); the capture of Timor and Bali (*bottom center*) enabled the Japanese to control the sea route from Australia to Java. Realizing that the situation was hopeless, Wavell left Java on 25 February. ABDACOM collapsed; British and American forces began evacuating. As the Japanese Eastern and Western Forces converged on Java, Dutch Rear Admiral K. W. F. M. Doorman took his worn-down Allied fleet out to meet them, but was overwhelmed in the Battle of the Java Sea. The Japanese then swarmed ashore on Java, forcing a Dutch capitulation on 9 March. A Japanese wedge had been driven between the British in the Indian Ocean and the American forces in the Pacific.

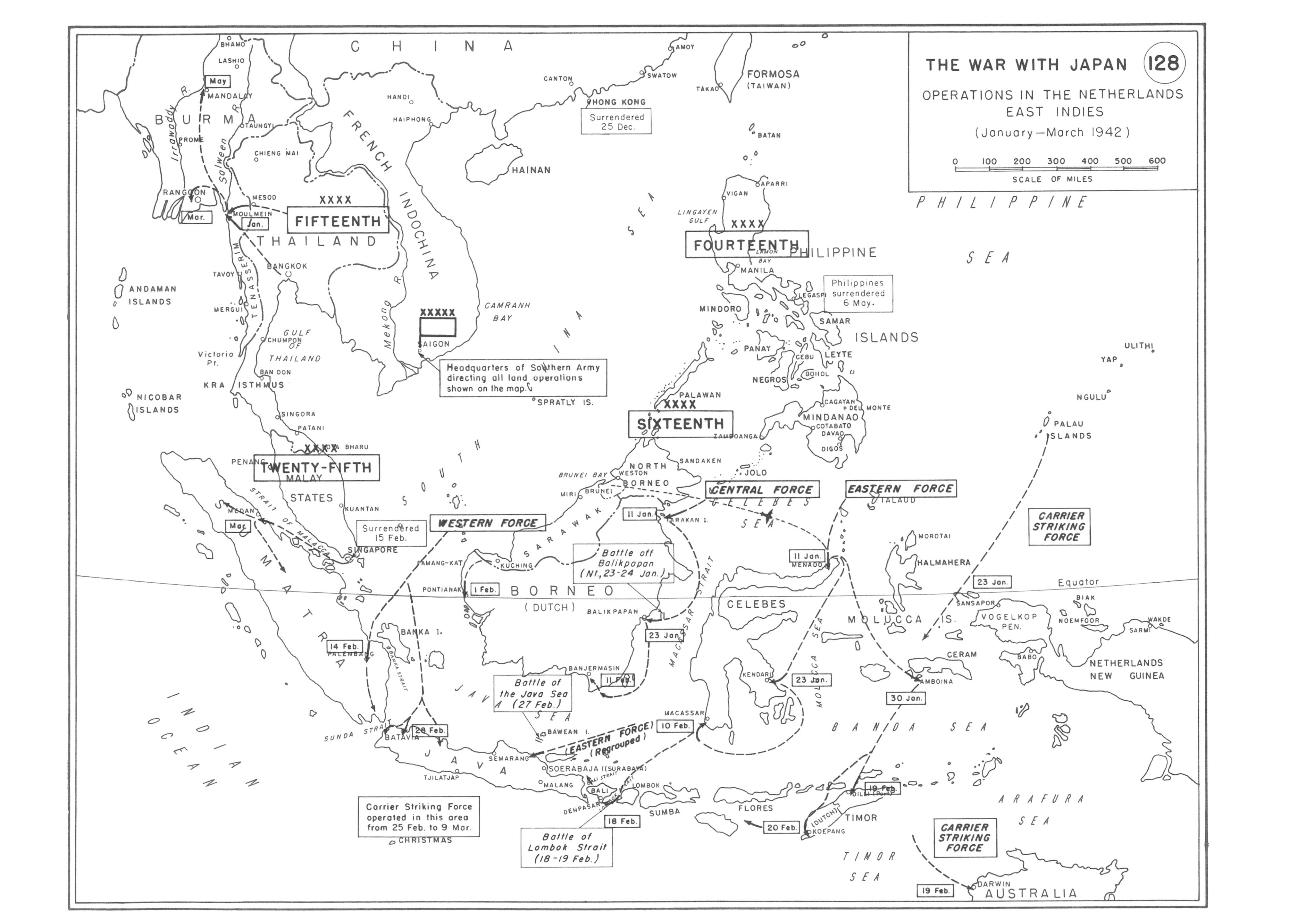

THE WAR WITH JAPAN
128
OPERATIONS IN THE NETHERLANDS EAST INDIES
(January—March 1942)
0 100 200 300 400 500 600
SCALE OF MILES
CHINA
BURMA
THAILAND
FRENCH INDOCHINA
FORMOSA (TAIWAN)
HAINAN
PHILIPPINE SEA
PHILIPPINE ISLANDS
SOUTH CHINA SEA
INDIAN OCEAN
JAVA SEA
BANDA SEA
ARAFURA SEA
TIMOR SEA
CELEBES SEA
MOLUCCA SEA
MACASSAR STRAIT
SUNDA STRAIT
BANKA STRAIT
STRAIT OF MALACCA
BALI STRAIT
LOMBOK STRAIT
GULF OF THAILAND
Surrendered 25 Dec.
Philippines surrendered 6 May.
Surrendered 15 Feb.
Headquarters of Southern Army directing all land operations shown on the map.
FIFTEENTH
FOURTEENTH
SIXTEENTH
TWENTY-FIFTH
XXXX
XXXXX
WESTERN FORCE
CENTRAL FORCE
EASTERN FORCE
EASTERN FORCE (Regrouped)
CARRIER STRIKING FORCE
Battle off Balikpapan (Nt., 23-24 Jan.)
Battle of the Java Sea (27 Feb.)
Battle of Lombok Strait (18-19 Feb.)
Carrier Striking Force operated in this area from 25 Feb. to 9 Mar.
May
Mar.
Jan.
11 Jan.
23 Jan.
30 Jan.
1 Feb.
10 Feb.
11 Feb.
14 Feb.
18 Feb.
19 Feb.
20 Feb.
28 Feb.
Equator
BHAMO
LASHIO
MANDALAY
TAUNGYI
PROME
RANGOON
MOULMEIN
MESOD
CHIENG MAI
TAVOY
MERGUI
TENASSERIM
BANGKOK
Victoria Pt.
KRA ISTHMUS
CHUMPON
BAN DON
SINGORA
PATANI
KOTA BHARU
PENANG
MALAY STATES
KUANTAN
SINGAPORE
ANDAMAN ISLANDS
NICOBAR ISLANDS
Irrawaddy R.
Salween R.
Mekong R.
HANOI
HAIPHONG
CAMRANH BAY
SAIGON
SPRATLY IS.
CANTON
HONG KONG
SWATOW
AMOY
TAKAO
BATAN
APARRI
VIGAN
LINGAYEN GULF
LAMON BAY
MANILA
MINDORO
LEGASPI
SAMAR
PANAY
CEBU
LEYTE
NEGROS
BOHOL
PALAWAN
CAGAYAN
DEL MONTE
MINDANAO
COTABATO
DAVAO
DIGOS
ZAMBOANGA
JOLO
SANDAKEN
NORTH BORNEO
BRUNEI BAY
WESTON
BRUNEI
MIRI
SARAWAK
KUCHING
PAMANG-KAT
PONTIANAK
BORNEO (DUTCH)
TARAKAN I.
BALIKPAPAN
BANJERMASIN
SUMATRA
MEDAN
PALEMBANG
BANKA I.
BATAVIA
TJILATJAP
JAVA
SEMARANG
SOERABAJA (SURABAYA)
MALANG
BAWEAN I.
BALI
DENPASAR
LOMBOK
SUMBA
FLORES
TIMOR
DILI (Port.)
(DUTCH)
KOEPANG
CHRISTMAS
MACASSAR
KENDARI
CELEBES
MENADO
TALAUD
MOROTAI
HALMAHERA
MOLUCCA IS.
SANSAPOR
CERAM
AMBOINA
VOGELKOP PEN.
BABO
BIAK
NOEMFOOR
WAKDE
SARMI
NETHERLANDS NEW GUINEA
PALAU ISLANDS
NGULU
YAP
ULITHI
DARWIN
AUSTRALIA

OPERATIONS IN SOUTH AND SOUTHWEST PACIFIC

★

As the Japanese invasion relentlessly crushed the hopelessly gallant Allied defense of the Netherlands East Indies, other Japanese task forces fanned out to seize the strategic island chains that were to form the defensive perimeter about their rich conquests.

As one part of this operation, the Japanese Fourth Fleet steamed south in late January to seize Rabaul (*center*) and Kavieng. Most of the available Australian forces (the territory shown here was under Australian jurisdiction) had been sent to Singapore and the East Indies; the few soldiers and planes remaining did what they could, and were overwhelmed. Rabaul had one of the finest natural harbors in the Pacific and ample terrain suitable for airfields. The Japanese rapidly developed it into a major advanced base.

From Rabaul, they continued their methodical, leapfrog advance as shown, constructing airfields as they moved southward, island by island. During the first part of 1942, the Japanese planners decided to extend their planned perimeter (*see map 113*) to include Port Moresby (*this map, lower left*), since air bases in that area would enable them to dominate northeastern Australia. A bold move in February or March would undoubtedly have overrun it with ease, but the Japanese preferred to carry their protective umbrella of land-based air power with them at all times. While they slowly chopped out their jungle airstrips, the Allies rallied.

These new Japanese conquests were incomplete in another sense. The Australians had forehandedly organized a special intelligence agency known as the Coastwatching Service. Picked men, most of them long-time residents of these islands, remained behind as the Australian forces withdrew. They were equipped with two-way radios; usually, the natives aided them. Their radioed warnings were invaluable to the scanty Allied forces. As a sideline, they rescued shot-down Allied aviators.

During this period, the Americans were struggling to secure their supply line to Australia (*see map 130*). Alarmed by Japanese activity in New Guinea and the Solomons, Admiral Ernest J. King—Commander in Chief, United States Fleet, and Chief of Naval Operations—ordered a carrier task force to move to the assistance of Australian naval units operating south of that area. These combined forces attempted an air strike on Rabaul. Their approach (*this map, center*) was detected by Japanese reconnaissance planes on 20 February, and—though American carrier planes broke up the ensuing Japanese bomber attacks—the strike was called off since surprise had been lost. Reinforced by another carrier, the American task force launched a surprise air strike across the Owen Stanley Mountains of eastern New Guinea on 10 March, inflicting some damage on Japanese shipping off Lae and Salamaua.

A more serious operation followed. The Japanese finally launched an amphibious operation to seize Port Moresby and, in addition, to establish seaplane bases at Tulagi (*lower right*) and in the Louisiades (*lower center*). During this operation, they hoped to trap the Allied naval forces opposing them between a carrier force (two big aircraft carriers with their escorts from their Carrier Striking Force) and the strong escort (which included one light carrier) which would accompany their Transport Force.

Intercepted radio messages warned the Allies of this offensive. (American cryptographers had broken the Japanese codes even before the beginning of hostilities.) One American carrier launched its planes against Tulagi on 4 May. Most of the Japanese ships assigned to that phase of the operation had come and gone; a few small craft were sunk or damaged. Several days of complicated maneuvers followed (the Battle of the Coral Sea). This was a new type of sea battle, waged by exchanges of air strikes, in which the opposing surface ships never made direct contact. Their carrier forces crippled (the Japanese lost one small carrier, the Americans one large one), both sides finally withdrew. Tactically, the Americans were the worse hurt; technically, it was a draw; strategically—since it saved Port Moresby and the Louisiades—it was an Allied victory. Unconvinced, the Japanese Army took over the task their Navy had fumbled; a reinforced engineer regiment landed at Gona (*lower left*) and moved inland, capturing Kokoda—the key to the best pass through the Owen Stanley Mountains—by 29 July.

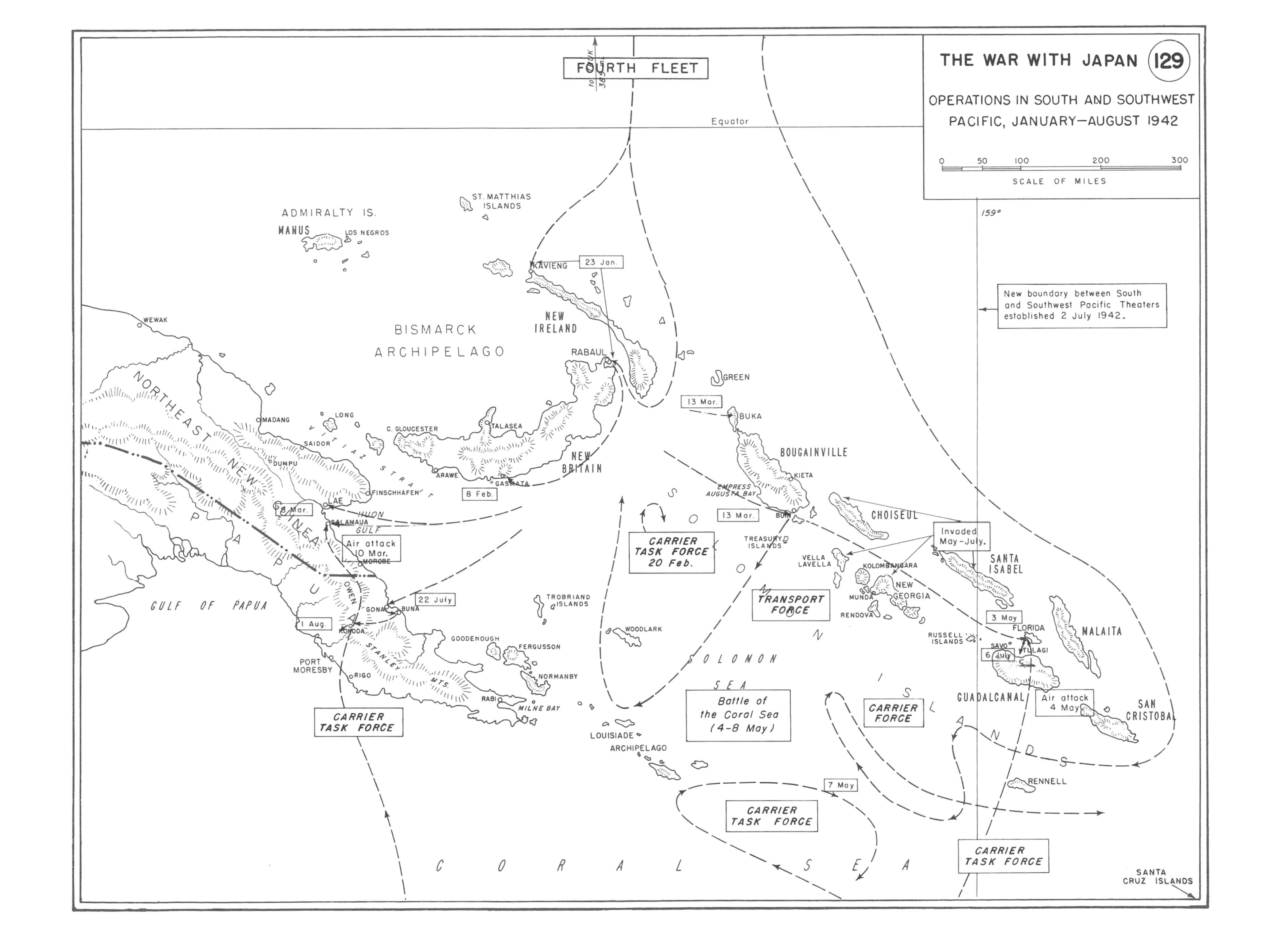

THE WAR WITH JAPAN
129
OPERATIONS IN SOUTH AND SOUTHWEST PACIFIC, JANUARY–AUGUST 1942
0 50 100 200 300
SCALE OF MILES
FOURTH FLEET
Equator
159°
New boundary between South and Southwest Pacific Theaters established 2 July 1942.
ADMIRALTY IS.
MANUS
LOS NEGROS
ST. MATTHIAS ISLANDS
KAVIENG
23 Jan.
NEW IRELAND
BISMARCK ARCHIPELAGO
RABAUL
WEWAK
NORTHEAST NEW GUINEA
MADANG
LONG
SAIDOR
DUMPU
VITIAZ STRAIT
C. GLOUCESTER
TALASEA
ARAWE
GASMATA
NEW BRITAIN
8 Feb.
FINSCHHAFEN
LAE
8 Mar.
HUON GULF
SALAMAUA
Air attack 10 Mar.
MOROBE
PAPUA
OWEN STANLEY MTS.
GULF OF PAPUA
22 July
GONA
BUNA
1 Aug.
KOKODA
PORT MORESBY
RIGO
GOODENOUGH
FERGUSSON
NORMANBY
RABI
MILNE BAY
TROBRIAND ISLANDS
WOODLARK
CARRIER TASK FORCE
GREEN
13 Mar.
BUKA
BOUGAINVILLE
KIETA
EMPRESS AUGUSTA BAY
13 Mar.
BUIN
TREASURY ISLANDS
CARRIER TASK FORCE 20 Feb.
SOLOMON SEA
LOUISIADE ARCHIPELAGO
Battle of the Coral Sea (4–8 May)
TRANSPORT FORCE
CHOISEUL
Invaded May–July.
VELLA LAVELLA
KOLOMBANGARA
NEW GEORGIA
MUNDA
RENDOVA
SANTA ISABEL
3 May
FLORIDA
MALAITA
RUSSELL ISLANDS
SAVO
6 July
TULAGI
GUADALCANAL
Air attack 4 May
SAN CRISTOBAL
SOLOMON ISLANDS
CARRIER FORCE
RENNELL
7 May
CARRIER TASK FORCE
CARRIER TASK FORCE
CORAL SEA
SANTA CRUZ ISLANDS

THE ALLIED REORGANIZATION

★

The break-up of ABDACOM forced a reorganization of the Allied command in the Pacific. The Japanese advance had cut off the British in India from Australia and New Zealand. At the same time, American forces were building up in Australia. Discussions among Allied leaders produced the system shown here. The United States assumed responsibility for the Pacific, the British for India and the Indian Ocean. China remained a special case—an area of American strategic responsibility, where Chiang Kai-Shek retained the supreme command, with Stilwell as his chief of staff. (The American creation, for administrative reasons, of a China-Burma-India Command Area resulted in something of a command monstrosity, wherein Stilwell—commanding general of United States Army forces in that area, and commander of the Chinese forces in India and Burma—could be simultaneously responsible to his American superiors, Chiang, and the British commander in India.)

The Pacific was divided into three commands: the Southwest Pacific Area, under MacArthur; the Pacific Ocean Areas, under Admiral Chester W. Nimitz; and the minor Southeast Pacific Area (*off map, east*). Nimitz's area was subdivided as shown. This organization remained largely unchanged for the first two years of the war. The one major boundary change (*lower center*) was made to give Nimitz responsibility for the southern Solomons at the beginning of the Guadalcanal campaign (*see map 132*).

The American supply line to Australia was rapidly strengthened in early 1942. Hawaii was heavily reinforced, and strong Allied garrisons were established at islands along and astride this route. This involved construction of a whole series of air, naval, and logistical bases.

The Japanese triumphs over England, Holland, and the United States had come far sooner and far more cheaply than they had dared to hope. Possessed by a conviction of invincibility, they began to consider expanding their perimeter, instead of rapidly consolidating its defenses. This desire was stimulated by Lt. Col. James H. Doolittle's surprise air raid on Tokyo (*not shown*) on 18 April with sixteen air corps medium bombers, launched by an American carrier task force. Realizing that their capital was vulnerable to air attacks, the Japanese planners took action: a major expedition would be launched against Midway, to draw the American Pacific Fleet into battle and destroy it. As a diversion, a smaller Japanese force would seize Attu and Kiska in the western Aleutians (*this map, upper center*), making its strike one day ahead of the main force. Later, once the Japanese had established bases at Port Moresby and Tulagi, further operations could be launched to isolate Australia and New Zealand by capturing New Caledonia, Fiji, and Samoa.

The Japanese fleets put to sea, confident of quick and overwhelming victory. But—while facing their greatest battle—they split their formidable Carrier Striking Force. Two of their big carriers had gone to the Coral Sea. The four that were assigned to the Midway operation had just returned from a highly successful raid into the Indian Ocean (25 March–8 April), which had, however, apparently resulted in the loss of a considerable number of veteran naval aviators. According to Japanese accounts, their replacements were relatively untrained.

Once again, intercepted radio messages alerted the Americans; Nimitz quickly concentrated and readied his three available carriers. The Battle of Midway was another intricate struggle between distant aircraft carriers, the American ships being supported by marine and army aircraft from the Midway field. Japanese tactics were clumsy—they had overwhelming superiority in battleships and cruisers, but failed to commit them while the carrier battle was deadlocked. That battle ended with all four Japanese carriers and their planes lost. One American carrier was sunk. The Japanese Navy had lost its long-range striking power; except for the Battle of the Philippine Sea, it would never again venture far beyond the protection of land-based aircraft.

The Japanese did have one consolation. Under cover of a hit-and-run raid on Dutch Harbor (*upper right*), their Aleutian expedition occupied the empty islands of Attu and Kiska on 6–7 June.

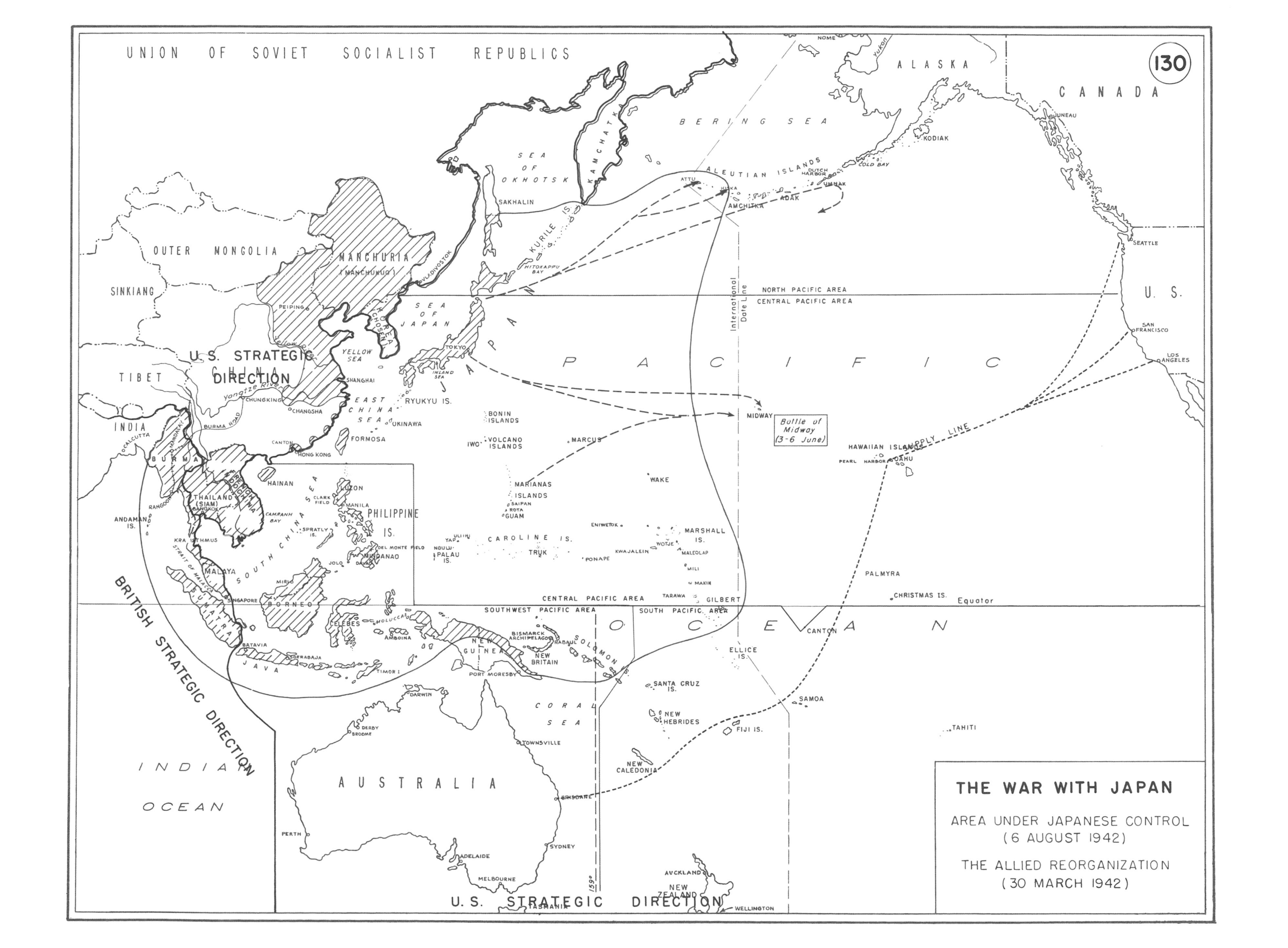
130
THE WAR WITH JAPAN
AREA UNDER JAPANESE CONTROL
(6 AUGUST 1942)
THE ALLIED REORGANIZATION
(30 MARCH 1942)
UNION OF SOVIET SOCIALIST REPUBLICS
ALASKA
CANADA
U. S.
BERING SEA
SEA OF OKHOTSK
KAMCHATKA
SAKHALIN
KURILE IS.
ALEUTIAN ISLANDS
ATTU
KISKA
AMCHITKA
ADAK
DUTCH HARBOR
UMNAK
KODIAK
COLD BAY
NOME
JUNEAU
SEATTLE
SAN FRANCISCO
LOS ANGELES
OUTER MONGOLIA
SINKIANG
TIBET
INDIA
MANCHURIA (MANCHUKUO)
VLADIVOSTOK
KOREA CHOSEN
SEA OF JAPAN
JAPAN
TOKYO
INLAND SEA
PEIPING
YELLOW SEA
U.S. STRATEGIC DIRECTION
CHINA
SHANGHAI
CHUNGKING
CHANGSHA
Yangtze River
BURMA ROAD
CANTON
HONG KONG
EAST CHINA SEA
RYUKYU IS.
OKINAWA
FORMOSA
BURMA
MANDALAY
CALCUTTA
RANGOON
ANDAMAN IS.
THAILAND (SIAM)
BANGKOK
FRENCH INDO CHINA
HAINAN
KRA ISTHMUS
STRAIT OF MALACCA
MALAYA
SINGAPORE
SUMATRA
SOUTH CHINA SEA
CAMRANH BAY
SPRATLY IS.
LUZON
CLARK FIELD
MANILA
PHILIPPINE IS.
DEL MONTE FIELD
MINDANAO
JOLO
DAVAO
BORNEO
MIRI
CELEBES
MOLUCCAS
AMBOINA
BATAVIA
SOERABAJA
JAVA
TIMOR I.
BONIN ISLANDS
IWO
VOLCANO ISLANDS
MARCUS
MARIANAS ISLANDS
SAIPAN
ROTA
GUAM
ULITHI
YAP
NGULU
PALAU IS.
CAROLINE IS.
TRUK
PONAPE
WAKE
ENIWETOK
KWAJALEIN
WOTJE
MARSHALL IS.
MALEOLAP
MILI
MAKIN
TARAWA
GILBERT
PACIFIC
OCEAN
International Date Line
NORTH PACIFIC AREA
CENTRAL PACIFIC AREA
MIDWAY
Battle of Midway (3-6 June)
HAWAIIAN ISLANDS
PEARL HARBOR
OAHU
SUPPLY LINE
PALMYRA
CHRISTMAS IS.
Equator
CANTON
SOUTHWEST PACIFIC AREA
SOUTH PACIFIC AREA
BISMARCK ARCHIPELAGO
RABAUL
NEW BRITAIN
NEW GUINEA
PORT MORESBY
SOLOMON
ELLICE IS.
SANTA CRUZ IS.
NEW HEBRIDES
FIJI IS.
SAMOA
TAHITI
NEW CALEDONIA
CORAL SEA
DARWIN
DERBY
BROOME
TOWNSVILLE
AUSTRALIA
BRISBANE
PERTH
ADELAIDE
SYDNEY
MELBOURNE
TASMANIA
159°
AUCKLAND
NEW ZEALAND
WELLINGTON
BRITISH STRATEGIC DIRECTION
INDIAN OCEAN
U. S. STRATEGIC DIRECTION

AREA UNDER JAPANESE CONTROL

The Japanese wave of conquest had come on in full flood to Midway; thereafter, it could only ebb. On the map, their new empire looked impressive; in cold actuality, it was a patchwork imperium, built of far more ramshackle materials than either Allied or Japanese leaders recognized. To begin with, Japanese war plans had been predicated upon a short, limited war. Neither their armed forces nor their armament industry had been organized for a long war of attrition. (For example, Japan had begun the war with an aircraft industry capable of doing little more than maintaining her air force at its prewar strength, let alone expanding it.) Her merchant marine was weak; it could manage its mission of hauling troops and supplies on outbound voyages to her far-flung perimeter, and of returning loaded with the raw materials so badly needed by Japanese industry, only so long as it suffered merely minor losses. Finally, the loss of the big carriers, with their planes and trained pilots, had abruptly thrown Japan on the defensive on its ocean front. New ships would have to be built, which meant a hopeless race against superior American industry.

However, there remained one front where the Japanese felt capable of continuing their offensive—the Bismarck–New Guinea–Solomons area. They could no longer hope to launch their planned operation against New Caledonia, Fiji, and Samoa, but the possession of Port Moresby and the southern Solomons now was even more important. From such bases, their land-based aircraft could strike at the American supply line to Australia, or at Allied counteroffensives in that area. Consequently, the overland advance against Port Moresby (*see text, map 129*) began. At the same time, airfield construction was pushed throughout this area; one of the new fields was located on Guadalcanal (*see map 132, lower right*).

The Allied build-up in the Pacific had been rapid. Most of the Australian troops serving in the Middle East were ordered home; Australia and New Zealand raised new forces. American troops and planes likewise poured in. Approximately four times as many Americans went to the Pacific as to Europe in early 1942, despite the fact that Germany had been proclaimed the primary enemy. This diversion of troops involved an even greater diversion of scarce shipping, since to land and support an American unit in Australia took over twice the ship tonnage that a similar force bound for Europe would require. The driving force behind this American mustering was the United States Navy, as personified by Admiral King. Through long years of planning and service, the Navy had come to regard the Pacific as its own theater and any war against the Japanese as its particular war. To wage such a war, it wanted an immediate, massive concentration of army troops and aircraft, even if this meant the delay of the European offensive against Germany. Army planners, generally speaking, were willing to oppose any further Japanese advances which might imperil American interests, but wished to commit only the necessary minimum of ground and air forces. The Navy pressed for more aggressive operations—the Japanese must be constantly engaged and kept off-balance until the United States was ready to launch its major Pacific offensive.

This difference of opinion was further perplexed by irritations resulting from the division of the Pacific into two major commands. MacArthur was emotionally, as well as geographically, oriented toward a campaign that would involve the early liberation of the Philippines. The Navy, following its prewar planning, visualized the coming major Pacific offensive as driving due west from Hawaii. MacArthur and Nimitz were in constant competition for whatever forces were available; each regarded his area as the vital one.

This lack of unity of command was to confuse American operations in the Pacific. Nevertheless, considering the powerful interests and personalities involved, it is difficult to see how such unity could have been achieved. Fortunately, the enemy was even more divided in his counsels.

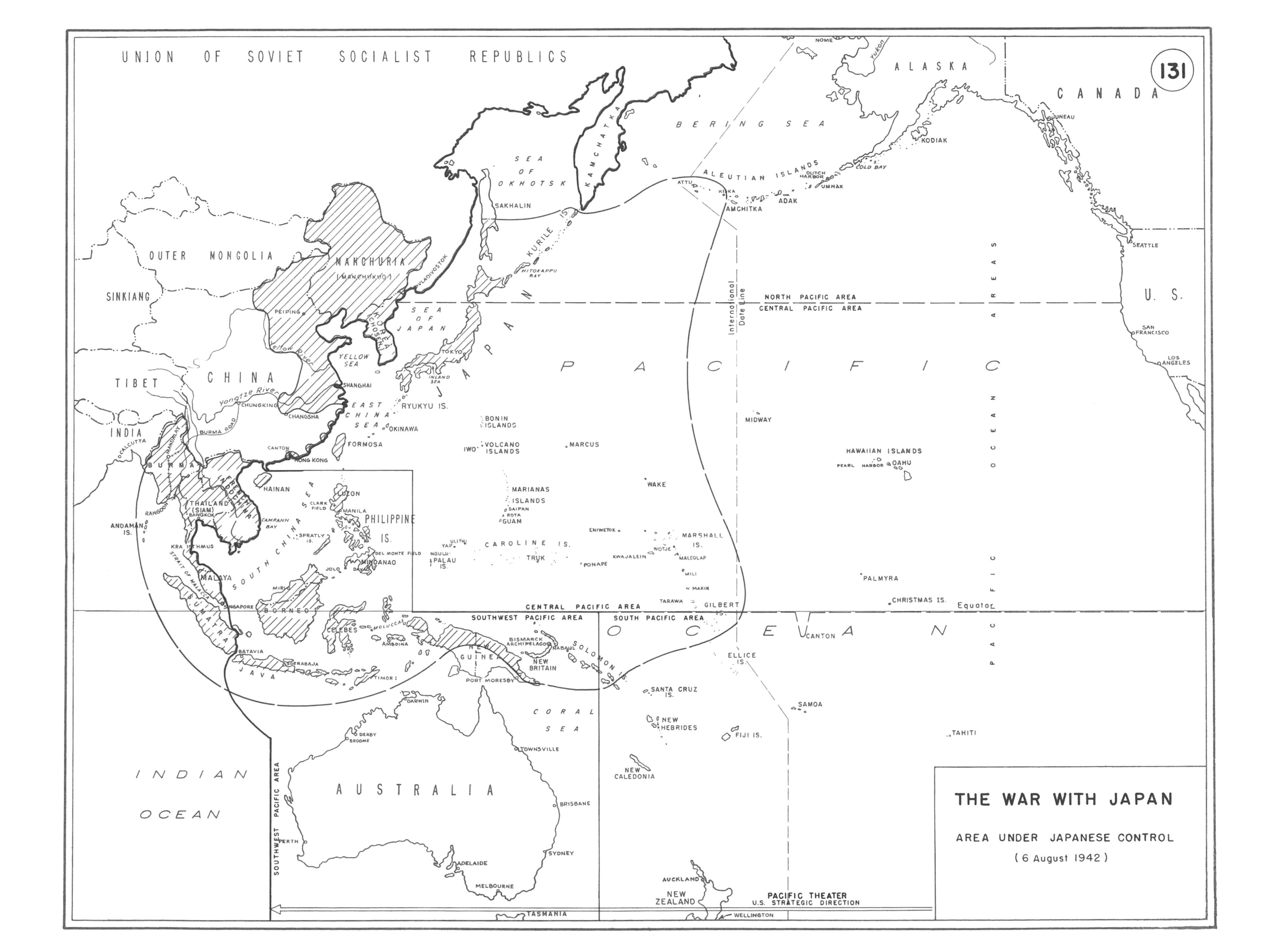
131
THE WAR WITH JAPAN
AREA UNDER JAPANESE CONTROL
(6 August 1942)
UNION OF SOVIET SOCIALIST REPUBLICS
OUTER MONGOLIA
SINKIANG
TIBET
CHINA
INDIA
MANCHURIA
(MANCHUKUO)
KOREA
(CHOSEN)
SEA OF OKHOTSK
SAKHALIN
KAMCHATKA
KURILE IS.
HITOKAPPU BAY
SEA OF JAPAN
JAPAN
TOKYO
INLAND SEA
YELLOW SEA
EAST CHINA SEA
RYUKYU IS.
OKINAWA
FORMOSA
PEIPING
VLADIVOSTOK
Yellow River
Yangtze River
CHUNGKING
CHANGSHA
SHANGHAI
CANTON
HONG KONG
BURMA ROAD
CALCUTTA
MANDALAY
BURMA
RANGOON
ANDAMAN IS.
THAILAND (SIAM)
BANGKOK
FRENCH INDOCHINA
HAINAN
CAMRANH BAY
KRA ISTHMUS
STRAIT OF MALACCA
MALAYA
SINGAPORE
SUMATRA
SOUTH CHINA SEA
SPRATLY IS.
LUZON
CLARK FIELD
MANILA
PHILIPPINE IS.
DEL MONTE FIELD
MINDANAO
DAVAO
JOLO
MIRI
BORNEO
CELEBES
MOLUCCAS
AMBOINA
BATAVIA
SURABAJA
JAVA
TIMOR
BERING SEA
ALASKA
NOME
Yukon
KODIAK
COLD BAY
DUTCH HARBOR
UMNAK
ALEUTIAN ISLANDS
ATTU
KISKA
AMCHITKA
ADAK
CANADA
JUNEAU
SEATTLE
U. S.
SAN FRANCISCO
LOS ANGELES
International Date Line
NORTH PACIFIC AREA
CENTRAL PACIFIC AREA
PACIFIC OCEAN AREAS
PACIFIC OCEAN
MIDWAY
HAWAIIAN ISLANDS
PEARL HARBOR
OAHU
BONIN ISLANDS
VOLCANO ISLANDS
IWO
MARCUS
WAKE
MARIANAS ISLANDS
SAIPAN
ROTA
GUAM
ULITHI
YAP
NGULU
PALAU IS.
CAROLINE IS.
TRUK
PONAPE
ENIWETOK
KWAJALEIN
WOTJE
MARSHALL IS.
MALEOLAP
MILI
MAKIN
TARAWA
GILBERT IS.
PALMYRA
CHRISTMAS IS.
Equator
CANTON
ELLICE IS.
SAMOA
TAHITI
SOUTHWEST PACIFIC AREA
SOUTH PACIFIC AREA
NEW GUINEA
PORT MORESBY
BISMARCK ARCHIPELAGO
RABAUL
NEW BRITAIN
SOLOMON IS.
SANTA CRUZ IS.
NEW HEBRIDES
FIJI IS.
NEW CALEDONIA
CORAL SEA
DARWIN
DERBY
BROOME
TOWNSVILLE
AUSTRALIA
BRISBANE
SYDNEY
PERTH
ADELAIDE
MELBOURNE
TASMANIA
INDIAN OCEAN
AUCKLAND
NEW ZEALAND
WELLINGTON
PACIFIC THEATER
U.S. STRATEGIC DIRECTION

GUADALCANAL CAMPAIGN

In demanding prompt offensive action in the Pacific, the United States Navy was only preaching what it had already practiced. Shortly after Pearl Harbor, it had used its few available ships in raids against Japanese-held islands in the central Pacific. Though these did the Japanese no appreciable damage, they were valuable training exercises in the handling of carrier task forces and had an excellent effect upon American public morale. In the Battles of the Coral Sea and Midway, American fleets had closed boldly with stronger Japanese naval forces.

After Midway, for the first time since Pearl Harbor, the Americans possessed a degree of naval superiority in the Pacific. This superiority was, however, so marginal that the loss of one or two aircraft carriers would come close to canceling it; consequently, the Navy could not yet launch its long-planned major Pacific offensive. American planners therefore sought to develop an operation by which the modest forces at their disposal could inflict maximum punishment upon the Japanese, while improving the overall Allied strategic position in the Pacific.

King and MacArthur urged an offensive in the Bismarck–New Guinea–Solomons area to destroy the growing Japanese threat to the American supply line to Australia. But, aside from agreeing that such action would be desirable and should be taken as soon as possible, the Army and Navy found themselves completely at odds as to how this was to be done, and who was to do it. The Army favored a quick, direct blow at Rabaul; since the action would take place within the Southwest Pacific Area, MacArthur would naturally command the forces involved. The Navy proposed to fight its way up the Solomons, island by island, to Rabaul; since the operation would be primarily of a naval and amphibious character, Nimitz would command. (King's plan provided that Nimitz was to take over all of MacArthur's ships and aircraft; it assigned the Army the mission of garrisoning the various islands after the Navy and Marines had captured them.) General Marshall needed all his tact and patience to reach a solution, placed as he was between the outraged MacArthur and the irascible King. On 2 July, he and King finally signed a joint directive, ordering that an offensive be mounted at once to seize the New Britain–New Guinea–New Ireland area.

This offensive was to consist of three "tasks." The first—to be carried out by Vice Adm. Robert L. Ghormley, commanding the South Pacific Area—would be the seizure of the Santa Cruz Islands (*off map, bottom right corner*), Tulagi (*lower right*), and adjacent islands. This would begin as soon as possible after 1 August. Ghormley would be reinforced by some of MacArthur's aircraft and warships; other aircraft from Australian bases would interdict Japanese air and naval activity west of Ghormley's objectives.

MacArthur would take command for Task Two (the seizure of the rest of the Solomons, Lae and Salamaua [*left center*], and the northwest coast of New Guinea [*off map, west*]) and Task Three (the capture of the Rabaul area). The Joint Chiefs of Staff reserved the authority to withdraw any naval units after the completion of any phase of the operation, in case the carriers were in jeopardy or an emergency developed elsewhere. Finally, the boundary between the Southwest and South Pacific Areas (*see map 130*) was shifted westward to facilitate Ghormley's control of Task One.

Both Ghormley and MacArthur objected that this offensive was being launched too soon with insufficient forces, but the discovery that the Japanese were building an airfield on Guadalcanal caused the JCS to reject their protests. Preparations were rushed, and shipping was in short supply. As a result, D-Day had to be postponed until 7 August.

Ghormley organized his forces into three major commands: the supporting land-based aircraft; the Amphibious Force (a convoy—carrying the reinforced 1st Marine Division—and its escort, fire support group, and mine sweepers); and the Air Support Force (three aircraft carriers and their escorting battleship, cruisers, and destroyers). Early on 7 August, this armada approached Guadalcanal.

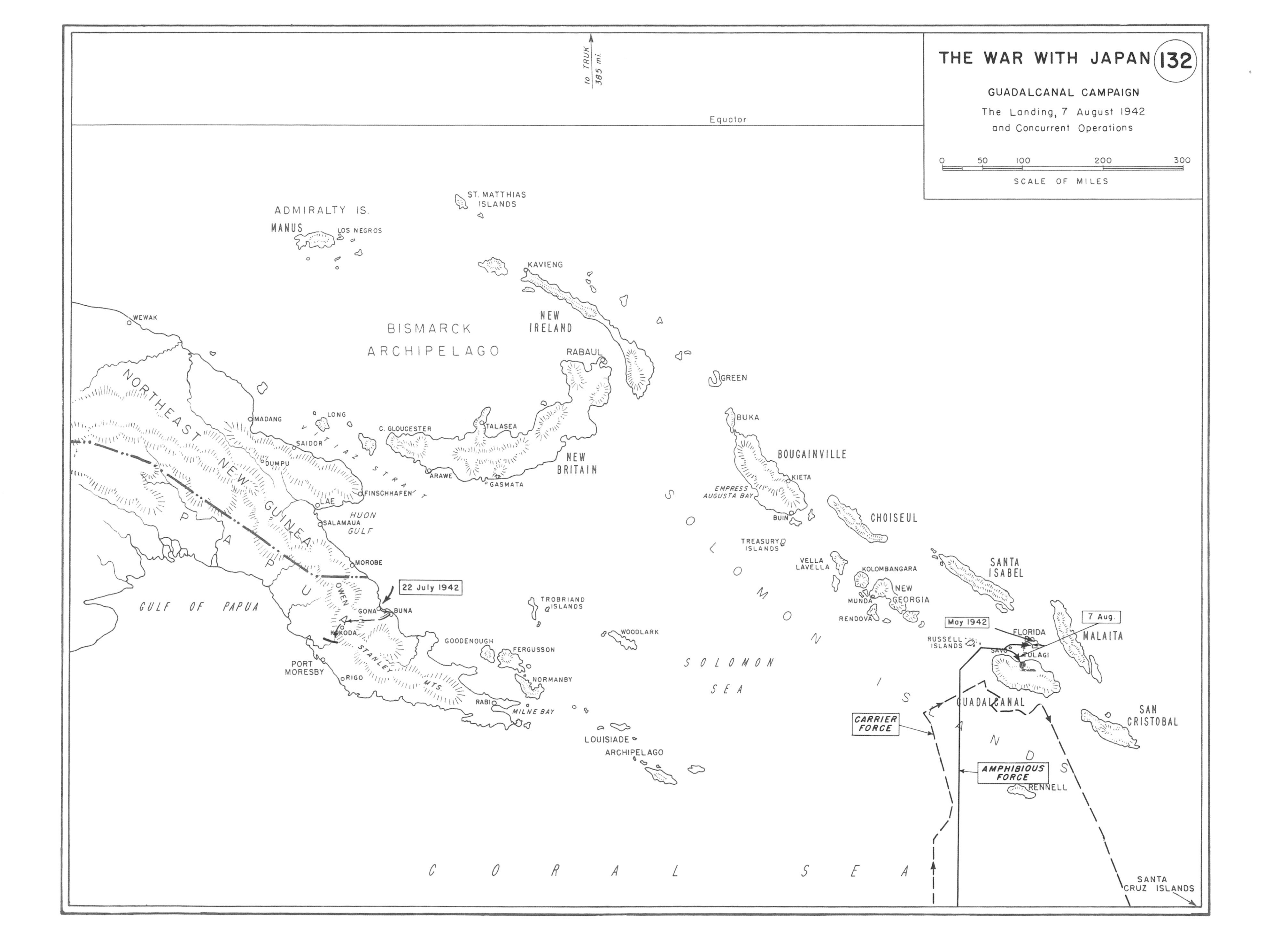
THE WAR WITH JAPAN
132
GUADALCANAL CAMPAIGN
The Landing, 7 August 1942
and Concurrent Operations
0
50
100
200
300
SCALE OF MILES
to TRUK
385 mi.
Equator
ADMIRALTY IS.
MANUS
LOS NEGROS
ST. MATTHIAS
ISLANDS
KAVIENG
NEW
IRELAND
BISMARCK
ARCHIPELAGO
RABAUL
GREEN
BUKA
BOUGAINVILLE
KIETA
EMPRESS
AUGUSTA BAY
BUIN
CHOISEUL
TREASURY
ISLANDS
VELLA
LAVELLA
KOLOMBANGARA
NEW
GEORGIA
MUNDA
RENDOVA
SANTA
ISABEL
May 1942
7 Aug.
FLORIDA
MALAITA
RUSSELL
ISLANDS
SAVO
TULAGI
GUADALCANAL
SAN
CRISTOBAL
CARRIER
FORCE
AMPHIBIOUS
FORCE
RENNELL
SANTA
CRUZ ISLANDS
WEWAK
NORTHEAST NEW GUINEA
MADANG
LONG
SAIDOR
VITIAZ STRAIT
DUMPU
C. GLOUCESTER
TALASEA
ARAWE
GASMATA
NEW
BRITAIN
FINSCHHAFEN
LAE
SALAMAUA
HUON
GULF
MOROBE
22 July 1942
GONA
BUNA
KOKODA
PAPUA
OWEN STANLEY MTS.
GULF OF PAPUA
PORT
MORESBY
RIGO
GOODENOUGH
FERGUSSON
NORMANBY
RABI
MILNE BAY
TROBRIAND
ISLANDS
WOODLARK
LOUISIADE
ARCHIPELAGO
SOLOMON ISLANDS
SOLOMON
SEA
CORAL SEA

GUADALCANAL CAMPAIGN

★

The Amphibious Force had two immediate objectives: the small island complex of Tulagi-Tanambogo-Gavutu, which sheltered the best-developed and largest anchorage in the southern Solomons, and the still incomplete airfield on Guadalcanal. Planning for these operations had been thoroughly handicapped by the lack of adequate hydrographic charts and maps. Information was scanty and frequently erroneous, even when obtained from former residents of the islands. As one result of this lack of knowledge, the marines landing on Guadalcanal were assigned Mount Austen (*lower center*) as one of their D-Day objectives. (Mount Austen was actually some nine miles inland through tangled jungle from Beach Red.) There was equal misinformation as to the Japanese strength in this area. Intelligence estimates placed it at approximately 7,000, 5,000 of whom were believed to be on Guadalcanal. Actual Japanese strength appears to have been about 1,500 men in the Tulagi area and 2,230 on Guadalcanal; of these, 600 and 1,700, respectively, were labor troops.

The Solomons are tropical islands, covered with heavy rain forests, and combining the most unpleasant features of jungles, swamps, and mountains. Their climate is dominated by heat, humidity, and heavy rain; malaria and dengue fever are endemic; skin infections are common. Only native trails led inland from the beaches, though Guadalcanal had a rough track running through the coconut plantations along its northern coast.

Since this operation would require several simultaneous assault landings, Maj. Gen. Alexander A. Vandegrift had organized his 1st Marine Division and its attached units into relatively self-contained task forces. Combat Groups A and B (these "combat groups" were the equivalent of a regimental combat team, plus certain specialized units such as an amphibious tractor company) were to seize the airfield on Guadalcanal. Combat Group C (*not shown*) formed the division's floating reserve. A smaller force (four reinforced battalions) was to seize Tulagi, Tanambogo, and Gavutu. (Some dominating terrain on the south coast of Florida was also occupied, to protect the flanks of the forces landing on the three islands.)

Since the haste with which the whole operation had gotten under way—plus providential bad weather which blinded Japanese reconnaissance planes—had prevented any warning, the Japanese were taken utterly by surprise. At 0613, 7 August, the cruisers and destroyers of the Amphibious Force's fire support elements opened fire on Japanese shore installations; carrier planes from the Air Support Force, which had remained south of Guadalcanal (*see map 132*), joined the attack. Combat Group A (*this map*) began an unopposed landing at Beach Red at 0650; at 0930, Combat Group B followed, passing through Group A at 1115 to seize Mount Austen. About 1330, a battalion of Group A moved west toward the Ilu River. By dusk, each group—its men heavily loaded with weapons and supplies, short of water and salt tablets—had advanced about a mile. General Vandegrift, realizing that Mount Austen was too distant, thereupon ordered both groups to attack the next morning to seize the Lunga Point area. Jumping off at 0930 on the 8th, the marines had the airfield and the situation well in hand by 1600. The outnumbered Japanese had offered only the slightest resistance before fleeing, leaving the airfield undamaged and abandoning large quantities of food, weapons, and equipment. There were no American casualties. The success of this operation had been dimmed only by the failure of the logistical arrangements at Beach Red, where a lack of beach personnel and suitable landing craft left the unloading of supplies in a muddle. The result was that the beach soon became congested, and none of the waiting transports was able to completely discharge its cargo—a state of affairs that was to have a grim aftermath on the 9th, when Japanese naval forces arrived and precipitated the Battle of Savo Island (*see text, map 134*). Small-scale Japanese air raids on the 7th and 8th caused further delay.

But, for the time being, General Vandegrift, unaware of how small the Japanese forces opposing him actually were, set up a perimeter defense to protect the newly captured airfield.

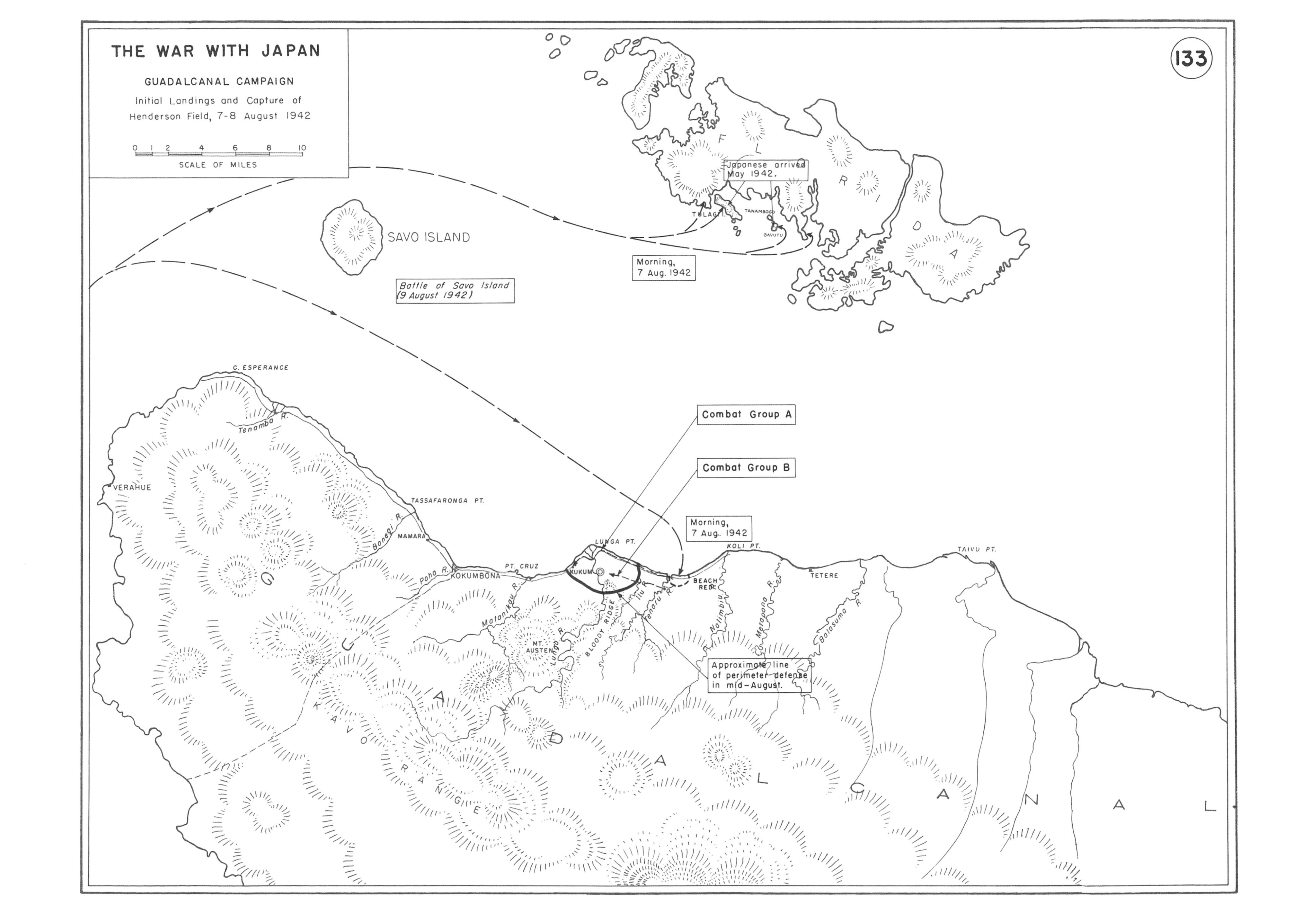
133
THE WAR WITH JAPAN
GUADALCANAL CAMPAIGN
Initial Landings and Capture of
Henderson Field, 7-8 August 1942
0 1 2 4 6 8 10
SCALE OF MILES
SAVO ISLAND
Battle of Savo Island
(9 August 1942)
Japanese arrived
May 1942.
TULAGI
TANAMBOGO
GAVUTU
Morning,
7 Aug. 1942
F L O R I D A
C. ESPERANCE
Tenombo R.
VERAHUE
TASSAFARONGA PT.
Bonegi R.
MAMARA
Poha R.
KOKUMBONA
PT. CRUZ
Matanikau R.
MT. AUSTEN
Lunga R.
KUKUM
LUNGA PT.
BLOODY RIDGE
Ilu R.
Tenaru R.
BEACH RED
Combat Group A
Combat Group B
Morning,
7 Aug. 1942
KOLI PT.
Nalimbiu R.
Metapona R.
TETERE
Balasuma R.
TAIVU PT.
Approximate line
of perimeter defense
in mid-August.
KAVO RANGE
G U A D A L C A N A L

GUADALCANAL CAMPAIGN

★

On Guadalcanal, there had been little to fight besides jungle, insects, and heat; in the Tulagi area, it was different.

The assaults on Tulagi, Gavutu, and Tanambogo formed an intricate pattern—in part, because the shortage of landing craft made it impossible to attack all objectives simultaneously. The assault on the causeway-linked islands of Gavutu and Tanambogo was further complicated by offshore reefs which forced the adoption of the circuitous approach shown here.

Initially, the attack went according to plan. Elements of a reinforced battalion (detached from the floating reserve) landed on Florida Island and seized the Haleta and Halavo peninsulas as shown. They found no Japanese (and were withdrawn in the late afternoon of 7 August). At H-Hour (0800), the Marine 1st Raider Battalion began splashing ashore on Tulagi at Beach Blue, followed by a battalion previously detached from Combat Group A. Once ashore, the Raiders pushed toward the southeastern end of the island, while the other battalion advanced toward its northwestern tip. There was little resistance at first; then, about a mile from its objective, the Raider Battalion developed an extensive system of Japanese cave and dugout positions. Here, the marines got their first lesson in the brutal facts of war in the Pacific theater: the Japanese was an expert burrower; his defenses could absorb amazing amounts of bombing and shelling; however hopeless his position, he did not surrender; and—once he was dug in—killing him was a slow and difficult job. When it became obvious that Tulagi could not be cleared before dark, the Raider Battalion set up a defensive position (*dashed red line*) across the island, holding it against several uncoordinated Japanese counterattacks during the night.

Meanwhile, the Marine 1st Parachute Battalion (serving as infantry) had cleared most of Gavutu after a stiff fight, but could not force the causeway between Gavutu and Tanambogo. The detachment that had been withdrawn from the Haleta area therefore attempted to land on the north shore of Tanambogo, but was repulsed with severe casualties.

Attacks were renewed on the morning of 8 August. Tulagi was cleared by 1500, and the last Japanese strong points on Gavutu wiped out, but Tanambogo's garrison held out until two light tanks were brought into action. American losses were reported as 144 killed and missing and 194 wounded.

So far—except for the unloading problem on Guadalcanal—the operation had been competently handled. The Japanese had launched a number of air attacks during the 7th and 8th, but—forewarned by a coastwatcher on Bougainville (*off map, northwest*)—American carrier planes and antiaircraft fire had beaten them off. Nevertheless, the expedition commander, Vice Adm. Jack Fletcher, apprehensive over the safety of his aircraft carriers, abruptly withdrew the Air Support Force southeastward on the evening of 8 August. (Fletcher had previously warned Rear Adm. Richmond K. Turner, the Amphibious Force commander, that he would withdraw the carriers before 10 August—even though Turner had protested that it would take four days to unload the transports. No one had warned Vandegrift.) Thus abandoned, Turner announced that he would be forced to withdraw the ships of the Amphibious Force on the morning of 9 August.

To increase Turner's worries, aerial reconnaissance had warned him during the day that a large Japanese naval task force was moving southward from Rabaul (*off map, northwest*). Turner's defensive dispositions for the night of the 8th were clumsy, and some of his subordinates lax. The Japanese squadron slipped through his inadequate patrols, completely surprised the unready Allied cruisers, and sank four of them in the Battle of Savo Island. Fortunately, the Japanese commander—like Fletcher—feared a possible trap; he failed to push home his attack and destroy the huddled and defenseless transports, which represented most of the available shipping in the South Pacific. Turner was tougher; regardless of the risks of further Japanese air and surface attack, he held his shattered fleet off Guadalcanal until the afternoon of the 9th, unloading what additional supplies he could.

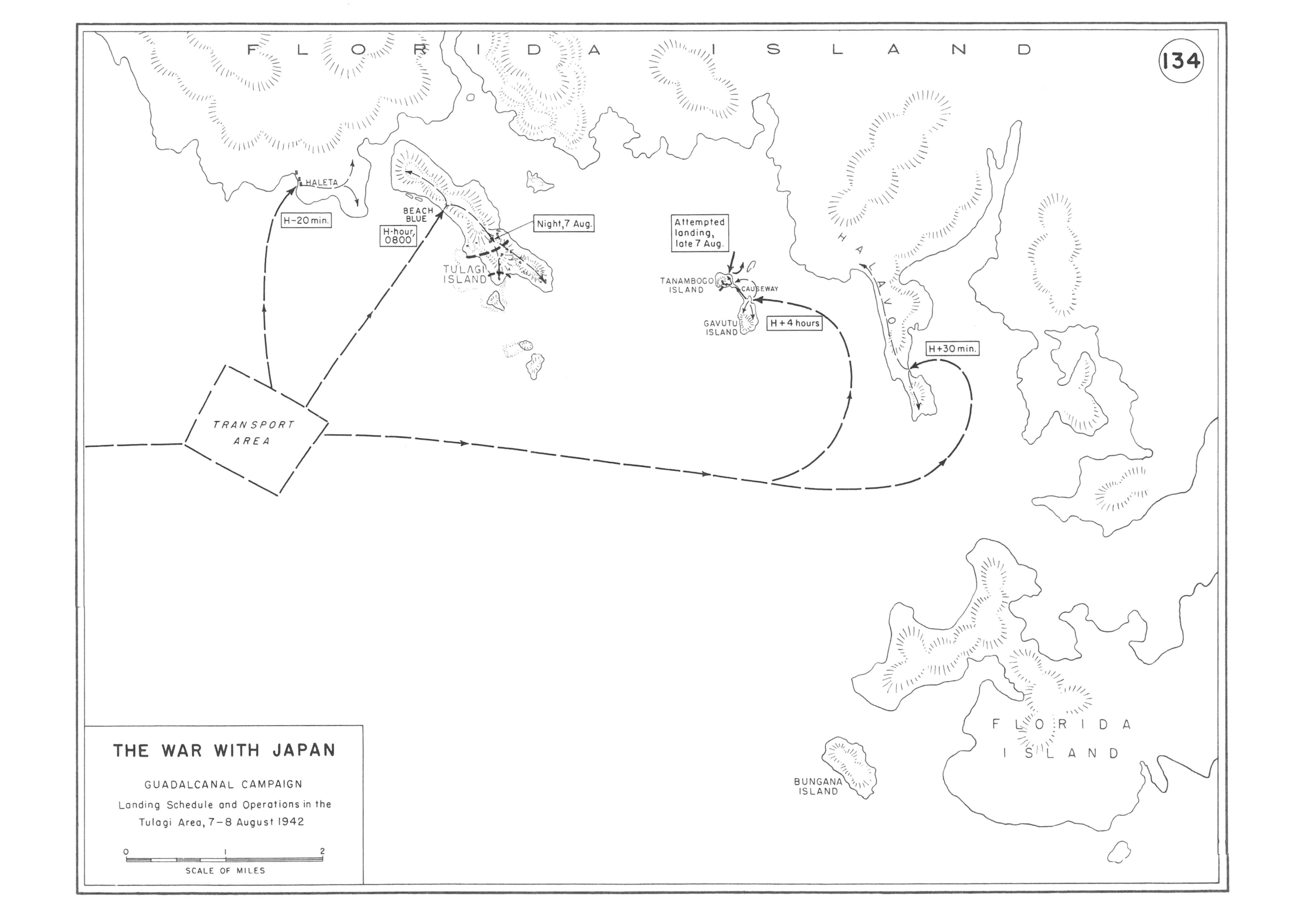
134
FLORIDA ISLAND
HALETA
H-20 min.
BEACH BLUE
H-hour, 0800
TULAGI ISLAND
Night, 7 Aug.
Attempted landing, late 7 Aug.
TANAMBOGO ISLAND
CAUSEWAY
GAVUTU ISLAND
H+4 hours
HALAVO
H+30 min.
TRANSPORT AREA
FLORIDA ISLAND
BUNGANA ISLAND
THE WAR WITH JAPAN
GUADALCANAL CAMPAIGN
Landing Schedule and Operations in the Tulagi Area, 7-8 August 1942
0
1
2
SCALE OF MILES

GUADALCANAL CAMPAIGN

★

Vandegrift's marines found themselves isolated—with ammunition enough for four days of heavy combat, rations (one-third of which were captured Japanese food) for thirty days, and eighteen spools of barbed wire. Their coastal defense guns, radar sets, and heavy construction equipment were in the holds of the vanishing transports. As a climax, the fleet had departed with approximately 1,400 marines still aboard!

Though Admiral Ghormley considered Vandegrift's position serious, he approved Fletcher's premature withdrawal of the aircraft carriers, considering them too irreplaceable to risk in the routine support of the Guadalcanal garrison. He began (12 August) to get a trickle of supplies to Vandegrift by means of a few attack transports (old destroyers converted to cargo ships) which ran in and unloaded under cover of darkness. He overlooked the urgency of developing the captured airfield (renamed Henderson Field) as a base from which bombers could operate against the Rabaul area.

On Guadalcanal, meanwhile, Vandegrift put his marines on reduced rations, strengthened his defenses, and—using captured Japanese equipment—lengthened and roughly completed Henderson Field (17 August). On 20 August, Marine Corps dive bombers and fighters took station there; navy dive bombers and obsolescent army fighters followed. These fliers operated under great handicaps, Ghormley having supplied only the most primitive equipment. Planes had to be fueled by hand pumps from gasoline drums—a time-devouring and risky process when the field was under attack.

Initially, the marines experienced only a few minor clashes with the Japanese remaining on Guadalcanal, though enemy planes and warships kept the American beachhead under sporadic bombardment. Japanese commanders were concentrating on their operation against Port Moresby; the hasty withdrawal of the American fleet and the lack of air support subsequently given Vandegrift had convinced them that American operations on Guadalcanal represented only a reconnaissance in force—and that there might not be more than 1,000 Americans on the island. Almost as a routine matter, they began building up their forces there. About 18 August, the first echelon of the so-called Ichiki Force (approximately 1,000 men) landed from Japanese cruisers and destroyers near Taivu Point (*center, right*). Probably out of arrogant self-confidence, Colonel Ichiki immediately moved to attack the American position; or—a marine patrol having ambushed one of his detachments on the 19th—he may have considered it essential to seize the initiative before the Americans attacked him. Assaulting the American position behind the mouth of the Ilu River at about 0310, 21 August, he met a costly repulse. Later that morning, an American counterattack enveloped his left flank and almost annihilated his little force.

A strong Japanese naval task force had moved down well to the east of the Solomons from Rabaul on 19 August to cover the movement of a second Guadalcanal-bound troop convoy. Fletcher engaged the Japanese fleet in another long-range clash (Battle of the Eastern Solomons, 24 August) in which neither side displayed much aggressiveness. The Japanese, however, lost another carrier—a loss that was balanced when a Japanese submarine sank an American carrier on 15 September, leaving Ghormley with only one serviceable warship of that type.

By gradual infiltration, the Japanese built up a force of some 5,000 in the Taivu area, with another 1,000 near Kokumbona (*center, left*). Their commander, General Kawaguchi, planned a coordinated air-naval-ground attack on the beachhead; his ground forces would strike it on three sides, as shown. Kawaguchi put his men to work chopping a trail through the jungle to the Bloody Ridge sector (*lower center*) of Vandegrift's perimeter. Native scouts, patrols, and aircraft detected the movement, and Vandegrift stationed his Raiders and paratroopers (now consolidated into one battalion) on Bloody Ridge. Kawaguchi's assault (13–14 September) was a masterpiece of mismanaged ferocity: the Japanese aircraft arrived early and did little damage; the attack across the Ilu River withered in front of the American defenses there; the assault on Bloody Ridge was beaten off in savage night fighting; the attack from Kokumbona arrived a day late and failed quickly; supporting Japanese warships shot at both sides with fine impartiality. On the 14th, the Japanese retreated, abandoning weapons and equipment.

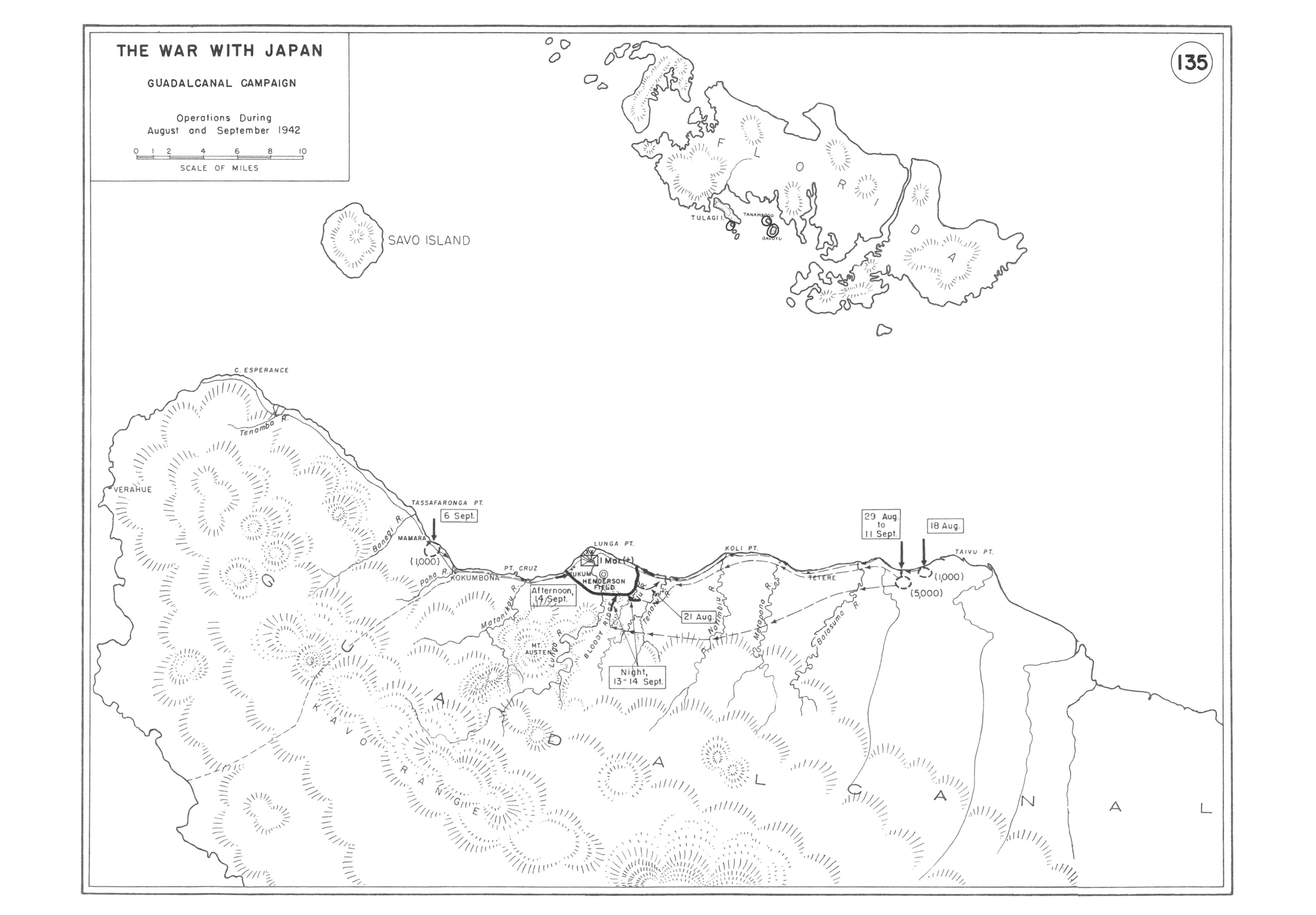
135
THE WAR WITH JAPAN
GUADALCANAL CAMPAIGN
Operations During
August and September 1942
0 1 2 4 6 8 10
SCALE OF MILES
SAVO ISLAND
FLORIDA
TULAGI I.
TANAMBOGO
GAVUTU
C. ESPERANCE
Tenombo R.
VERAHUE
TASSAFARONGA PT.
6 Sept.
MAMARA
(1,000)
Bonegi R.
Poha R.
KOKUMBONA
PT. CRUZ
Afternoon, 14 Sept.
Matanikau R.
MT. AUSTEN
Lunga R.
BLOODY RIDGE
LUNGA PT.
1 Mar(+)
KUKUM
HENDERSON FIELD
Tenaru R.
21 Aug.
Night, 13-14 Sept.
KOLI PT.
Nalimbiu R.
Metapona R.
TETERE
Balasuma R.
29 Aug. to 11 Sept.
18 Aug.
TAIVU PT.
(1,000)
(5,000)
GUADALCANAL
KAVO RANGE

GUADALCANAL CAMPAIGN

★

The Japanese now reconsidered their problems in the Southwest Pacific. Guadalcanal was draining away forces needed for the capture of Port Moresby. Therefore, General Hyakutake's Seventeenth Army was ordered to clear the island; the Japanese Navy promised full support. Through September and early October, Japanese troops moved steadily down from Rabaul to land on Guadalcanal during the night, when American planes from Henderson Field could not interfere. Since the weakened American naval forces seldom ventured into the Solomons area after dark, only one convoy was intercepted (Battle of Cape Esperance [*upper left*]). This method of reinforcement, however, was too slow for the Japanese, who began a determined effort to knock out Henderson Field so that they could bring in and unload large cargo vessels during the day. Air and naval bombardments were reinforced by newly landed Japanese medium artillery, firing from the Kokumbona area. (Fortunately, Japanese artillery techniques were primitive.) A bombardment by Japanese battleships and cruisers during the nights of 13–14 October actually put the field out of operation, but the few remaining planes—operating off a newly opened grass runway and fueled with the last gasoline available—somehow remained in action.

Meanwhile, the 7th Marine Regiment (the remaining regiment of the 1st Marine Division) was put ashore on Guadalcanal on 18 September, along with considerable quantities of supplies, the first reinforcements and ammunition Vandegrift had received. On 13 October, the 164th Infantry Regiment (Americal Division) likewise arrived. (Ghormley had wanted to use any available ground forces to establish a new base in the Santa Cruz Islands [*off map, southeast*], but Maj. Gen. Millard F. Harmon, who commanded the Army forces in the South Pacific Area, finally persuaded him to reinforce Guadalcanal instead.) Knowing that this regiment was en route, Vandegrift extended his perimeter to command the mouth of the steep-banked Matanikau River (*center, left*), the only point where heavy equipment could be gotten across it.

By mid-October, Hyakutake had concentrated all of the Japanese 2d Division, part of the 38th Division, several battalions of infantry, and a tank company on Guadalcanal; in addition, he had the survivors of Ichiki's and Kawaguchi's forces. Believing that the American forces on the island numbered only about 7,500, he left most of the 38th Division in the Rabaul area.

His plan of attack provided for a tank-infantry secondary attack across the mouth of the Matanikau to seize Kukum. Simultaneously, the main attack would strike out of the jungle to the east of Mt. Austen. (Either in the original plan, or as an afterthought—Japanese accounts are extremely vague—a second enveloping column was given the mission of cutting in behind the American defenses along the Matanikau.) Meanwhile, a strong Japanese fleet moved toward the Santa Cruz Islands to intercept any American effort to reinforce Guadalcanal.

Hyakutake's main attack forces had to cut their way through the jungle; progress was extremely slow, and all weapons heavier than machine guns had to be abandoned; contact with the secondary attack force seems to have been lost. The latter attacked on 23 October, hit strong American defenses, and was butchered. The main force (and the smaller column on its left) finally emerged from the jungle late on the 24th. It attacked that night and the next, was defeated, and staggered back into the jungle. Vandegrift now advanced toward the Poha River (*center, left*) to force the Japanese back out of artillery range of the airfield, but this operation had to be suspended to mop up some 1,500 Japanese who landed near Tetere on 2 November. The Japanese fleet, meanwhile, had met and defeated a weaker American force north of the Santa Cruz Islands on 26 October, but failed to pursue.

Subsequent action around Guadalcanal consisted largely of a series of naval and air clashes, brought on by Japanese efforts to land more troops. A series of clashes from 12 through 15 November (Battle of Guadalcanal) ended in the defeat of a major Japanese task force and the destruction of the convoy it was covering. In another night clash (Battle of Tassafaronga, 30 November), a small squadron of Japanese destroyers defeated an American cruiser task force. During this same period, elements of the 2d Marine and Americal Divisions reinforced Vandegrift.

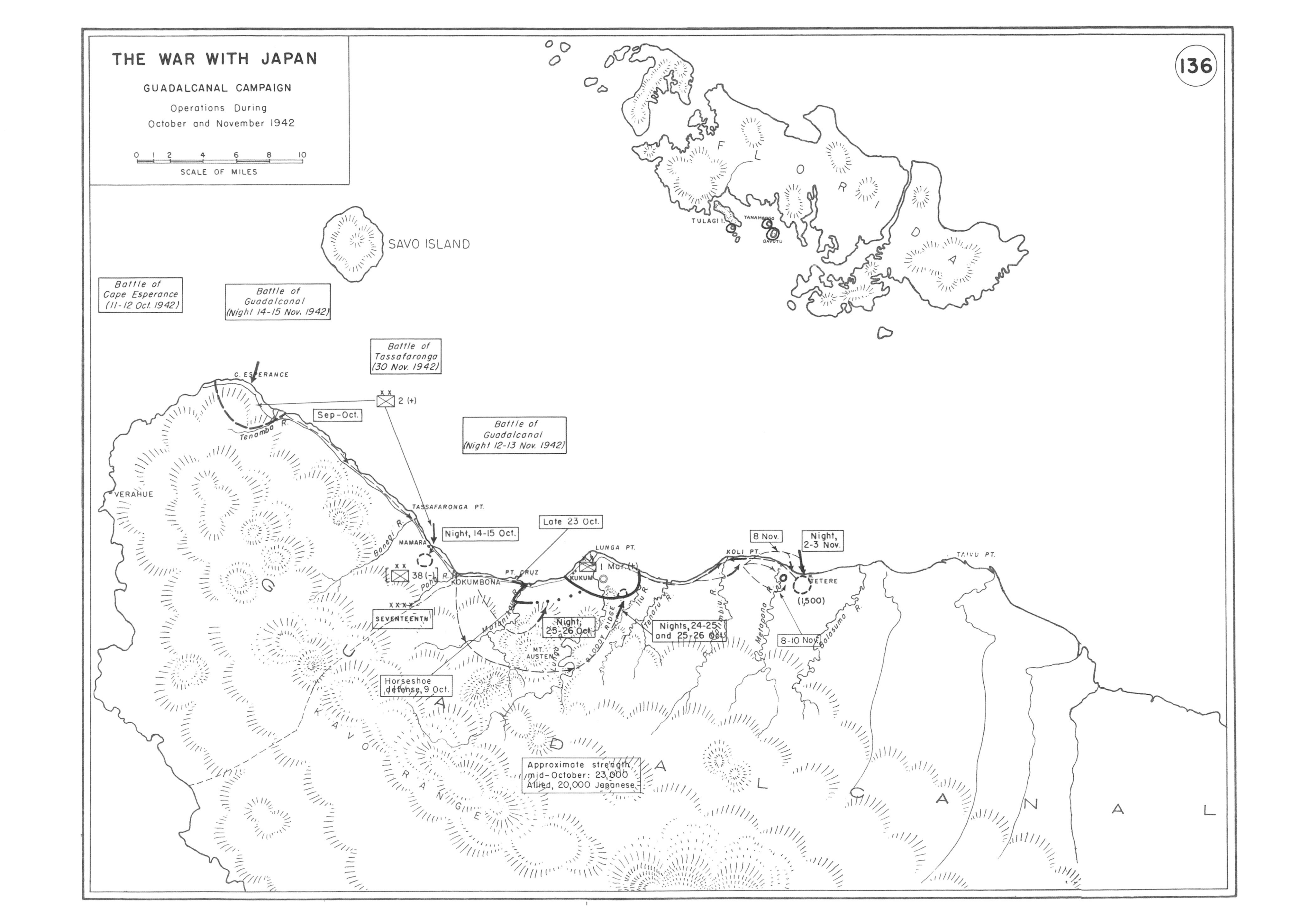

THE WAR WITH JAPAN
GUADALCANAL CAMPAIGN
Operations During
October and November 1942
0 1 2 4 6 8 10
SCALE OF MILES
136
FLORIDA
TULAGI I.
TANAMBOGO
GAVUTU
SAVO ISLAND
Battle of Cape Esperance (11-12 Oct. 1942)
Battle of Guadalcanal (Night 14-15 Nov. 1942)
Battle of Tassafaronga (30 Nov. 1942)
Battle of Guadalcanal (Night 12-13 Nov. 1942)
C. ESPERANCE
2 (+)
Sep-Oct.
Tenamba R.
VERAHUE
TASSAFARONGA PT.
Night, 14-15 Oct.
Late 23 Oct.
MAMARA
Bonegi R.
38 (-)
Poha R.
KOKUMBONA
PT. CRUZ
XXXX
SEVENTEENTH
LUNGA PT.
KUKUM
1 Mar. (+)
Matanikau R.
Night, 25-26 Oct.
MT. AUSTEN
Lunga R.
BLOODY RIDGE
Ilu R.
Tenaru R.
Nights, 24-25 and 25-26 Oct.
Horseshoe defense, 9 Oct.
KOLI PT.
8 Nov.
Night, 2-3 Nov.
TETERE
(1,500)
Metapona R.
Balasuma R.
8-10 Nov.
TAIVU PT.
KAVO RANGE
Approximate strength, mid-October: 23,000 Allied, 20,000 Japanese.
GUADALCANAL

JAPANESE EVACUATION OF GUADALCANAL

The opening of the Guadalcanal campaign coincided with preparations for the invasion of North Africa and the build-up of American air power in England. As the situation on Guadalcanal and New Guinea worsened, King, MacArthur, and Harmon called for additional reinforcements, especially aircraft, for the Pacific. This led to a long controversy over the priorities to be assigned the various theaters, the Navy demanding that the Pacific be reinforced, if need be, at the expense of the other theaters. The crisis raised by the Japanese Seventeenth Army offensive in October tipped the decision in favor of the Pacific. The 25th and 43d Divisions were ordered to the South Pacific Area; Nimitz sent all available aircraft from the Central Pacific; and repair work on damaged warships was speeded up. On 18 October, Vice Adm. William F. Halsey replaced Ghormley. Great efforts were made to secure sufficient shipping. Meanwhile, Vandegrift repulsed Hyakutake, the Japanese Navy failed to press its advantage after the Battle of Santa Cruz, and the crisis passed. The incoming reinforcements and supplies created a mammoth logistical jam throughout the South Pacific's rudimentary ports.

During early December, the 1st Marine Division was withdrawn from Guadalcanal and sent to Australia for rehabilitation (after which it was to be assigned to MacArthur, who had been requesting a division trained for amphibious operations). General Patch, commanding the Americal Division, took over the command on Guadalcanal with the mission to "eliminate all Japanese forces" there. His forces (reorganized on 2 January as the XIV Corps) consisted of the Americal, 2d Marine, and 25th Divisions, plus some smaller units. Allied air strength had increased, Henderson Field was being expanded and improved, and additional air strips were under construction at Koli Point and Kukum. The logistical situation was gradually improving.

The situation of the Japanese had grown steadily worse. Furtive night runs by destroyers and submarines brought only a trickle of replacements and supplies; disease and hunger riddled them. By December, they were incapable of offensive action, but—to the end—held their defenses with a fatalistic bravery.

Patch planned to capture the dominating terrain of Mt. Austen immediately. That accomplished, one division would move across the ridges from Mt. Austen to envelop Kokumbona, another would drive westward along the shore, and the third would guard the airfields. Initial operations (17 December–3 January; *not shown*) by the Americal Division pocketed the Japanese in the Mt. Austen area, where troops from the 25th Division wiped them out (10–23 January).

Meanwhile, most of the 25th Division (Maj. Gen. Collins) had moved off in the attack against Kokumbona, while elements of the 2d Marine and Americal Divisions passed through each other in successive attacks down the coastal trail. The 25th Division reached the sea west of Kokumbona on 23 January, but only a few Japanese were trapped, and it soon became evident that they were retreating toward Cape Esperance. Though troubled by reports that another Japanese force was massing at Rabaul, Patch sent a reinforced regiment toward Cape Esperance in pursuit, while a reinforced battalion was embarked on landing craft and landed at Verahue (*left center*) to drive on Cape Esperance from the southwest. The two columns met on 9 February, but found only a few stragglers. The Japanese Navy had carried out a brilliant evacuation during the nights of 1, 4, and 7 February, picking up between 11,000 and 13,000 troops at Cape Esperance, despite air attacks.

Guadalcanal was the first major defeat the Japanese Army had suffered. For the Americans, it was an operation launched on the proverbial shoestring—one that could have easily been a disastrous failure. That it was not was due in large measure to Japanese mistakes. Possessing a definite preponderance in air, ground, and naval strength in the beginning, they had never brought it to bear effectively. Strategically and tactically, they committed their forces piecemeal, failed to exploit their victories, and persisted stubbornly in their misconceptions. Their Navy expected their Army to recover Guadalcanal—yet it failed to halt the build-up of American ground forces on that island, with the result that they always outnumbered the Japanese.

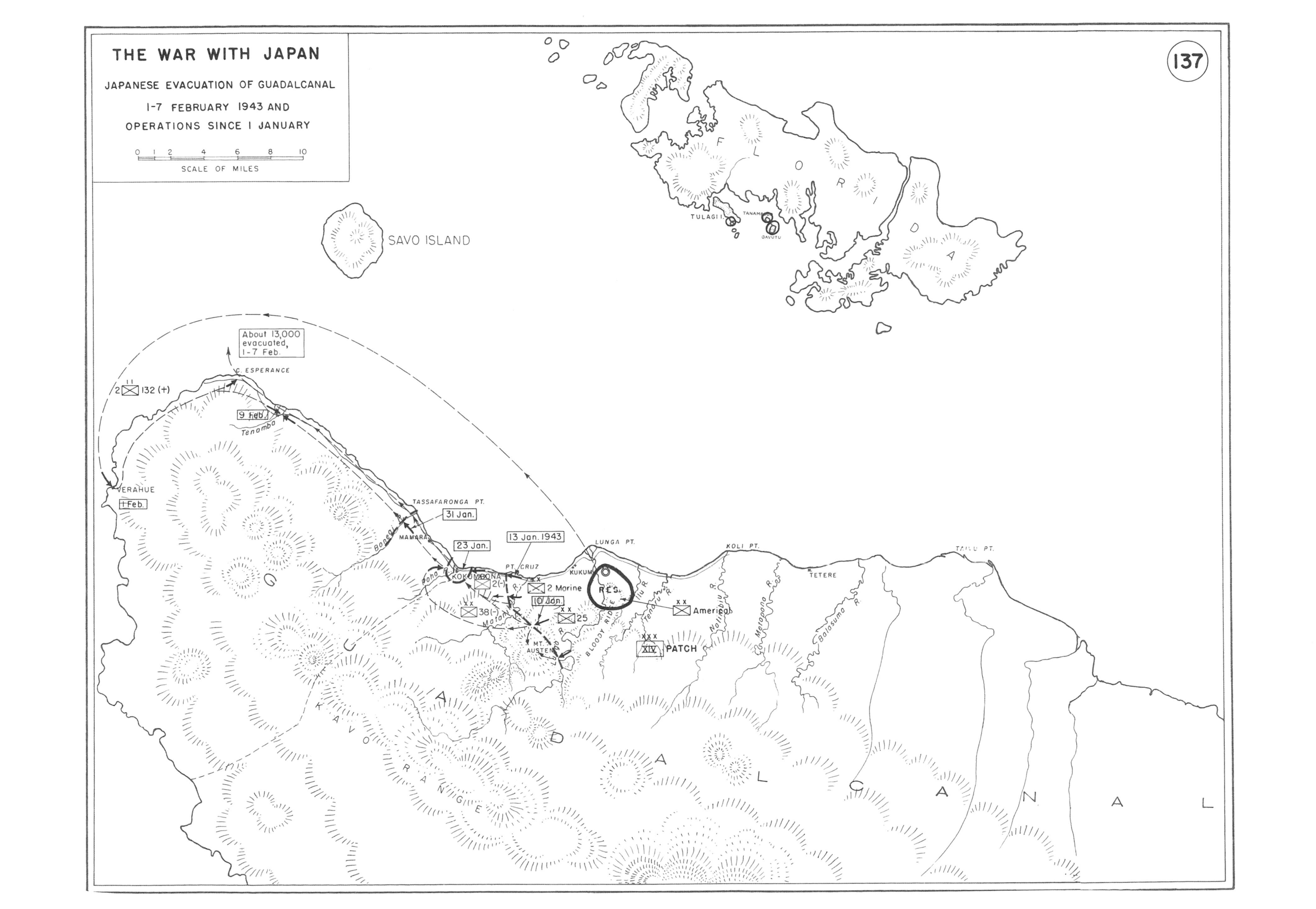
137
THE WAR WITH JAPAN
JAPANESE EVACUATION OF GUADALCANAL
1-7 FEBRUARY 1943 AND
OPERATIONS SINCE 1 JANUARY
0 1 2 4 6 8 10
SCALE OF MILES
SAVO ISLAND
FLORIDA
TULAGI I.
GAVUTU
About 13,000 evacuated, 1-7 Feb.
C. ESPERANCE
2 132 (+)
9 Feb.
Tenambo
VERAHUE
1 Feb.
TASSAFARONGA PT.
31 Jan.
MAMARA
Bonegi R.
23 Jan.
13 Jan. 1943
LUNGA PT.
KOLI PT.
TETERE
PT. CRUZ
KUKUM
KOKUMBONA
Poha R.
2(-)
2 Marine
10 Jan.
38(-)
25
Matan R.
MT. AUSTEN
Lunga R.
BLOODY RIDGE
Ilu R.
Tenaru R.
Americal
XIV
PATCH
Nalimbiu R.
Metapona R.
Balasuma R.
KAVO RANGE
GUADALCANAL

NEW GUINEA CAMPAIGN

As previously noted, the Japanese had occupied Lae and Salamaua (*both center, left*) in March 1942. Having strengthened these advance bases, they prepared for an amphibious offensive, based on Rabaul, to seize Port Moresby (*bottom center*). In Japanese hands, Port Moresby would be a serious threat to the vital Brisbane-Melbourne sector of Australia.

Initial American troop movements to Australia in early 1942 had consisted largely of air corps units and their supporting elements, in the vain hope that these would enable Wavell to hold the Netherlands East Indies. These forces, plus a handful of Australian troops, were all that were available when MacArthur reached Australia (17 March) from Bataan. Later, he received the American 32d and 41st Divisions and the Australian 6th and 7th Divisions (which had been recalled from the Middle East). MacArthur considered these forces insufficient, but—even so—decided that the best way to defend Australia was to hold New Guinea.

The Japanese advance on Port Moresby was delayed about a month while their Carrier Striking Force raided into the Indian Ocean. On its return, two large carriers were detached to support the Port Moresby operation, but this first offensive was turned back in the Battle of the Coral Sea (*see map 129*). Plans for a second offensive were nullified by Japanese aircraft carrier losses at Midway. MacArthur took advantage of the time thus gained to strengthen Port Moresby and develop a new base at Milne Bay (*this map, bottom center*). With the initiation of the American offensive in the South Pacific (*see text, map 132*), he pressed the occupation of Buna (*this map, lower center*) and the development of an airfield in the adjacent Dobodura area, to support the projected attacks on Lae and Salamaua during the second phase of that offensive. Air and naval forces of MacArthur's command supported Ghormley during the first phase of the offensive, chiefly by air strikes on the Rabaul area.

The Japanese, however, forestalled him at Buna, landing there the night of 21 July and driving inland—against the desperate resistance of the tiny Australian forces in the area—to seize Kokoda and its small airstrip on 12 August. Then, to the complete surprise of Allied intelligence, the Japanese continued their advance through the wild mountains south of Kokoda. They got to within thirty miles of Port Moresby by 13 September, but Allied aircraft had disrupted their communications, and the situation of the Japanese forces on Guadalcanal had worsened. Consequently, they were recalled to Buna until the situation on Guadalcanal could be restored. As part of their drive on Port Moresby, the Japanese had also made an unsuccessful amphibious assault on Mime Bay (25 August–5 September). Allied troops then converged on the Buna area by air (airfields were rapidly improvised at Wanigela and Pongani [*both bottom center*]), by difficult mountain trails, and by small boats along the northern coast. Fighting continued around Buna from 19 November through 22 January (*see map 139*).

Elsewhere, a Japanese attempt (9–30 January; *action not shown*) to seize the mountain airfield at Wau (*center, left*) was thwarted when Australian troops were flown in at the last minute. A large Japanese convoy, bound for Lae and Salamaua, was shattered (*action not shown*) by Allied aircraft in the Bismarck Sea during 2–4 March. From June through September, MacArthur cleared the Lae-Salamaua area by feinting an attack on the Japanese forces at Salamaua and then seizing Lae behind them with a skillful converging airborne-amphibious-ground attack. Exploiting his success, he next seized the Huon Peninsula.

Meanwhile, amphibious operations, as shown, had covered the north flank of the Allied advance. On 26 December, the rehabilitated 1st Marine Division seized Cape Gloucester, and army units occupied Long Island (*both center*), threatening communications between Rabaul and New Guinea. Throughout this campaign, the Allied air forces did magnificent work in gaining air superiority and in transporting troops and supplies across New Guinea's jungle mountains.

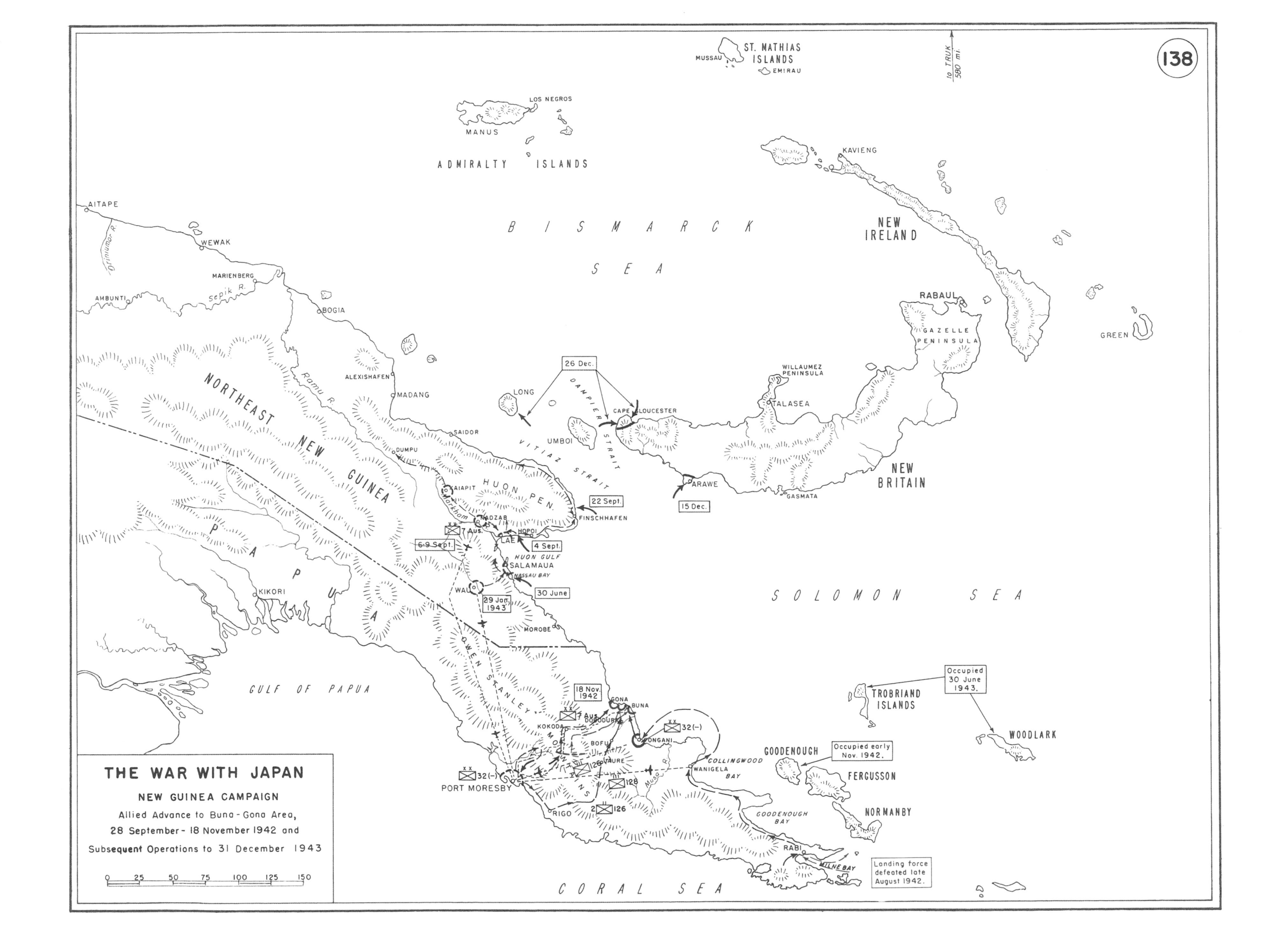

138
THE WAR WITH JAPAN
NEW GUINEA CAMPAIGN
Allied Advance to Buna-Gona Area,
28 September - 18 November 1942 and
Subsequent Operations to 31 December 1943
0 25 50 75 100 125 150
to TRUK 580 mi.
ST. MATHIAS ISLANDS
MUSSAU
EMIRAU
LOS NEGROS
MANUS
ADMIRALTY ISLANDS
KAVIENG
NEW IRELAND
GREEN
BISMARCK SEA
RABAUL
GAZELLE PENINSULA
NEW BRITAIN
WILLAUMEZ PENINSULA
TALASEA
GASMATA
ARAWE
15 Dec.
CAPE GLOUCESTER
26 Dec.
DAMPIER STRAIT
LONG
UMBOI
VITIAZ STRAIT
AITAPE
Drinumor R.
WEWAK
MARIENBERG
Sepik R.
AMBUNTI
BOGIA
Ramu R.
ALEXISHAFEN
MADANG
SAIDOR
DUMPU
NORTHEAST NEW GUINEA
HUON PEN.
KAIAPIT
Markham
NADZAB
7 Aus.
6-9 Sept.
HOPOI
LAE
4 Sept.
22 Sept.
FINSCHHAFEN
HUON GULF
SALAMAUA
NASSAU BAY
30 June
WAU
29 Jan. 1943
MOROBE
PAPUA
KIKORI
GULF OF PAPUA
OWEN STANLEY MOUNTAINS
18 Nov. 1942
GONA
BUNA
7 Aus.
DOBODURA
KOKODA
32(-)
ONGANI
BOFU
JAURE
126
128
2
RIGO
PORT MORESBY
Musa R.
COLLINGWOOD BAY
WANIGELA
SOLOMON SEA
Occupied 30 June 1943.
TROBRIAND ISLANDS
WOODLARK
GOODENOUGH
Occupied early Nov. 1942.
FERGUSSON
NORMANBY
GOODENOUGH BAY
RABI
MILNE BAY
Landing force defeated late August 1942.
CORAL SEA

PAPUAN CAMPAIGN

★

Organized around the major strong points shown, the Japanese position in the Buna area was a complex of mutually supporting bunkers, concealed by dense tropical vegetation and sited to cover every avenue of approach. Its garrison numbered approximately 6,500—about half of them exhausted survivors of the abortive drive on Port Moresby, the rest fresh troops newly arrived from Rabaul. This area was a hot and humid mixture of jungle and swamp, infested with insects and leeches. Scrub typhus, malaria, dengue fever, dysentery, and skin infections were endemic.

Many of the Australian troops had been fighting continuously for two months. The 32d Division went into its first battle here with many of its men already weakened by sickness and short rations. Practically untrained for jungle warfare, it was short of both engineer equipment and medical supplies. Initially, it was without artillery, until the Australians loaned it several guns; eventually, one of its own howitzers was sent forward. Its logistical support was extremely sketchy. At first, supplies came by small boats from Milne Bay or were air-dropped. Later, airstrips in the Dobodura area (*lower center*) were utilized, but the situation was never satisfactory until late December, when small freighters began bulk deliveries. An early supply crisis, created when Japanese planes sank most of the available small boats (16–17 November), handicapped operations for weeks.

On 18 November, the Allied advance reached the outposts of the Japanese position. The next morning they attacked, and immediately found themselves halted by heavy fire from an unseen enemy. Allied infantry—armed only with rifles, grenades, and machine guns, and supported by a few mortars and pieces of artillery—were thrust against a strong, carefully prepared defensive system. Lack of training and the confusing terrain made direct air support ineffective. The Navy refused to risk its ships in the uncharted waters off Buna. Lateral communications between the different Allied units was blocked by swamps and streams, while the Japanese shifted their forces swiftly along the coastal trail, or by landing craft from point to point. Radio equipment proved unreliable; losses and sickness mounted; morale sagged.

Maj. Gen. Edwin F. Harding organized his available forces (the 127th Infantry was still en route, and Lt. Gen. Edmund F. Herring had transferred two battalions of the 126th to the Australian sector) into two combat teams—the Urbana and Warren Forces (*note, bottom right*). He could gain but little ground; in the Australian zone, however, one of the American battalions scored the first appreciable Allied success when it established a roadblock behind the forward Japanese position on 30 November as shown.

Impatient for a quick victory, MacArthur sent Lt. Gen. Robert L. Eichelberger to Buna to take command of the American forces there. Eichelberger relieved Harding (2 December), replaced the commanders of the Warren and Urbana Forces, and put Brig. Gen. Albert W. Waldron in command of the 32d Division. Eichelberger was an aggressive leader, but he also profited from the gradual improvement taking place in the logistical system, the fact that the surviving Allied troops were becoming combat veterans, and the inroads starvation was making in the Japanese ranks. During a generally unsuccessful attack on 5 December, a platoon of the Urbana Force penetrated to the sea east of Buna. On 9 December, the Australians stormed Gona. The decisive attack, however, was launched on the 18th in the Cape Endaiadere sector, Warren Force being reinforced by two battalions of fresh Australian infantry and eight Australian light tanks. The tanks cracked line after line of bunkers in a series of coordinated assaults. By 3 January, the Buna-Endaiadere area was pinched out between this advance and the Urbana Force (now reinforced by the 127th Infantry), which had punched another corridor to the sea on 29 December. Subsequently, the Australian 7th Division, reinforced by the 163d Infantry (41st Division), finished clearing the Sananda area by 22 January.

It was a costly campaign: in addition to normal casualties (Australian and American, 8,546; Japanese, probably 13,000–15,000), some 2,334 Americans were disabled by disease. But it was also educational—as to both the strength of a Japanese defensive system and the methods of reducing it.

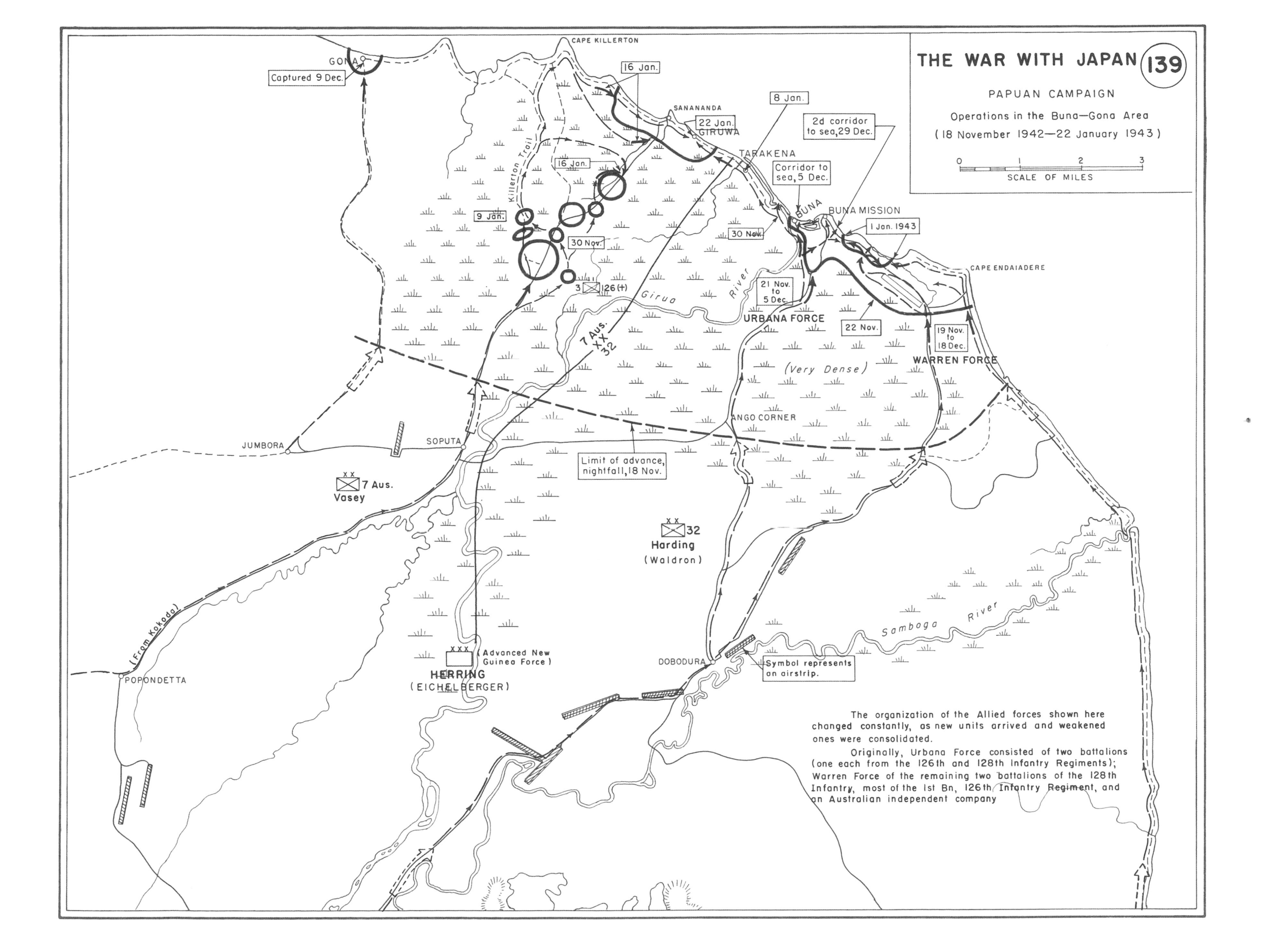
THE WAR WITH JAPAN
139
PAPUAN CAMPAIGN
Operations in the Buna–Gona Area
(18 November 1942–22 January 1943)
0 1 2 3
SCALE OF MILES
GONA
Captured 9 Dec.
CAPE KILLERTON
16 Jan.
SANANANDA
22 Jan.
GIRUWA
8 Jan.
TARAKENA
2d corridor to sea, 29 Dec.
Corridor to sea, 5 Dec.
BUNA
BUNA MISSION
1 Jan. 1943
CAPE ENDAIADERE
Killerton Trail
16 Jan.
9 Jan.
30 Nov.
3 126(+)
30 Nov.
Girua River
21 Nov. to 5 Dec.
URBANA FORCE
22 Nov.
19 Nov. to 18 Dec.
WARREN FORCE
7 Aus. XX 32
(Very Dense)
ANGO CORNER
JUMBORA
SOPUTA
Limit of advance, nightfall, 18 Nov.
7 Aus.
Vasey
32
Harding
(Waldron)
Samboga River
(From Kokoda)
POPONDETTA
(Advanced New Guinea Force)
HERRING
(EICHELBERGER)
DOBODURA
Symbol represents an airstrip.
The organization of the Allied forces shown here changed constantly, as new units arrived and weakened ones were consolidated.
Originally, Urbana Force consisted of two battalions (one each from the 126th and 128th Infantry Regiments); Warren Force of the remaining two battalions of the 128th Infantry, most of the 1st Bn, 126th Infantry Regiment, and an Australian independent company

OPERATIONS IN THE SOLOMON ISLANDS

★

In November, 1942, before the Allies had achieved complete victory in Papua (*left center*) and Guadalcanal (*lower right*), Japan adopted a more determined defense in both New Guinea and the Solomons as a prelude to recapturing Guadalcanal and seizing Port Moresby. Ground and air reinforcements were moved to the Rabaul area, and a new army (the Eighteenth) assumed control of New Guinea operations—the Seventeenth now being restricted to the Solomons. In January 1943, this overly optimistic plan was scuttled by Allied successes at Buna and Guadalcanal; now the Japanese—more realistically—decided to hold in the Huon Gulf area (*center, left*) and at New Georgia (*center, right*).

On the Allied side, General Marshall, on 1 December, urged implementation of the second and third tasks of the 2 July directive (*see text, map 132*). This set off a debate which raged for four months—primarily among JCS planners. The major issue revolved about command—already assigned in the earlier directive to MacArthur, in whose area the operations in both the Solomons and New Guinea would lie. But to Admiral King, control of the Pacific Fleet and command were indivisible: if MacArthur controlled the operations, the strategic flexibility afforded by the fleet would be jeopardized, he inferred. Exasperated Army planners observed that air and ground forces also provided flexibility. The argument had not been settled by the time the JCS went to the Casablanca Conference (January) where—for the first time—the Americans adopted the policy of counterbalancing British demands for continued Mediterranean operations with proposals for expanded Pacific operations. The conference gave a green light to continuation of the drive on Rabaul, which the JCS confidently predicted would fall in 1943. But, in March, upon receipt of MacArthur's plan for such a drive, it became apparent that, without sizable reinforcements (not authorized at Casablanca), MacArthur could not take Rabaul in 1943. As a result, a less ambitious program was substituted: CARTWHEEL (an advance in 1943 to Bougainville by Halsey and to western New Britain by MacArthur). Strategic direction of both advances was assigned to MacArthur; Nimitz, however, would still control Halsey's forces and the fleet. The map depicts the implementation of this plan. (The operations along the New Guinea coast have already been discussed [*see text, map 138*].)

MacArthur initially intended that Halsey would jump directly from Guadalcanal to Bougainville, but Halsey, having already occupied the Russell Islands, convinced him that air bases in the central Solomons were a prerequisite to a Bougainville assault. Thus, in the latter part of 1943, Halsey, utilizing elements of six army and marine divisions, executed a series of amphibious operations designed to secure air bases and bypass Japanese Seventeenth Army forces in the central Solomons. The battles were typical of operations in the South Pacific. Hampered by the weather, unhealthy climatic conditions, a resourceful enemy, and lack of communications, Halsey exploited air and naval power to the maximum in establishing a string of bases (*this map; center, right*) pointing toward Rabaul. Operations culminated in the landing at Empress Augusta Bay on Bougainville in November, after Halsey had misled the Japanese with an earlier, diversionary landing on Choiseul. In the northward drive, Halsey's naval forces and the Japanese had fought four surface engagements (Vella Lavella, Vella Gulf, Kolombangara, and Kula Gulf). On the whole, the honors were about even.

Back in April, the Japanese I-Go operation (an attempt to destroy Allied air and naval power through concentrated air strikes in New Guinea and the Solomons) had failed to blunt MacArthur's offensives. In early November, worried over the threat to Rabaul, Japan moved most of her carrier aircraft and powerful surface elements from Truk (*off map, top center*) to Rabaul. But Halsey's and MacArthur's air forces, supported by carriers provided by Nimitz, won this battle for control of the air and forced the Japanese to withdraw their remaining carrier aircraft and surface forces to Truk. Allied air forces now stepped up their attacks on Rabaul. In August, the JCS had recognized the possibilities of isolating that fortress, and had ordered it to be bypassed. MacArthur could now contain Rabaul and continue his drive north and west.

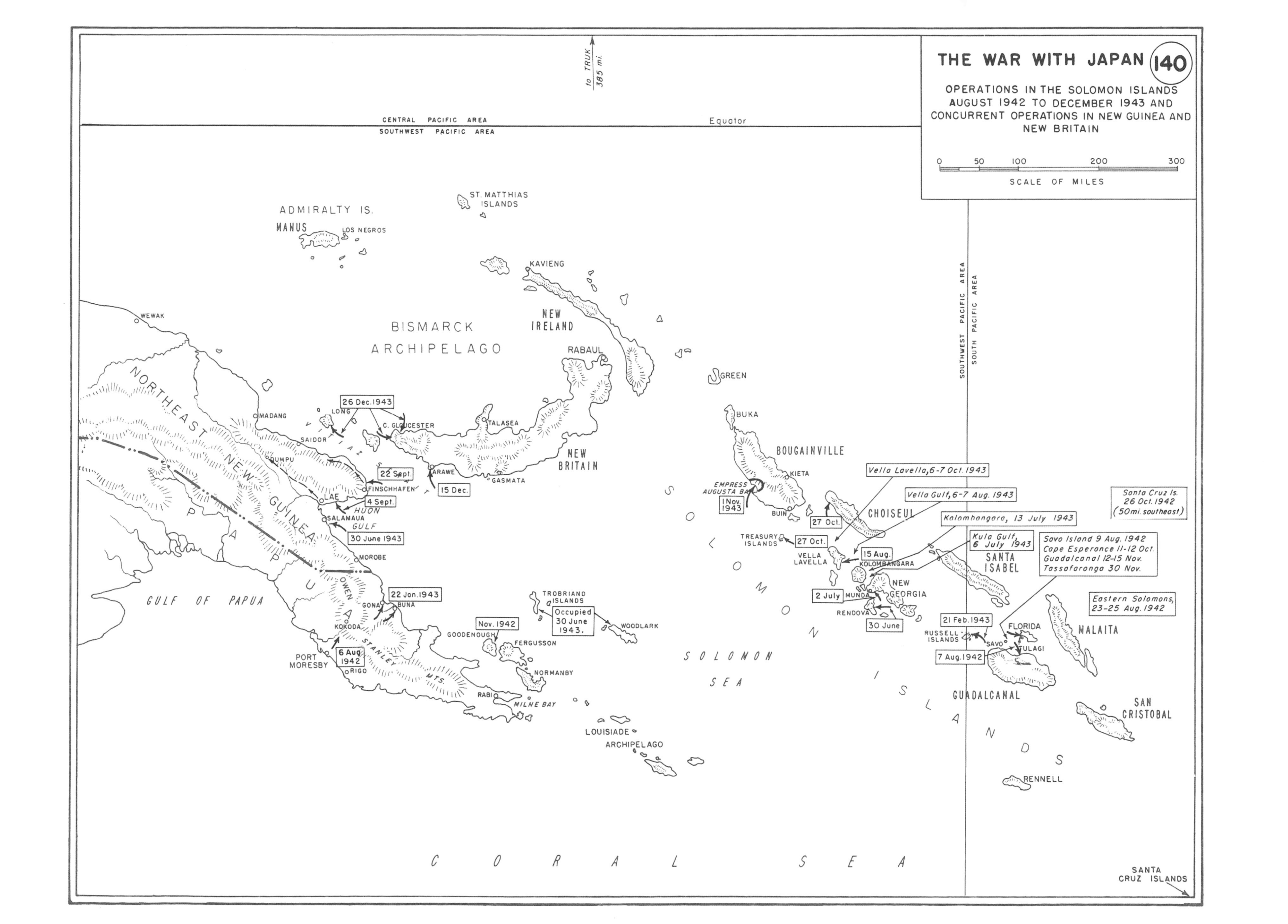
THE WAR WITH JAPAN 140
OPERATIONS IN THE SOLOMON ISLANDS
AUGUST 1942 TO DECEMBER 1943 AND
CONCURRENT OPERATIONS IN NEW GUINEA AND
NEW BRITAIN
0 50 100 200 300
SCALE OF MILES
to TRUK 385 mi.
CENTRAL PACIFIC AREA
SOUTHWEST PACIFIC AREA
Equator
SOUTH PACIFIC AREA
ADMIRALTY IS.
MANUS
LOS NEGROS
ST. MATTHIAS ISLANDS
KAVIENG
NEW IRELAND
BISMARCK ARCHIPELAGO
RABAUL
GREEN
BUKA
BOUGAINVILLE
KIETA
EMPRESS AUGUSTA BAY
1 Nov. 1943
BUIN
WEWAK
NORTHEAST NEW GUINEA
MADANG
26 Dec. 1943
LONG
C. GLOUCESTER
TALASEA
NEW BRITAIN
SAIDOR
DUMPU
VITIAZ STRAIT
22 Sept.
ARAWE
15 Dec.
GASMATA
FINSCHHAFEN
4 Sept.
LAE
HUON GULF
SALAMAUA
30 June 1943
MOROBE
PAPUA
GULF OF PAPUA
22 Jan. 1943
GONA
BUNA
KOKODA
OWEN STANLEY MTS.
PORT MORESBY
6 Aug. 1942
RIGO
TROBRIAND ISLANDS
Occupied 30 June 1943.
WOODLARK
Nov. 1942
GOODENOUGH
FERGUSSON
NORMANBY
RABI
MILNE BAY
LOUISIADE ARCHIPELAGO
SOLOMON SEA
SOLOMON ISLANDS
Vella Lavella, 6-7 Oct. 1943
Vella Gulf, 6-7 Aug. 1943
Kolombangara, 13 July 1943
Kula Gulf, 6 July 1943
27 Oct.
CHOISEUL
TREASURY ISLANDS
27 Oct.
VELLA LAVELLA
15 Aug.
KOLOMBANGARA
SANTA ISABEL
NEW GEORGIA
2 July
MUNDA
RENDOVA
30 June
Santa Cruz Is. 26 Oct. 1942 (50 mi. southeast)
Savo Island 9 Aug. 1942
Cape Esperance 11-12 Oct.
Guadalcanal 12-15 Nov.
Tassafaronga 30 Nov.
Eastern Solomons, 23-25 Aug. 1942
21 Feb. 1943
RUSSELL ISLANDS
SAVO
FLORIDA
TULAGI
7 Aug. 1942
MALAITA
GUADALCANAL
SAN CRISTOBAL
RENNELL
CORAL SEA
SANTA CRUZ ISLANDS

CHINA-BURMA THEATER

★

The Japanese conquests of Burma (*see map 127*) left China practically isolated. Allied leaders consequently feared that general war-weariness and the cessation of foreign aid might force China out of the war. Great plans to reestablish land communication between India and China therefore were set afoot. This required the liberation of Burma—an operation of considerable magnitude in itself (*see maps 142 and 151*).

In the meantime, an air transport system was organized to fly in the most essential supplies from bases in the Assam region of India (*this map, lower left*) to Kunming (*lower center*) across the "Hump"—some 500 miles of Himalayan Mountain wilderness. For some unknown reason, the Japanese never made a serious effort to break up this vulnerable system.

Operations in China proper are poorly documented, and so can be covered only in the most general fashion. Even available American accounts are frequently highly partisan. It should be remembered that in many ways the struggle between China and Japan was hardly "war" in the Western understanding of the word—just as the Chinese Army was far from being a modern army. Throughout this period, a constant, fluctuating struggle went on between Chiang Kai-Shek and the Chinese Communists, who were based in the Sian area (*center*). The latter, while presenting themselves to the outside world as pure-hearted "agrarian reformers" devoted only to freeing China from the Japanese, applied most of their energy to undermining Chiang, who replied in kind. The average American, anxious to get on with the war, and innocent of any real knowledge of China or Communism, was at a major disadvantage in this environment.

The one American combat force in China was Maj. Gen. Claire Chennault's United States China Air Task Force (later the Fourteenth Air Force). Beginning in July 1942, Chennault carried on a growing air offensive against Japanese shipping off the China coast and Japanese installations in China, Burma, Thailand, Indochina, and Formosa. In early June 1944, B-29's of the XX Bomber Command began operating from bases deep in China, striking targets as distant as southern Japan. All these American air operations were straitjacketed by the fact that all supplies—especially aviation gasoline—had to be flown in over the Hump.

Other than the American air activity, the overall situation had hardly changed since 1939. The Japanese held most of the railroads, major ports, and important industrial and agricultural areas. Occasionally they conducted minor offensives to seize crops, suppress guerrilla outbreaks, or give new troops combat indoctrination. Chinese operations were largely limited to guerrilla activity, vastly publicized at the time, but apparently of no great importance. In some areas, there had been no fighting for years—allegedly, the opposing commanders sometimes reached mutually profitable understandings. Anxious to develop an efficient Chinese Army, Stilwell requested the allocation of a large part of the Hump system's cargo space for weapons and equipment. This put him at loggerheads with Chennault, who managed to retain control of most of the cargo capacity, claiming that the existing Chinese forces would suffice, if given sufficient air support.

In April 1944, the China stalemate exploded. Apparently fearful that the defeats they had suffered in the Southwest Pacific would endanger their control of the South China Sea, the Japanese launched a series of offensives to consolidate their position on the Asiatic mainland. These offensives (*striped red areas*) swept the Chinese off the principal north-south rail lines in central and southern China, giving the Japanese continuous land communications between northern Manchuria and Singapore. Seven of Chennault's airfields were overrun, forcing him farther into the interior. During these painful reverses, Stilwell was recalled to the United States; his former command was divided into the India-Burma theater (under Lt. Gen. Daniel I. Sultan) and the China theater (Maj. Gen. Albert C. Wedemeyer). Late in November, the Japanese advanced on Kweiyang (*lower center*), but were checked by American-trained Chinese troops flown in from Burma.

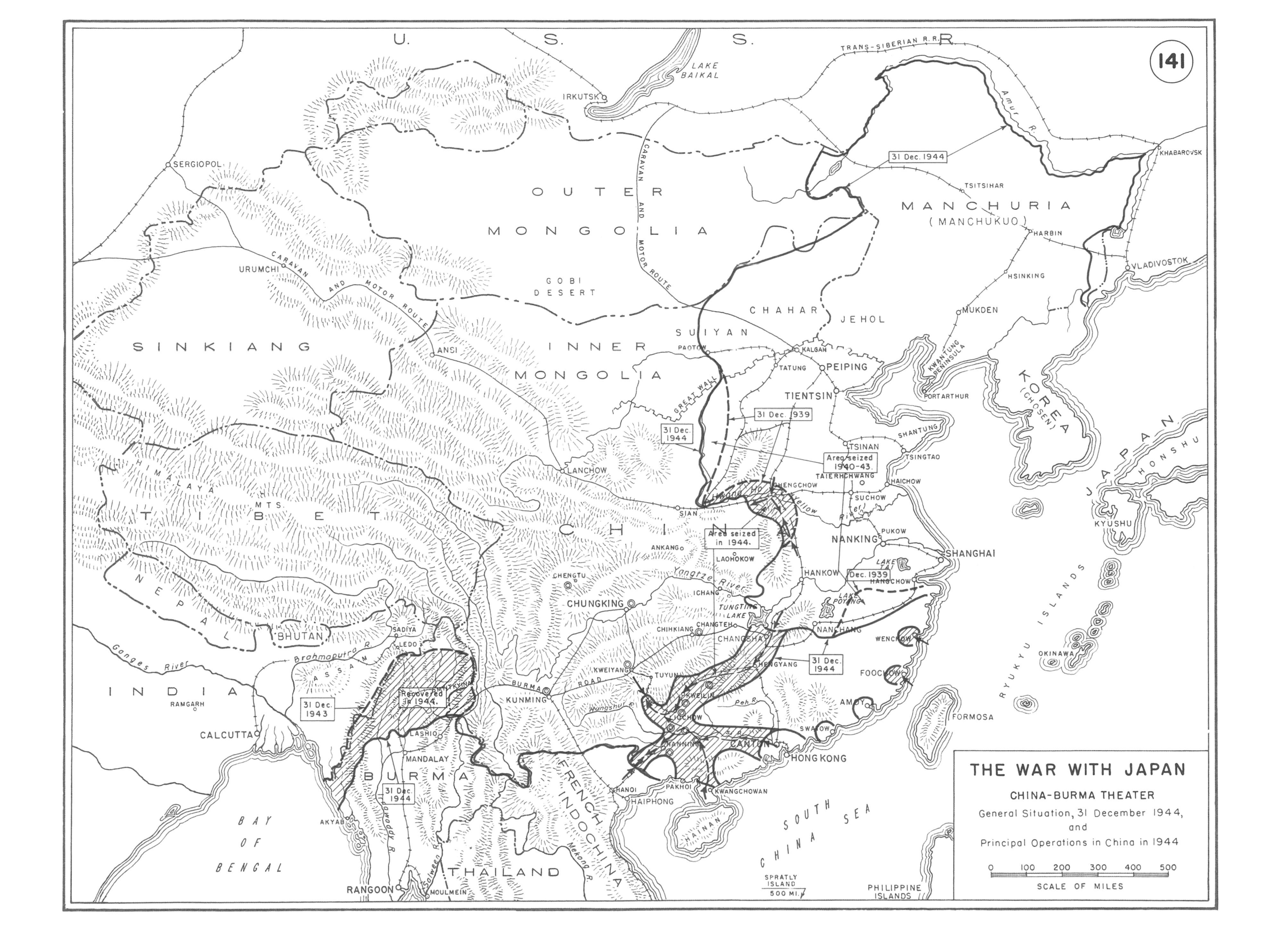

141
THE WAR WITH JAPAN
CHINA-BURMA THEATER
General Situation, 31 December 1944,
and
Principal Operations in China in 1944
0 100 200 300 400 500
SCALE OF MILES
31 Dec. 1944
31 Dec. 1939
Area seized 1940-43.
Area seized in 1944.
Dec. 1939
31 Dec. 1943
Recovered in 1944.
U. S. S. R.
TRANS-SIBERIAN R.R.
LAKE BAIKAL
IRKUTSK
SERGIOPOL
OUTER MONGOLIA
CARAVAN AND MOTOR ROUTE
GOBI DESERT
URUMCHI
SINKIANG
ANSI
INNER MONGOLIA
SUIYAN
CHAHAR
JEHOL
MANCHURIA
(MANCHUKUO)
TSITSIHAR
HARBIN
HSINKING
MUKDEN
KHABAROVSK
VLADIVOSTOK
Amur R.
KWANTUNG PENINSULA
PORT ARTHUR
KOREA
(CHOSEN)
JAPAN
HONSHU
KYUSHU
RYUKYU ISLANDS
OKINAWA
FORMOSA
PAOTOW
KALGAN
TATUNG
PEIPING
TIENTSIN
GREAT WALL
TSINAN
SHANTUNG
TSINGTAO
TAIERHCHWANG
HAICHOW
CHENGCHOW
SUCHOW
Yellow River
Hwang Ho
LANCHOW
SIAN
CHINA
TIBET
HIMALAYA MTS.
NEPAL
BHUTAN
ANKANG
LAOHOKOW
NANKING
PUKOW
SHANGHAI
LAKE TAI
HANGCHOW
HANKOW
Yangtze River
ICHANG
TUNGTING LAKE
LAKE POYANG
CHENGTU
CHUNGKING
CHIHKIANG
CHANGTEH
CHANGSHA
NANCHANG
WENCHOW
HENGYANG
FOOCHOW
KWEIYANG
TUYUN
KWEILIN
LIUCHOW
NANNING
Peh R.
Hungshui R.
AMOY
SWATOW
CANTON
HONG KONG
KWANGCHOWAN
PAKHOI
HANOI
HAIPHONG
HAINAN
SOUTH CHINA SEA
SPRATLY ISLAND 500 MI.
PHILIPPINE ISLANDS
BURMA ROAD
KUNMING
FRENCH INDOCHINA
Mekong R.
THAILAND
BURMA
MYITKYINA
LASHIO
MANDALAY
Irrawaddy R.
Salween R.
RANGOON
MOULMEIN
AKYAB
BAY OF BENGAL
SADIYA
LEDO
ASSAM
Brahmaputra R.
INDIA
Ganges River
RAMGARH
CALCUTTA

BURMA CAMPAIGN

★

Following the Allied retreat from Burma (*see map 127*), Wavell attempted a counteroffensive (September, 1942–May, 1943; *action not shown*) down the coast against Akyab (*this map, lower left*), but was unsuccessful.

The Allies then slowly gathered strength. The American Tenth Air Force had begun moving into India in March 1942. In December, 1942, American engineers began the construction of a highway from Ledo (*upper center*) into northern Burma. Throughout India, a vast complex of improved road and rail communications, airfields, and supply installations proliferated. Concurrently, Stilwell reorganized and trained the Chinese troops that had retreated into India after the fall of Burma, flying in replacements from China. Brigadier Orde C. Wingate, an eccentric specialist in irregular warfare, now urged the use of small columns of specially trained troops—supplied by air drops—in operations against Japanese communications deep in Burma. Wavell authorized this force, and Wingate led these "Chindits" on a foray (February-April, 1943) against the railroad north of Mandalay. Air resupply proved highly effective, but Wingate's erratic tactics resulted in the loss of a third of his force, without compensating damage to the Japanese. Allied air forces carried out vigorous raids against the Japanese communications.

The *Quadrant* Conference (Quebec, 1943) resulted in the decision to clear northern Burma and reestablish land communication with China as soon as the 1943 monsoon season ended. In its final form, this plan included four operations: an attack toward Akyab by the XV Corps, the seizure of Myitkyina (*upper center*) by Stilwell, a deep penetration by Wingate's Chindits to aid Stilwell's advance, and an advance to the Chindwin River by the IV Corps. Wingate's activities had greatly impressed the JCS, who hastily improvised the 5307th Composite Unit (Provisional)—better known as Merrill's Marauders—for service in Burma. The Japanese, meanwhile, strengthened their forces in Burma. Expecting an Allied offensive, they decided to strike first to seize the British bases at Imphal and Kohima (*center, left*).

Stilwell's attack opened in October, 1943. In February, when the Marauders came into line, Stilwell used them in a series of wide enveloping movements to get in the rear of the Japanese opposing his Chinese. These maneuvers were successful, the Marauders capturing Myitkyina airfield on 17 May, but the Japanese waged an indomitable fight for the town itself. The Chindits had blocked the southern approaches to Myitkyina, but were finally forced to withdraw.

The Akyab offensive began in November. In February, the Japanese delivered a major counterattack, but were roughly repulsed. In early March, the Japanese Fifteenth Army struck at Imphal and Kohima, isolating both towns. The British garrisons, supplied by air, held out successfully, and counterattacks threw the Japanese back. Their advance, as usual in Japanese operations, had combined aggressive tactics with shoestring logistical support. By 1 July, sickness, hunger, and battle casualties had crippled them; as the monsoon season worsened, they retreated in growing confusion.

During this period, fresh Chinese forces attacked down the Burma Road, but were checked at the walled towns of Lungling and Tengchung. Myitkyina finally fell on 3 August. Thereafter, operations paused until the end of the rains. The Marauders were disbanded, but the newly created Mars Force took their place. On 2 December, the British captured Kalewa (*center, left*), linking up the next day with Sultan's right flank. (Sultan had succeeded Stilwell.) Bhamo (*center*) fell on the 15th. The Chinese had previously, with help from the Fourteenth Air Force, stormed Tengchung and Lungling. By the end of the year, the Japanese were withdrawing along most of the front (*heavy red line*), and Allied pressure was steadily increasing.

Note: On this map, upper center, Tengyueh *should be* Tengchung.

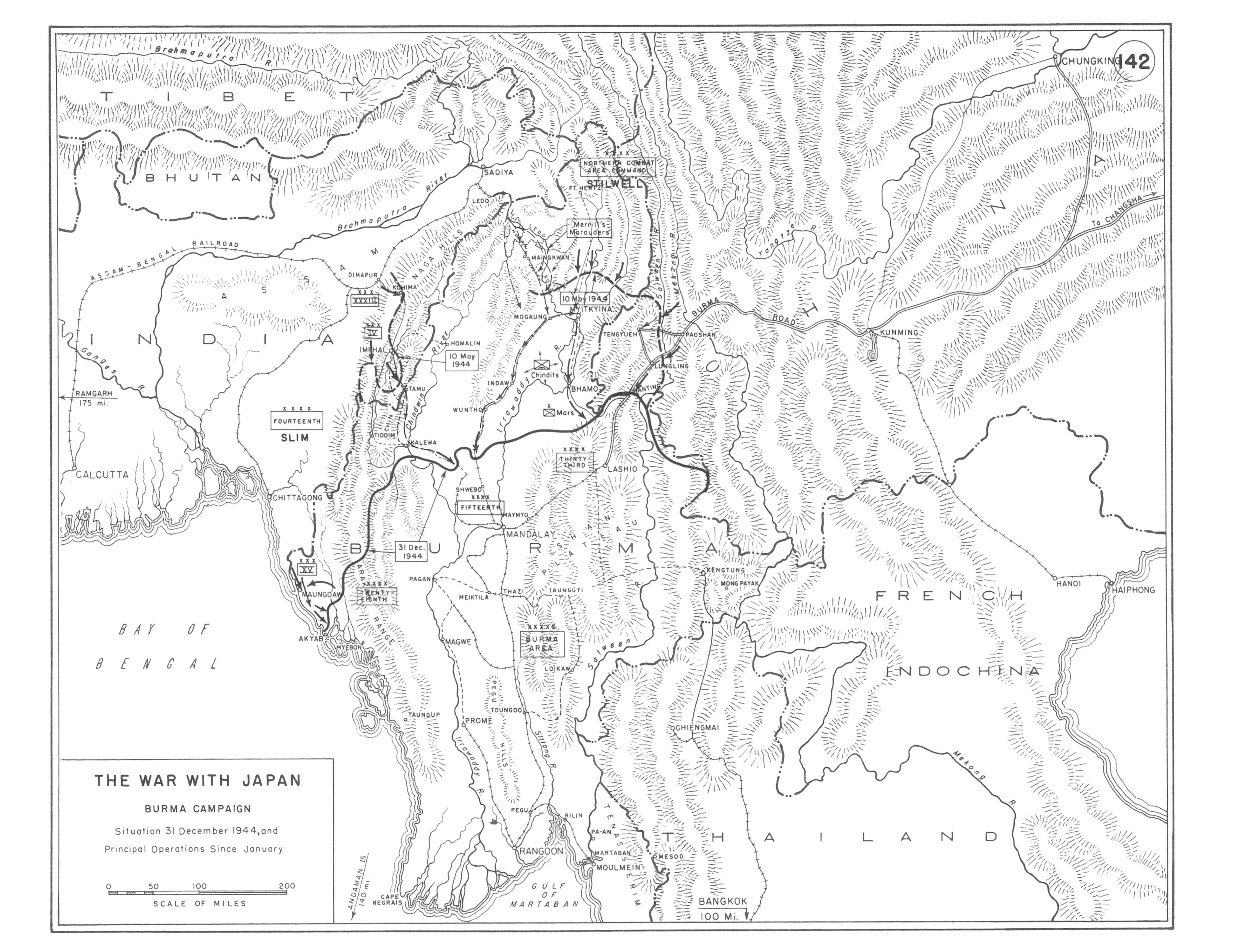
142
THE WAR WITH JAPAN
BURMA CAMPAIGN
Situation 31 December 1944, and
Principal Operations Since January
0 50 100 200
SCALE OF MILES
TIBET
BHUTAN
INDIA
ASSAM
BURMA
CHINA
FRENCH
INDOCHINA
THAILAND
BAY OF BENGAL
GULF OF MARTABAN
Brahmaputra R.
Brahmaputra River
Ganges R.
Irrawaddy R.
Chindwin River
Salween R.
Mekong R.
Yangtze R.
Sittang R.
ASSAM-BENGAL RAILROAD
BURMA ROAD
NAGA HILLS
ARAKAN RANGE
PEGU HILLS
SHAN PLATEAU
TENASSERIM
NORTHERN COMBAT AREA COMMAND
STILWELL
Merrill's Marauders
10 May 1944
10 May 1944
31 Dec. 1944
FOURTEENTH
SLIM
FIFTEENTH
THIRTY-THIRD
TWENTY-EIGHTH
BURMA AREA
XXXIII
IV
XV
Chindits
Mars
CHUNGKING
To CHANGSHA
KUNMING
SADIYA
LEDO
FT. HERTZ
MAINGKWAN
DIMAPUR
KOHIMA
IMPHAL
TAMU
TIDDIM
KALEWA
HOMALIN
MOGAUNG
MYITKYINA
TENGYUEH
PAOSHAN
LUNGLING
WANTING
BHAMO
INDAW
WUNTHO
SHWEBO
MAYMYO
MANDALAY
LASHIO
PAGAN
MEIKTILA
THAZI
TAUNGGYI
KENGTUNG
MONG PAYAK
MAGWE
LOIKAW
TAUNGUP
PROME
TOUNGOO
PEGU
BILIN
PA-AN
RANGOON
MARTABAN
MOULMEIN
MESOD
CHIENGMAI
CAPE NEGRAIS
ANDAMAN IS. 140 mi.
BANGKOK 100 Mi.
CALCUTTA
RAMGARH 175 mi.
CHITTAGONG
MAUNGDAW
AKYAB
MYEBON
HANOI
HAIPHONG

LANDINGS IN THE GILBERT ISLANDS

By approving CARTWHEEL in March 1943, the JCS gave impetus to the Allied drive back to the Philippines. But, as yet, no Allied advance had been initiated in the Central Pacific. At the TRIDENT Conference (Washington) in May, the JCS presented an overall plan for operations in the Pacific, which the CCS generally accepted.

This basic strategic plan specified the seizure—in conjunction with the British and Chinese—of a foothold on the China coast near Hong Kong as a base from which Japan could be taken under air attack, and invaded if necessary. American forces would get to Hong Kong by opening a line of communications to the Celebes Sea (*center, left*) and recapturing part of the Philippines. The plan specified that the main drive westward should be made through the Central Pacific, and a subsidiary one up through New Guinea. For the next nine months, this approach was debated between the JCS and MacArthur. The latter felt firmly that the Central Pacific advance was too long, could gain no vital strategic objectives, would entail costly island assaults, and would fail to exploit land-based air power; he wanted the major effort made up through New Guinea. But the JCS believed the central route would be easier to support logistically, was better hygienically, would exploit the fleet's mobility, and would strike Japan's vulnerable eastern flank. In October, the JCS added another reason—the Army Air Corps' new B-29 bomber could strike Japan proper from the Marianas.

So, ultimately, the Allies returned to the Philippines by the two routes delineated on the map. (MacArthur's operations from 15 February to 22 April [*see text, map 144*] and the meeting of the two-pronged advance in the Philippines on 20 October [*see text, maps 145–148*] will be described subsequently.) After the landing at St. Matthias (*this map; center, right*) on 20 March, the South Pacific Area was pinched out, and Halsey, returning to the Central Pacific Area, assumed command of the Third Fleet.

Meanwhile, in September, the Japanese had reluctantly revised their strategy. Recognizing the tremendous growth in American air and sea power and their own excessive losses in shipping and aircraft, they decided to contract their defensive perimeter to gain time for rebuilding an offensive capability. The new line would extend from the Kuriles (*off map, top center*) through the Bonins–Marianas–Carolines–western New Guinea–Netherlands East Indies to Burma. Outposts forward of this line would trade space for time.

Admiral Nimitz's drive across the Pacific began with landings in the Gilberts (*right center*) in November 1943. Unable to obtain sufficient troops to implement the TRIDENT decision to seize the Marshalls, he had substituted the Gilberts when the JCS made available one marine division from MacArthur's area. Japanese concern for Bougainville had immobilized their fleet at Truk just when it might have caused Nimitz trouble by attacking his landing force in the Gilberts. Nevertheless, the operation was costly; at Tarawa, the marines had a vicious fight on their hands before finally wiping out the Japanese defenders. But the Gilberts taught the Americans many valuable lessons about amphibious warfare, and the subsequent seizure of Kwajalein in January was a model amphibious landing. About this time, carrier raids on Truk revealed that island's weakness and partial abandonment, so the western Carolines were bypassed, and Nimitz moved into the Marianas instead. It was while Admiral Raymond Spruance's Fifth Fleet lay off Saipan (*center*) that the Japanese fleet finally decided to give battle. The Battle of the Philippine Sea ended disastrously for Japan, for it practically destroyed her painfully rebuilt carrier pilot groups. Most of the fleet escaped, but it was no longer a serious threat.

Before seizing the Saipan bastion, however, Nimitz had lent carrier support to MacArthur so that he could leap beyond land-based aircraft range and take Hollandia (*lower center*). Then, while MacArthur—in a brilliantly executed series of amphibious landings—moved along the northern New Guinea coast, Nimitz swung south to the Palaus, thus completing the isolation of Truk and getting into position to support MacArthur's projected landing on Mindanao in November.

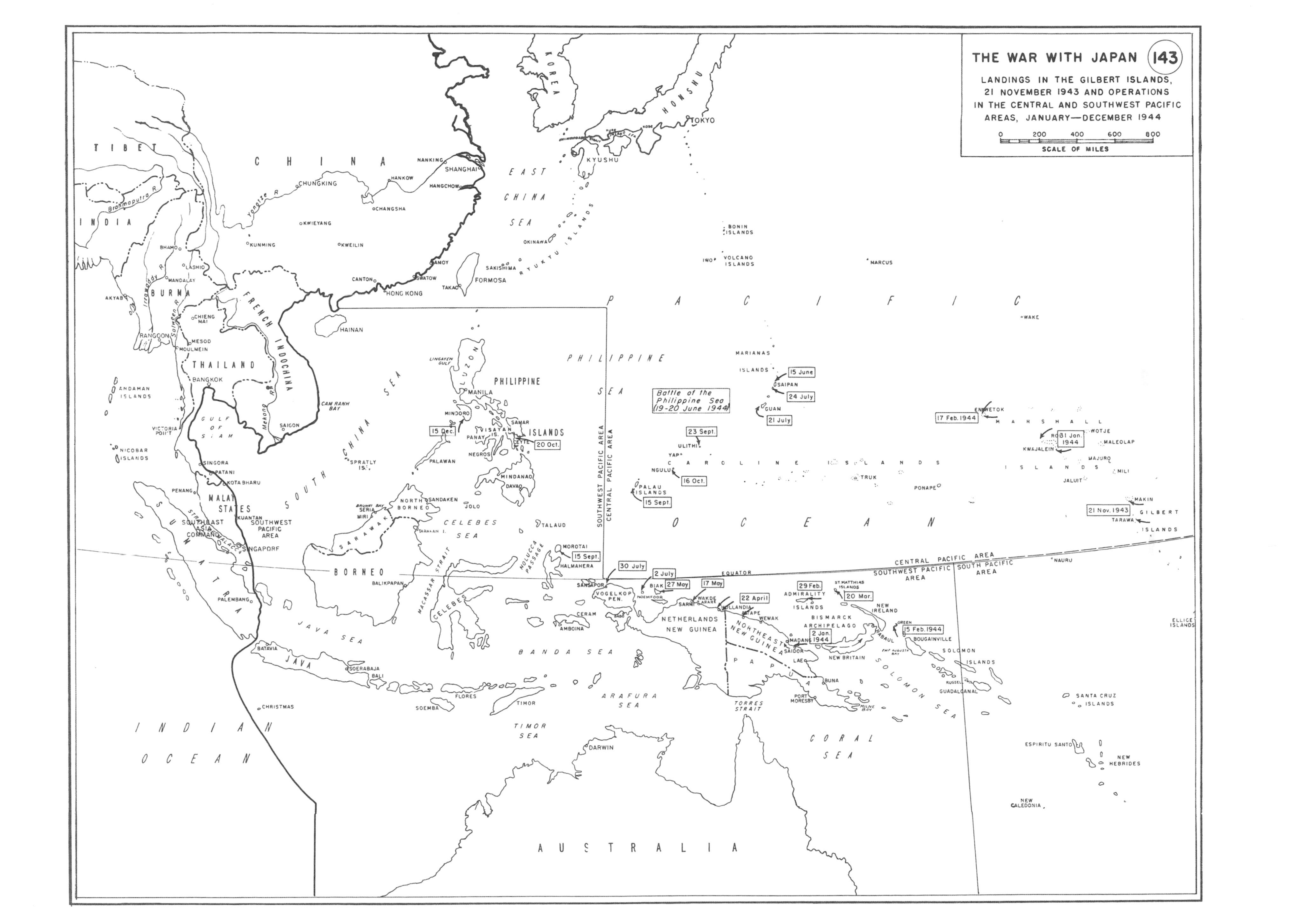
THE WAR WITH JAPAN
143
LANDINGS IN THE GILBERT ISLANDS, 21 NOVEMBER 1943 AND OPERATIONS IN THE CENTRAL AND SOUTHWEST PACIFIC AREAS, JANUARY—DECEMBER 1944
0 200 400 600 800
SCALE OF MILES
PACIFIC
OCEAN
PHILIPPINE SEA
SOUTH CHINA SEA
EAST CHINA SEA
CELEBES SEA
BANDA SEA
JAVA SEA
ARAFURA SEA
TIMOR SEA
CORAL SEA
SOLOMON SEA
INDIAN OCEAN
CHINA
TIBET
INDIA
BURMA
THAILAND
FRENCH INDOCHINA
MALAY STATES
KOREA
HONSHU
KYUSHU
TOKYO
FORMOSA
PHILIPPINE ISLANDS
BORNEO
SUMATRA
JAVA
CELEBES
NETHERLANDS NEW GUINEA
NORTHEAST NEW GUINEA
PAPUA
AUSTRALIA
Battle of the Philippine Sea (19-20 June 1944)
15 June
SAIPAN
24 July
GUAM
21 July
23 Sept.
ULITHI
16 Oct.
PALAU ISLANDS
15 Sept.
20 Oct.
LEYTE
15 Dec.
MINDORO
15 Sept.
MOROTAI
30 July
SANSAPOR
2 July
NOEMFOOR
27 May
BIAK
17 May
WAKDE
22 April
HOLLANDIA
29 Feb.
ADMIRALTY ISLANDS
20 Mar.
2 Jan. 1944
SAIDOR
15 Feb. 1944
GREEN
17 Feb. 1944
ENIWETOK
31 Jan. 1944
KWAJALEIN
21 Nov. 1943
MAKIN
TARAWA
GILBERT ISLANDS
MARSHALL ISLANDS
CAROLINE ISLANDS
MARIANAS ISLANDS
CENTRAL PACIFIC AREA
SOUTHWEST PACIFIC AREA
SOUTH PACIFIC AREA
SOUTHEAST ASIA COMMAND
EQUATOR

OPERATIONS IN NEW GUINEA AND THE BISMARCK ARCHIPELAGO

★

MacArthur's first amphibious landing in 1944 was made by a regimental combat team at Saidor (*center, left*) in an effort to cut off the Japanese who had retreated from Lae and Salamaua. Eventually, this sizable Japanese force (12,000)—starving, dispirited, and harried by the Australian advance from Finschhafen—was forced to move inland to reach Madang. Saidor, whose earlier occupation had given Maj. Gen. George C. Kenney a good airfield from which he could support operations on Cape Gloucester (*center*), was reached by the Australians on 10 January. In February, the American landing force at Saidor withdrew, and the Australians, opposed by strong Japanese forces from Madang, consolidated their position until April. Then they renewed their advance up the coast, having been joined en route by an Australian battalion which had moved out of the Markham Valley to Dumpu.

Halsey's troops in the South Pacific spent the first few months of 1944 isolating and neutralizing enemy bases. On 15 February, he landed a small New Zealand force at Green Island (*upper right*) to obtain a site for an air base. A month later, he occupied Emirau (*top center*), after MacArthur had already jumped to the Admiralties (*top center*) and Halsey's projected landing at Kavieng (*top center*) had been canceled. Meanwhile, back on Bougainville (*off map, right*), the bulk of Halsey's forces had a real fight on their hands to hold their perimeter against determined—but piecemeal—Seventeenth Army attacks. Nevertheless, by May, the Japanese—cut off from Rabaul and starving—had reached desperate straits; wholesale desertion followed. In June, the South Pacific Area operations came under MacArthur's control. In November, the Australians assumed responsibility for the area, as well as for New Britain and eastern New Guinea; by then, the American troops were being moved forward for operations in the Philippines. The task given the Australians was to mop up the bypassed Japanese. No strategic threat, these Japanese—in sizable groups and in inaccessible places—nevertheless posed a nasty problem for the Australians. When the war ended, many of these Japanese were still in hiding.

Early 1944 was not pleasant on Cape Gloucester. Fighting the elements as much as the Japanese, the 1st Marine Division and the 112th Cavalry Regimental Combat Team finally established a common front across the island by March. The marine landing on Willaumez Peninsula forced the Japanese to begin a withdrawal toward Rabaul which the 40th Division, having relieved the marines in April, hastened. When relieved by the Australians in November, the Americans had the Japanese contained on the Gazelle Peninsula.

The most spectacular operation of this series was MacArthur's seizure of the Admiralties. After the JCS decision in August to bypass Rabaul, MacArthur planned to complete Rabaul's encirclement by seizing the Admiralties and Kavieng in March. But when Nimitz stated he could not provide the necessary assault shipping and carrier support because of operations in the Marshalls in February, the date was changed to April. In the meantime, Allied aircraft continued to bomb Rabaul and the Admiralties. On 23 February, Kenney was advised that aerial reconnaissance flights indicated that the Japanese had practically abandoned the Admiralties. The Southwest Pacific intelligence section disagreed, maintaining that the enemy had about 4,000 troops there (a remarkably accurate estimate). MacArthur made a characteristically bold decision to dispatch a 1,000-man reconnaissance force to Los Negros to verify the report, and decided to accompany the troops himself. The landing took place on 29 February (*top center*) and quickly established that, indeed, Kenney's estimate of 300 Japanese was wrong. But MacArthur ordered the rest of the 1st Cavalry Division forward and directed the reconnaissance force to hold "at any cost." This accelerated action advanced operations in the Southwest Pacific by at least a month. Quickly, the Admiralties were overrun, Kavieng was bypassed, and in April MacArthur jumped all the way to Aitape (*upper left*) and Hollandia beyond. Thus, the Japanese Eighteenth Army, surprised at the leap beyond land-based air range, was caught between the advancing Australians and the Aitape force. It was ultimately left—isolated and starving—for the Australians to mop up.

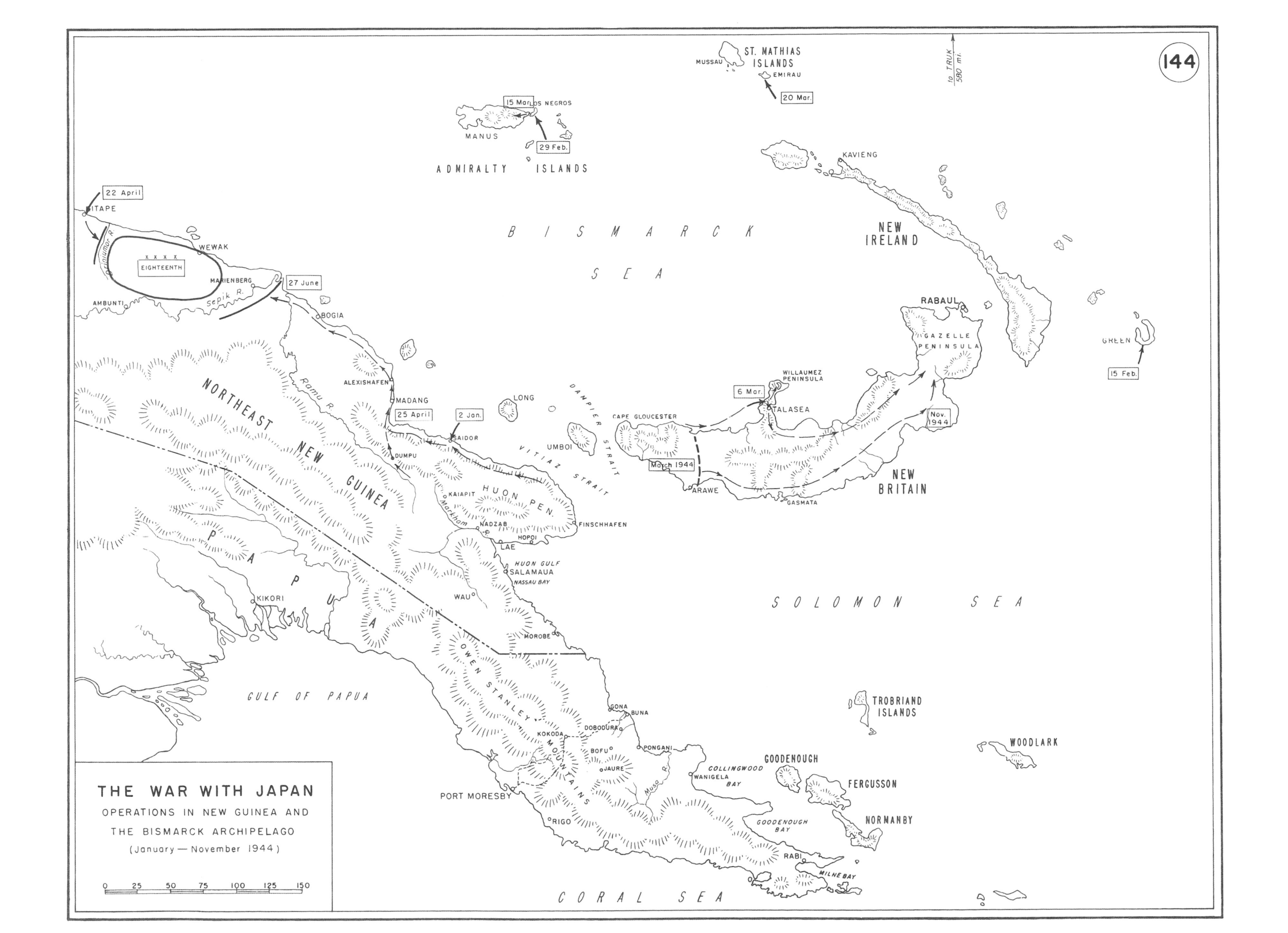
144
THE WAR WITH JAPAN
OPERATIONS IN NEW GUINEA AND
THE BISMARCK ARCHIPELAGO
(January — November 1944)
0 25 50 75 100 125 150
ST. MATHIAS ISLANDS
MUSSAU
EMIRAU
20 Mar.
to TRUK 580 mi.
15 Mar.
LOS NEGROS
29 Feb.
MANUS
ADMIRALTY ISLANDS
KAVIENG
NEW IRELAND
BISMARCK SEA
22 April
AITAPE
WEWAK
EIGHTEENTH
Driniumor R.
MARIENBERG
Sepik R.
27 June
AMBUNTI
BOGIA
RABAUL
GAZELLE PENINSULA
GREEN
15 Feb.
ALEXISHAFEN
MADANG
25 April
2 Jan.
SAIDOR
DUMPU
LONG
DAMPIER STRAIT
UMBOI
VITIAZ STRAIT
CAPE GLOUCESTER
6 Mar.
WILLAUMEZ PENINSULA
TALASEA
Nov. 1944
March 1944
ARAWE
GASMATA
NEW BRITAIN
NORTHEAST NEW GUINEA
Ramu R.
KAIAPIT
HUON PEN.
Markham
NADZAB
HOPOI
LAE
FINSCHHAFEN
HUON GULF
SALAMAUA
NASSAU BAY
WAU
PAPUA
KIKORI
MOROBE
SOLOMON SEA
GULF OF PAPUA
OWEN STANLEY MOUNTAINS
GONA
BUNA
DOBODURA
KOKODA
BOFU
JAURE
PONGANI
Musa R.
TROBRIAND ISLANDS
WOODLARK
GOODENOUGH
COLLINGWOOD BAY
WANIGELA
FERGUSSON
PORT MORESBY
RIGO
GOODENOUGH BAY
NORMANBY
RABI
MILNE BAY
CORAL SEA

LEYTE CAMPAIGN

★

It will be recalled that the 1943 strategic plan for the defeat of Japan envisioned an eventual landing on the China coast in the Hong Kong area (*see map 143*). Since that lodgment would depend upon controlling the South China Sea, Luzon and Formosa merited serious consideration as likely Allied objectives. As late as June 1944, JCS planners felt that Formosa was more vital to the basic strategy than Luzon, and some even advocated the complete bypassing of the Philippines. Nevertheless, in March 1944, a JCS directive specified that MacArthur land on Mindanao in November; it avoided the question of the next objective. But the debate continued, fed by intelligence reports that the Japanese were strengthening Formosan defenses, and by fears that China's collapse was imminent. When MacArthur and Nimitz were queried in June concerning a possible speed-up of Pacific operations in order to facilitate landing on Formosa before February, they both declared that acceleration of operations was not feasible. Further, they averred that, after seizure of the Palaus and Morotai, the next step should be a movement into the southern or central Philippines. This operation was approved, but debate continued over the choice of Luzon or Formosa as the next objective.

In support of the Palau and Morotai landings, Admiral Halsey's carriers launched air strikes in the central Philippines on 12–14 September. The lack of Japanese opposition led Halsey to conclude that "the area is wide open," and he accordingly recommended to Nimitz that the scheduled operations against the islands of Yap and Mindanao be canceled in favor of a direct thrust at Leyte. Concurring, Nimitz recommended seizure of Leyte and offered to lend MacArthur the XXIV Corps (already en route to Yap) and carrier air support—since the target would be beyond land-based air range. MacArthur immediately grasped the opportunity, and reported that he would invade Leyte on 20 October. The XXIV Corps was shunted to the Admiralties, and MacArthur's staff set to work revising plans. Once again, the flexibility of operations in the Pacific had been strikingly demonstrated.

The Japanese Leyte defenses (*this map*) were manned by the 16th Division, part of the Thirty-Fifth Army, which was responsible for defending Mindanao and the Visayas. By June 1944, Japan's military position had grown critical. To help protect her lines of communications to the Netherlands East Indies, she began reinforcing the Philippines, expecting to make her main defensive effort on Luzon. In defending the remainder of the islands, main reliance would be placed on air power—a concept which overlooked American superiority in the skies. On Leyte itself, the Japanese began preparing defensive positions in April, but were unable to decide whether to defend in depth or on the beaches. The result was an unsatisfactory compromise which did not provide flexibility.

The primary purpose of the Leyte campaign was to establish Allied air and logistic bases to support subsequent operations. Lt. Gen. Walter Krueger's plan of operations consisted of three phases. In the first, the 6th Ranger Battalion would secure the small islands (*right center*) guarding the entrance to Leyte Gulf, thus allowing safe passage for mine sweepers to clear the way for the assault. The second phase would comprise landings by the X and XXIV Corps (*upper center*), establishment of control over the strait between Leyte and Panaon Island (*bottom center*), and occupation of Leyte Valley (running from Carigara [*upper center*] to Abuyog [*center*]). The final phase would consist of securing the rest of the island and part of Samar (*top center*). In addition to the floating reserve shown, Krueger had two divisions in general reserve (one at Guam and one at Hollandia). The Sixth Army would be lifted and furnished direct naval support by the Seventh Fleet. Direct air support would be provided by Seventh Fleet escort carriers, while Kenney's bombers, China-based B-29's, and Halsey's Third Fleet carriers would neutralize enemy air power on Formosa, the East Indies, and Luzon. In addition, Halsey—subordinated to Nimitz, not to MacArthur—was to protect air and sea communications in the Visayas and destroy the Japanese fleet if it ventured forth to give battle.

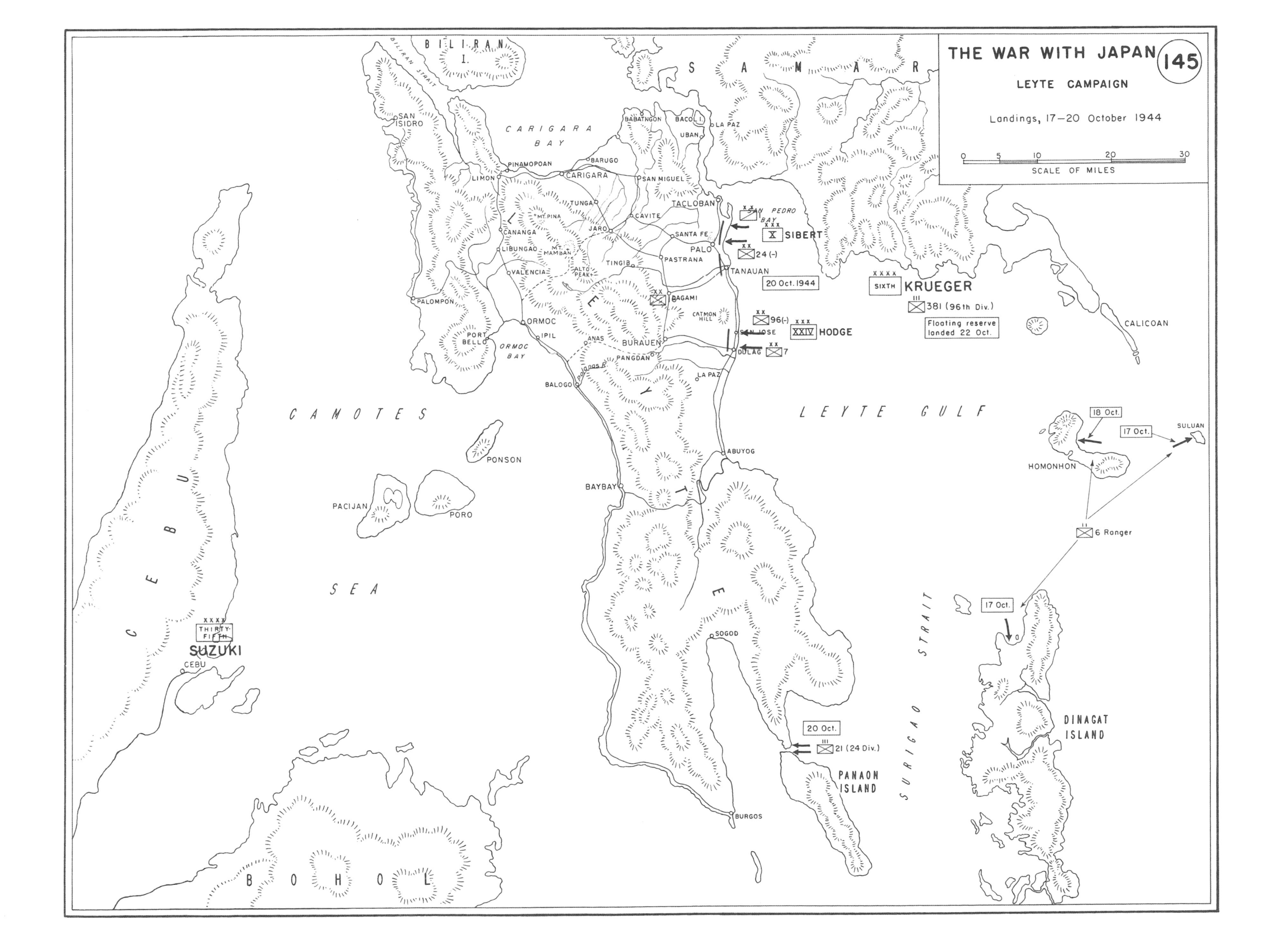
THE WAR WITH JAPAN
145
LEYTE CAMPAIGN
Landings, 17–20 October 1944
0 5 10 20 30
SCALE OF MILES
SAMAR
BILIRAN I.
BILIRAN STRAIT
SAN ISIDRO
CARIGARA BAY
BABATNGON
BACOL I.
LA PAZ
UBAN
BARUGO
PINAMOPOAN
CARIGARA
SAN MIGUEL
LIMON
TACLOBAN
TUNGA
MT. PINA
CAVITE
SAN PEDRO BAY
SIBERT
CANANGA
JARO
SANTA FE
24 (-)
LIBUNGAO
MT. MAMBAN
PALO
PASTRANA
VALENCIA
ALTO PEAK
TINGIB
TANAUAN
20 Oct. 1944
SIXTH
KRUEGER
381 (96th Div.)
Floating reserve landed 22 Oct.
PALOMPON
BAGAMI
CATMON HILL
96(-)
XXIV
HODGE
ORMOC
SAN JOSE
CALICOAN
PORT BELLO
IPIL
ANAS
BURAUEN
ORMOC BAY
PANGDAN
DULAG
7
BALOGO
LA PAZ
CAMOTES
LEYTE GULF
18 Oct.
17 Oct.
SULUAN
PONSON
ABUYOG
HOMONHON
BAYBAY
PACIJAN
PORO
6 Ranger
CEBU
SEA
17 Oct.
SOGOD
SURIGAO STRAIT
THIRTY-FIFTH
SUZUKI
20 Oct.
21 (24 Div.)
DINAGAT ISLAND
PANAON ISLAND
BURGOS
BOHOL
LEYTE

LEYTE CAMPAIGN

As the largest American convoy yet assembled in the Pacific moved north from the Admiralties, Halsey's carriers struck at Formosa and Luzon, while Seventh Fleet carrier aircraft protected the convoy and hit enemy shipping and airfields in the Visayas. Kenney's Morotai-based air forces joined in the attacks on Visayan targets within range. Exaggerated reports by Japanese airmen of losses inflicted on the Third Fleet off Formosa led to a false sense of security and the belief that the Philippines could not be invaded for two more months. (Actually, Halsey had dealt Japanese air power on Formosa a crippling blow.) As a result of this belief and a Japanese predisposition to consider Mindanao as the next Allied objective (even though naval intelligence had predicted an Allied landing in the Philippines for late October and surmised that Leyte might be the target), MacArthur's landing achieved complete strategic surprise.

The Rangers landed as planned on Dinagat and Suluan Islands (*see map 145, right center*), but rough weather delayed the assault on Homonhon until 18 October. Resistance was encountered only on Suluan, the other islands being unoccupied. Navigation lights were installed on the islands, and mine sweepers began clearing the entrances to Leyte Gulf. At 1000, 20 October, following a two-hour naval bombardment, assault waves of four divisions landed (*this map, center*) between Dulag and Tacloban and quickly secured beachheads. The 24th Division met considerable opposition, but elsewhere Japanese resistance was spotty. Thirty minutes earlier, the 21st Regimental Combat Team had easily secured Panaon Strait (*off map, south*).

General Krueger's troops quickly moved inland the next four days. The 1st Cavalry Division captured Tacloban (*upper center*) and its airfield (*red block*), landed at La Paz (on Samar), secured the northeastern coast of Leyte as far as Babatngon, and drove inland toward San Miguel. The 24th Division continued to meet stiff resistance until it took Palo and Hill 522; then it advanced more rapidly toward Jaro. The 96th Division initially bypassed the enemy strong point on Catmon Hill (*center*) and drove across swamps and rice paddies toward Dagami; the Japanese on Catmon Hill withdrew on the 26th when threatened with encirclement. The 7th Division seized Dulag and its airfield and then struck out for Burauen, capturing the three airfields en route.

Everywhere, the Japanese defense had appeared to be uncoordinated, though resistance was fierce in spots. In reality, the 16th Division—outnumbered and still organizing defense positions when the Sixth Army landed—had been fighting a delaying action back to the central mountain range, while reinforcements came ashore at Ormoc (*center, left*). On 21 October, General Yamashita (the Japanese commander in the Philippines) had decided to fight the battle for the Philippines on Leyte, and had ordered reinforcements moved there from Luzon and the Visayas. (Between 23 October and 11 December, the Japanese sent nine convoys to Ormoc and landed about 45,000 troops and 10,000 tons of matériel.)

Meanwhile, the Sixth Army continued its advance. In the north, the X Corps captured Carigara (*upper center*) on 2 November and then ran head-on into the strong Japanese position in the mountains southeast of Limon; in the south, the 7th Division pushed a battalion through Abuyog to Baybay (2 November) and then north toward Ormoc. But in the center, after Dagami fell on 30 October, the XXIV Corps made only slight gains against strong defenses in the mountains. During the last week in October and in early November, heavy tropical storms struck the area and turned many of the roads—already being taxed to the limit—into ribbons of mud.

By 7 November, Krueger's troops were poised for a drive on Ormoc, while Yamashita continued to reinforce the island. The construction of airfields and the logistic base had fallen well behind schedule. The airfield sites near Burauen were technically unsuitable, and the Tacloban and Dulag strips were unable to handle enough aircraft. As a result, there were insufficient ground-based planes on Leyte to either prevent the flow of Japanese reinforcements through Ormoc or provide the desired support of ground troops. Seventh Fleet carriers were of little assistance after the Battle for Leyte Gulf (*see map 147*), and Halsey's fleet, though it gave some support to operations on Leyte, could not compensate for the shortage of land-based aircraft.

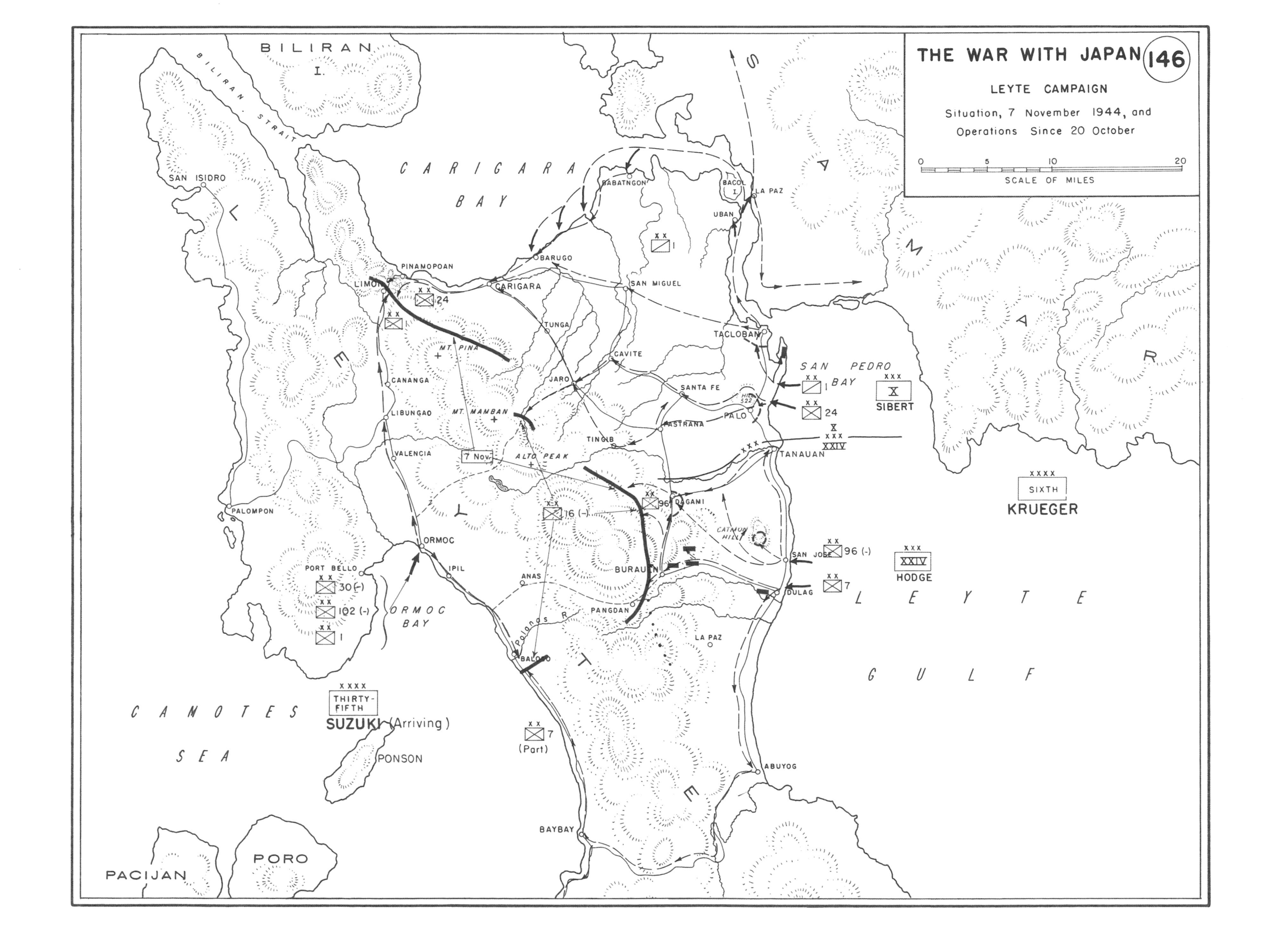
THE WAR WITH JAPAN
146
LEYTE CAMPAIGN
Situation, 7 November 1944, and
Operations Since 20 October
0
5
10
20
SCALE OF MILES
BILIRAN I.
BILIRAN STRAIT
CARIGARA BAY
SAN ISIDRO
BABATNGON
BACOL I.
LA PAZ
UBAN
BARUGO
PINAMOPOAN
CARIGARA
SAN MIGUEL
LIMON
24
1
TUNGA
TACLOBAN
MT. PINA
CAVITE
SAN PEDRO BAY
SIBERT
CANANGA
JARO
SANTA FE
HILL 522
PALO
LIBUNGAO
MT. MAMBAN
ASTRANA
TINGIB
XXIV
TANAUAN
VALENCIA
7 Nov.
ALTO PEAK
SIXTH
KRUEGER
PALOMPON
96
DAGANI
16 (-)
CATMON HILL
ORMOC
SAN JOSE
96 (-)
HODGE
PORT BELLO
IPIL
ANAS
BURAUEN
30 (-)
102 (-)
ORMOC BAY
PANGDAN
DULAG
7
Palanas R.
LA PAZ
BALOGO
THIRTY-FIFTH
SUZUKI (Arriving)
CAMOTES SEA
(Part)
PONSON
ABUYOG
BAYBAY
PORO
PACIJAN
S A M A R
L E Y T E
L E Y T E G U L F

BATTLE FOR LEYTE GULF

★

While the 16th Division was withdrawing before Krueger's superior forces, the weakened Japanese Navy was moving toward Leyte under orders to destroy the American landing forces and their supporting ships.

Imperial General Headquarters had devised the Sho-Go (meaning "Victory Operation") plan to meet probable American attacks. It had four variations; Sho-1 applied to an attack on the Philippines. This plan, recognizing the great inferiority of Japanese carrier air power, provided for support of the fleet by land-based aircraft. Accordingly, the Japanese made every effort to transfer large quantities of aircraft to the Philippines in late October, but Halsey's crippling strikes against Formosa and Luzon seriously impaired the effectiveness of this program.

The Sho-1 plan was based upon deception. The Main Body (*top center*) would lure Halsey's Third Fleet north, while the main surface elements (divided into 1st Attack Force [*left center*] and C Force [*bottom center*]) would come up from Borneo to close a giant pincer on the amphibious forces in Leyte Gulf. The 2d Attack Force (*lower center*) would join the southern prong. The Main Body contained all the carriers as bait (without many aircraft, however). Its sacrifice was considered justified if it succeeded in diverting Halsey's attention so that the surface elements could destroy the American ships in Leyte Gulf.

It is important to note that the Seventh Fleet was under MacArthur and the Third Fleet under Nimitz. Halsey had orders to support the landings—but also to destroy the enemy fleet if the opportunity arose. As will be seen, he considered this second part of his mission the more important.

The first naval action took place west of Palawan (*lower left*) early on 23 October, when two Seventh Fleet submarines sank two heavy cruisers of the 1st Attack Force. Alerted by this action and later submarine sightings off Mindoro, Halsey's search planes soon located C Force and the 1st Attack Force. At once, Third Fleet aircraft were launched in strikes against both Japanese forces. The 1st Attack Force suffered enough damage (one battleship sunk, other ships hit) in the Sibuyan Sea (*center*) to cause its commander (Vice Adm. Takeo Kurita) to reverse course. This movement affected the battle in two ways: it delayed the northern prong of the Japanese pincer, and—coupled with overly optimistic damage reports by Third Fleet pilots—it convinced Halsey that Kurita was no longer a threat. Halsey, having finally located the Main Body, then decided that it was the major threat and moved the entire Third Fleet (less one task force, 300 miles to the east refueling) northward that night. While Halsey took the bait, the Seventh Fleet battleships and cruisers—warned of the approach of the C and 2d Attack Forces—took position in Surigao Strait (*lower right*) and, in a brilliant action, practically wiped out C Force. The 2d Attack Force withdrew without giving battle.

Meanwhile, Kurita had again reversed course, moved through San Bernardino Strait, and surprised the Seventh Fleet escort carriers off Samar. (The Seventh Fleet thought Halsey was guarding San Bernardino Strait.) The slow carrier force tried to outrun Kurita, but though it put up a magnificent fight, was in danger of annihilation when Kurita suddenly broke off the action and withdrew. Misunderstanding, fear of land-based aircraft, and knowledge of C Force's destruction all contributed to this amazing decision. Meanwhile, Halsey, in answer to Seventh Fleet calls for help, finally sent his battleships south—but they arrived too late to engage Kurita. Aircraft from the task force returning from refueling did strike Kurita's force, however, as did the rest of Halsey's aircraft on the 26th and 27th. In the meantime, the Third Fleet had inflicted heavy damage on the Main Body off Cape Engano (*top center*).

Withdrawing the remnants of their once-proud fleet, the Japanese could take consolation only in having come perilously close to reaching MacArthur's soft-skinned transports. They had also revealed the desperateness of their situation by using Kamikaze tactics (suicide dive bombing) for the first time: against Halsey on the 24th, and against the Seventh Fleet on the 25th.

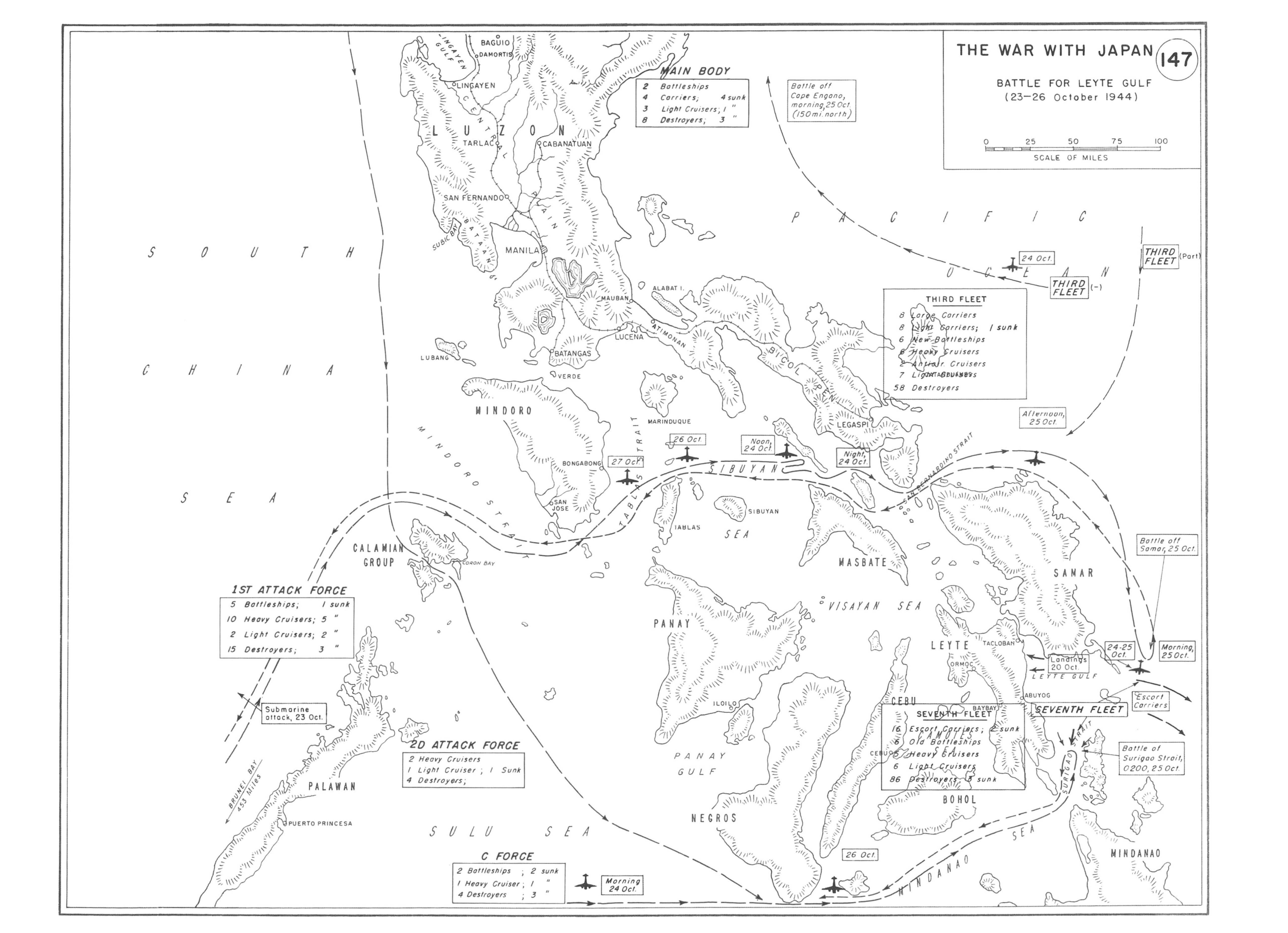
THE WAR WITH JAPAN
147
BATTLE FOR LEYTE GULF
(23–26 October 1944)
0 25 50 75 100
SCALE OF MILES
MAIN BODY
2 Battleships
4 Carriers; 4 sunk
3 Light Cruisers; 1 "
8 Destroyers; 3 "
Battle off Cape Engano, morning, 25 Oct. (150 mi. north)
THIRD FLEET (Port)
THIRD FLEET (-)
24 Oct.
THIRD FLEET
8 Large Carriers
8 Light Carriers; 1 sunk
6 New Battleships
58 Destroyers
Afternoon, 25 Oct.
P A C I F I C O C E A N
S O U T H C H I N A S E A
LUZON
CENTRAL PLAIN
LINGAYEN GULF
BAGUIO
DAMORTIS
LINGAYEN
TARLAC
CABANATUAN
SAN FERNANDO
SUBIC BAY
BATAAN
MANILA
ALABAT I.
MAUBAN
LUCENA
ATIMONAN
BATANGAS
VERDE
LUBANG
BICOL PEN.
LEGASPI
MINDORO
MARINDUQUE
MINDORO STRAIT
TABLAS STRAIT
BONGABONG
SAN JOSE
27 Oct.
26 Oct.
Noon, 24 Oct.
Night, 24 Oct.
SIBUYAN SEA
SIBUYAN
IABLAS
SAN BERNARDINO STRAIT
CALAMIAN GROUP
CORON BAY
MASBATE
SAMAR
Battle off Samar, 25 Oct.
VISAYAN SEA
PANAY
LEYTE
TACLOBAN
ORMOC
Landings 20 Oct.
LEYTE GULF
24-25 Oct.
Morning, 25 Oct.
ABUYOG
Escort Carriers
SEVENTH FLEET
16 Escort Carriers; 2 sunk
6 Old Battleships
6 Light Cruisers
86 Destroyers; 3 sunk
SEVENTH FLEET
CAMOTES SEA
CEBU
BAYBAY
Battle of Surigao Strait, 0200, 25 Oct.
SURIGAO STRAIT
BOHOL
1ST ATTACK FORCE
5 Battleships; 1 sunk
10 Heavy Cruisers; 5 "
2 Light Cruisers; 2 "
15 Destroyers; 3 "
Submarine attack, 23 Oct.
BRUNEI BAY 453 Miles
PALAWAN
PUERTO PRINCESA
2D ATTACK FORCE
2 Heavy Cruisers
1 Light Cruiser; 1 Sunk
4 Destroyers;
ILOILO
PANAY GULF
NEGROS
SULU SEA
C FORCE
2 Battleships ; 2 sunk
1 Heavy Cruiser ; 1 "
4 Destroyers ; 3 "
Morning 24 Oct.
26 Oct.
MINDANAO SEA
MINDANAO

LEYTE CAMPAIGN

Yamashita fully appreciated the implications of the Japanese defeat in the Battle of Leyte Gulf and suspected that the Japanese air arm had been seriously crippled. Accordingly, on 10 November, he recommended abandonment of Leyte and the concentration of strength for a defense of Luzon. But when his superiors balked, he renewed his efforts to reinforce Lt. Gen. Sosaku Suzuki. The latter planned to recapture Carigara and move forces down Leyte Valley to join up with another thrust coming from the mountains west of Dagami.

Meanwhile, Krueger was making plans for a two-pronged drive on Ormoc. However, apprehensive over the demonstrated Japanese capability to reinforce the island despite American air and naval superiority, he feared they might land in the X Corps' rear near Carigara. Consequently, when Krueger learned Suzuki's plan from a captured Japanese order, he postponed moving the rest of the 7th Division across the island to Balogo until the Sixth Army was reinforced. But the X Corps, leaving some troops along the coast to protect its rear, attacked the Japanese north of Limon (*upper left*). By 14 November, the 24th Division had managed to move two battalions to positions (*not shown*) in rear of the Japanese near the road leading south from Limon. Holding there against repeated counterattacks, they seriously interfered with Japanese supply efforts. On the 16th, the 32d Division relieved the tired 24th and continued the attack to seize Limon. By now, Suzuki had abandoned his optimistic plan for an offensive, but he fought desperately to hold Limon, the northern gateway to Ormoc. Not until 10 December was the 32d Division able to capture the village.

In the meantime, the 11th Airborne Division (arriving on the island to stage for another operation) had been assigned to the Sixth Army, and the 77th Division had arrived from Guam. While the 96th Division continued to press the remnants of the 16th Division west of Dagami, the 7th Division turned over its sector at Burauen to the 11th and moved across the island to Balogo on 22 November. The Seventh Fleet finally scraped together enough assault shipping to lift the 77th Division to Ipil (*lower center*) on 7 December. Three days later, the major part of the division entered Ormoc after a vigorous fight, while one battalion moved south to link up with the 7th Division, which had been slowly edging forward. On 9 December, an 11th Division column met a battalion from the 7th Division at Anas and completed the destruction of the Japanese 26th Division.

Suzuki, meanwhile—on orders from Tokyo—had made one final, but futile, offensive gesture. Fearing that aircraft from the Burauen, Dulag, and Tacloban airfields would soon interdict the vital lines of communications between the East Indies and Japan, Tokyo planners had directed that an offensive be launched to seize the Burauen fields and destroy facilities at the other two. Suzuki complied by making a ground and airborne attack on 6–7 December; but, though Japanese paratroopers did control the Burauen strips for a short time, the attack was too weak to be a real threat. Ironically, by the time of the attack, Krueger had already canceled plans to develop the Burauen airfields, and was building a new one at Tanauan.

After the seizure of Ormoc and Limon, the campaign moved swiftly to its conclusion. The 1st Cavalry and 32d Divisions drove south to link up with the 77th Division on 20 December at Libungao. On Christmas Day, the last Japanese port (Palompon) was seized by a battalion from the 77th Division. (This same day, Yamashita advised Suzuki that the Thirty-Fifth Army forces on Leyte had been written off as lost.) On the 26th, General Eichelberger's Eighth Army assumed responsibility for Leyte, so that Krueger could begin preparations for the next operation. For the next four months, the Eighth Army "patrolled" Leyte and Samar, eliminating isolated bands of Japanese.

Leyte never provided the major Allied air bases envisioned, but its seizure had other, more important results. By electing to fight a decisive battle there, the Japanese had committed their carefully hoarded fleet and a major part of their air arm; both suffered crippling losses. Nor could Yamashita afford the some 70,000 casualties the ground forces suffered. Total American Army casualties were 15,584.

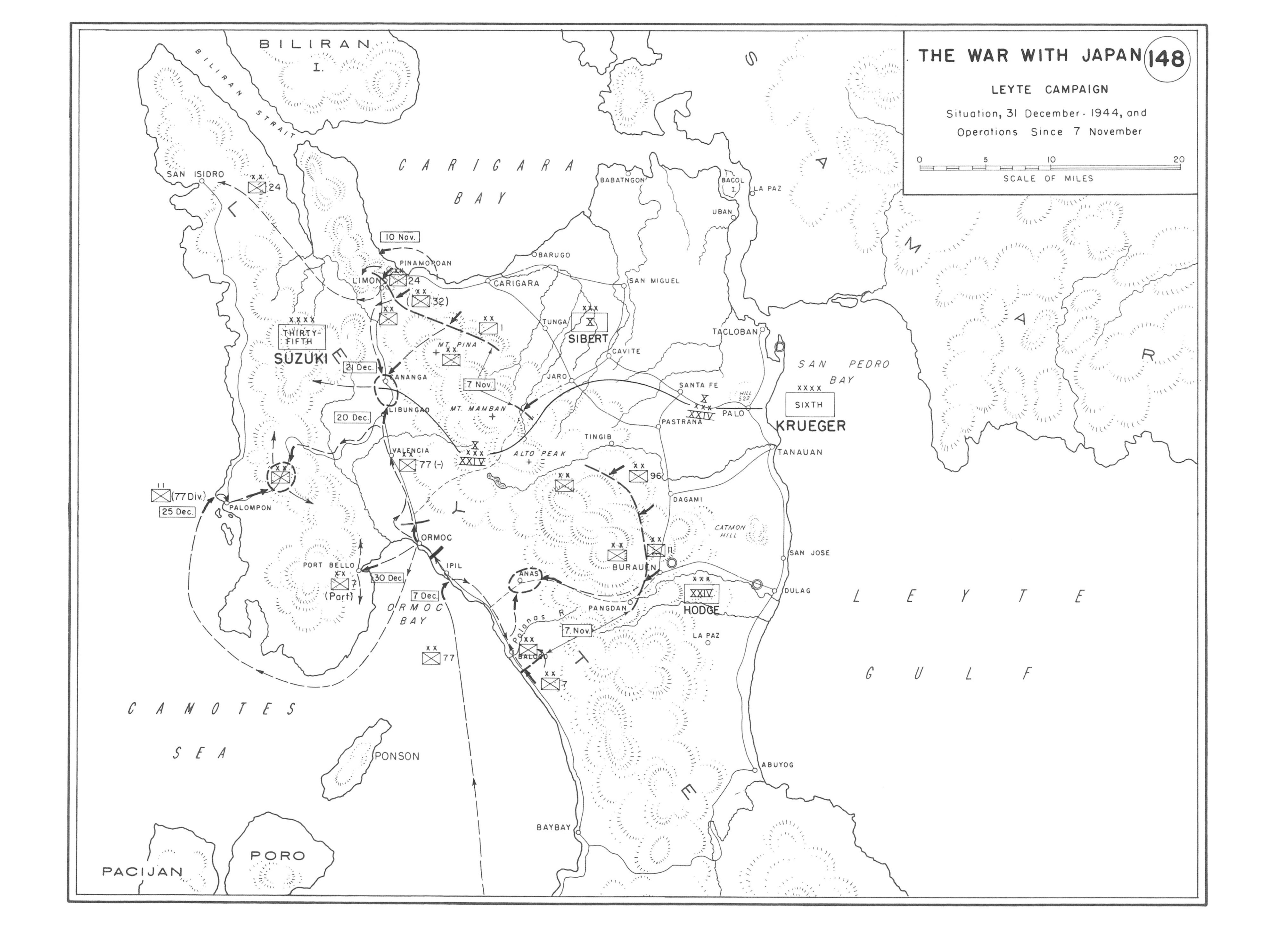
THE WAR WITH JAPAN
148
LEYTE CAMPAIGN
Situation, 31 December 1944, and
Operations Since 7 November
0
5
10
20
SCALE OF MILES
BILIRAN I.
BILIRAN STRAIT
CARIGARA BAY
SAN PEDRO BAY
LEYTE GULF
CAMOTES SEA
ORMOC BAY
SAMAR
LEYTE
SAN ISIDRO
PINAMOPOAN
LIMON
CARIGARA
BARUGO
BABATNGON
SAN MIGUEL
BACOL I.
LA PAZ
UBAN
TACLOBAN
TUNGA
CAVITE
JARO
SANTA FE
PALO
HILL 522
PASTRANA
TANAUAN
TINGIB
DAGAMI
CATMON HILL
SAN JOSE
DULAG
BURAUEN
PANGDAN
LA PAZ
ABUYOG
BAYBAY
BALOGO
Palanas R
ANAS
IPIL
ORMOC
PORT BELLO
VALENCIA
LIBUNGAO
CANANGA
MT. PINA
MT. MAMBAN
ALTO PEAK
PALOMPON
PONSON
PORO
PACIJAN
THIRTY-FIFTH
SUZUKI
SIBERT
SIXTH
KRUEGER
XXIV
HODGE
24
32
1
96
11
7
77
77 (-)
(77 Div.)
(Part)
10 Nov.
21 Dec.
7 Nov.
20 Dec.
25 Dec.
30 Dec.
7 Dec.
7 Nov.

SITUATION, DECEMBER 1944

★

The Leyte campaign concluded a year of unbroken Allied successes in the Pacific. The Japanese suffered defeat everywhere except in China (*see map 141*). There, they resumed offensive operations designed to establish a land corridor to French Indochina and to strengthen the China coast in anticipation of Allied landings. But even these operations had strategic defensive overtones, for the land corridor was conceived only as a substitute for the better water route to the Southern Resources Area. This route had already become unreliable by 1944—primarily because of attacks made by United States submarines on Japanese shipping— and was further threatened by MacArthur's seizure of Leyte, from which Allied air power could be projected over the South China Sea. (Japan's merchant shipping had declined from about 6,000,000 tons in December 1941, to about 2,500,000 tons in December 1944—submarines accounted for 60 percent of this destruction.)

Allied air power had played an important role in the Allied string of victories in 1944. In Burma and China, it provided tactical support for ground forces but, more important, began to demonstrate its capability for moving supplies and troops over difficult obstacles. In the Southwest Pacific Area, General MacArthur exploited air power to the maximum in his brilliant series of operations which leapfrogged—generally covered by Kenney's aircraft—along the New Guinea coast into the Philippines. In Admiral Nimitz's area, army aircraft pounded the Kurile Islands (*this map, upper center*) and supported the drive across the Pacific, but more spectacular achievements were credited to the highly mobile carrier force which was capable of launching 1,000-plane attacks. Finally, 1944 saw the creation of the Twentieth Air Force under JCS command; its B-29 bombers—stationed in the Marianas and the China-Burma-India theater—carried out thirty-nine attacks against Japanese targets during the year.

Allied logistical accomplishments were truly outstanding during this period. The flexibility of the supply system made it possible to support operations on the far-flung battlefields. In this respect, Nimitz's use of small-scale "floating bases," which enabled the fleet to stay at sea longer, was a revolutionary development.

The map indicates (*dashed red line*) the maximum extent of Japanese conquest that was reached in 1942; also shown (*shaded blue areas*) are the parts of the Japanese-dominated area over which the Allies had regained control by 31 December, 1944. The Japanese-held localities (*red circles*), which MacArthur and Nimitz had bypassed in their respective drives to the Philippines, are depicted to illustrate how effectively these areas had been isolated. (The Volcano Islands [*center*] were destined to be invaded in 1945. A few of the Japanese in the other islands were withdrawn by submarine, but most of them surrendered after the war.) Except for those in the Aleutians, the many Allied operations which contributed to the contraction of the Japanese perimeter have been discussed previously. (The Japanese had occupied Attu and Kiska [*upper center*] in June, 1942. Though these troops posed no great threat to the United States, public indignation at this occupation of American soil was too persistent to be ignored. Consequently, Attu was recaptured by the 7th Division in May 1943, and two months later the Japanese secretly evacuated Kiska. The campaign in the Aleutians was characterized mainly by the abominable weather which severely hampered all military operations.)

Thus, as 1944 drew to a close, all signs pointed to eventual Japanese defeat. American industry had augmented sea and air power to overwhelming proportions; huge, experienced amphibious forces stood poised for further advances—even against the Japanese home islands. But, with a typical display of fanaticism and tenacity, the Japanese refused to admit defeat. Some leaders still entertained a vague hope that the United States would tire of the war and seek a negotiated peace. Yamashita, more of a realist than his superiors, realized that after the disaster at Leyte it was no longer possible for Japan to win a decisive victory.

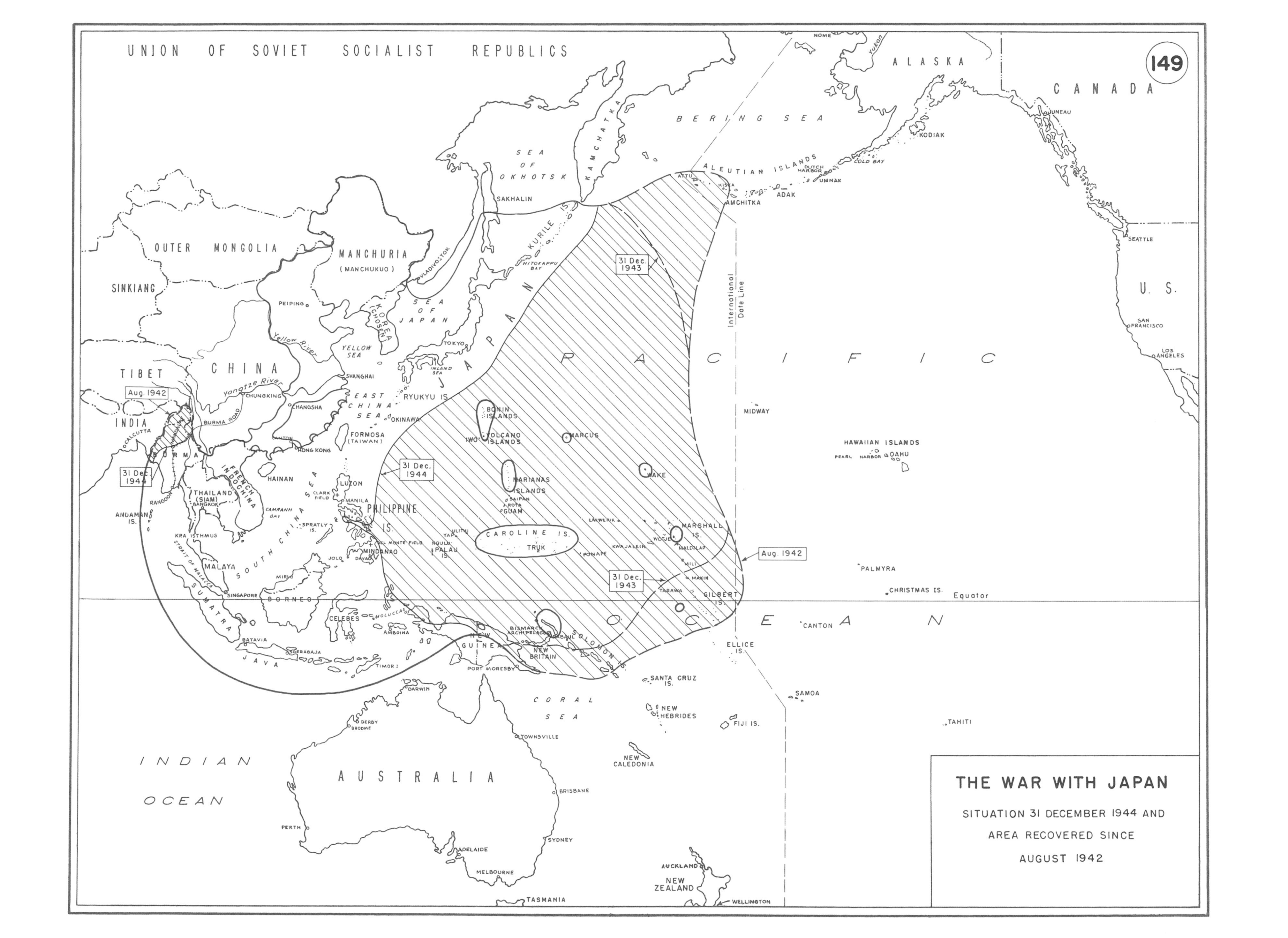
149
UNION OF SOVIET SOCIALIST REPUBLICS
ALASKA
CANADA
U. S.
BERING SEA
SEA OF OKHOTSK
KAMCHATKA
SAKHALIN
KURILE IS.
HITOKAPPU BAY
ALEUTIAN ISLANDS
ATTU
KISKA
AMCHITKA
ADAK
DUTCH HARBOR
UMNAK
COLD BAY
KODIAK
JUNEAU
SEATTLE
SAN FRANCISCO
LOS ANGELES
NOME
Yukon
OUTER MONGOLIA
SINKIANG
MANCHURIA
(MANCHUKUO)
VLADIVOSTOK
KOREA (CHOSEN)
SEA OF JAPAN
JAPAN
TOKYO
INLAND SEA
PEIPING
Yellow River
YELLOW SEA
TIBET
CHINA
Yangtze River
CHUNGKING
CHANGSHA
SHANGHAI
EAST CHINA SEA
RYUKYU IS.
OKINAWA
FORMOSA (TAIWAN)
CANTON
HONG KONG
INDIA
CALCUTTA
BURMA
BURMA ROAD
Aug. 1942
31 Dec. 1944
RANGOON
ANDAMAN IS.
THAILAND (SIAM)
BANGKOK
FRENCH INDOCHINA
HAINAN
KRA ISTHMUS
STRAIT OF MALACCA
MALAYA
SINGAPORE
SUMATRA
SOUTH CHINA SEA
CAMRANH BAY
SPRATLY IS.
CLARK FIELD
LUZON
MANILA
PHILIPPINE IS.
DEL MONTE FIELD
MINDANAO
DAVAO
JOLO
MIRI
BORNEO
CELEBES
MOLUCCAS
AMBOINA
BATAVIA
SOERABAJA
JAVA
TIMOR I
31 Dec. 1944
BONIN ISLANDS
IWO
VOLCANO ISLANDS
MARCUS
MARIANAS ISLANDS
SAIPAN
ROTA
GUAM
WAKE
31 Dec. 1943
ULITHI
YAP
NGULU
PALAU IS.
CAROLINE IS.
TRUK
PONAPE
ENIWETOK
KWAJALEIN
WOTJE
MALOELAP
MARSHALL IS.
MILI
MAKIN
TARAWA
GILBERT IS.
31 Dec. 1943
Aug. 1942
International Date Line
PACIFIC OCEAN
MIDWAY
HAWAIIAN ISLANDS
PEARL HARBOR
OAHU
PALMYRA
CHRISTMAS IS.
Equator
CANTON
ELLICE IS.
SAMOA
TAHITI
BISMARCK ARCHIPELAGO
RABAUL
NEW BRITAIN
NEW GUINEA
PORT MORESBY
SOLOMON IS.
SANTA CRUZ IS.
NEW HEBRIDES
FIJI IS.
NEW CALEDONIA
CORAL SEA
DARWIN
DERBY
BROOME
TOWNSVILLE
AUSTRALIA
BRISBANE
SYDNEY
PERTH
ADELAIDE
MELBOURNE
TASMANIA
AUCKLAND
NEW ZEALAND
WELLINGTON
INDIAN OCEAN
THE WAR WITH JAPAN
SITUATION 31 DECEMBER 1944 AND
AREA RECOVERED SINCE
AUGUST 1942

SITUATION, JANUARY 1945

★

This map depicts (on a larger scale than map 149) the extent to which the Allies had reestablished control—by 1 January, 1945—over the empire Japan had carved out in the first year of the war. It was in the New Guinea–Bismarck Archipelago–Solomons area that the bypassing technique had isolated the most Japanese. There, some 135,000 members of the armies which had opposed MacArthur and Halsey were hopelessly cut off and under pressure from Australian forces.

As the new year dawned, the Allies were readying new offensives against Japan's inner defenses. MacArthur was preparing to land on Luzon, while Halsey's powerful fleet was already launching strikes to cover this assault. The remainder of the Pacific Fleet was raiding to the north in the Bonin and Volcano Islands (*upper center*), concentrating on Iwo Jima—the next target for Nimitz's amphibious forces. Australian forces were preparing offensives against Borneo and the bypassed Japanese in New Guinea and the Solomons. In Burma, the British were slowly pushing Japanese forces back on Mandalay. The Americans now had twenty-seven divisions deployed in the Pacific (Australia provided four more; New Zealand, one), and MacArthur's combined command alone numbered almost 1,500,000 men. The bulk of the United States Navy (some 37,000 aircraft and 61,000 vessels) was under the control of Nimitz. In the air, the Allies had overwhelming superiority. (Japan's desperate answer was the suicide mission—the Kamikaze.) But perhaps more important than the individual build-up of ground, air, and naval forces was the welding of these services into an efficient fighting machine, which the Japanese were powerless to stop. Japan, however, was not willing to quit; the war would last only eight more months, but in this short period the Allies would encounter some of the bitterest fighting of the entire conflict.

The Joint Chiefs of Staff had decided, in July 1944, to invade Leyte, but the debate over the next objective—Luzon or Formosa—was by no means resolved by then. Until September, opinion in Washington was predominantly in favor of Formosa; in the field, Nimitz—apparently somewhat reluctantly—preferred Formosa, while MacArthur was solidly in favor of Luzon.

MacArthur believed that if Luzon were seized, Formosa could be bypassed; but, failing that, he averred that Formosa, in any event, could not be taken until Luzon was in Allied hands. He also pointed out that the liberation of all the Philippines was an American obligation—if not a political necessity. Admiral King, on the other hand, held that a seizure of Formosa would facilitate MacArthur's return to Luzon. He argued that the basic strategic plan of 1943 could not be implemented without seizing Formosa. Finally, he maintained—and General Marshall at first agreed—that if Formosa were bypassed, the next objective should be Japan itself. Army Air Corps planners, who wanted B-29 bases in eastern China, sided with King.

Events in September had a decisive influence on the debate. When the Leyte invasion date was advanced to October, MacArthur at once stated that he could land on Luzon in December, thus not interfering with a projected February operation in Formosa. When Nimitz's plan for a Formosa–China coast operation was received in Washington, the logisticians immediately pointed out that it could not be supported logistically without withdrawing troops from Europe and possibly canceling a Luzon assault as well. Then Stilwell advised the JCS that the Japanese were rapidly overrunning the Allied airfields in China which the air planners had expected to use for B-29 bases. The combination of these factors killed the Formosa operation. Only King continued to oppose a landing in Luzon, and eventually—when reassured by MacArthur that the carrier forces would not be tied up in support of the Sixth Army longer than the assault phase—he agreed to the operation. Hence, on 3 October, the JCS directed MacArthur to invade Luzon about 20 December, 1944.

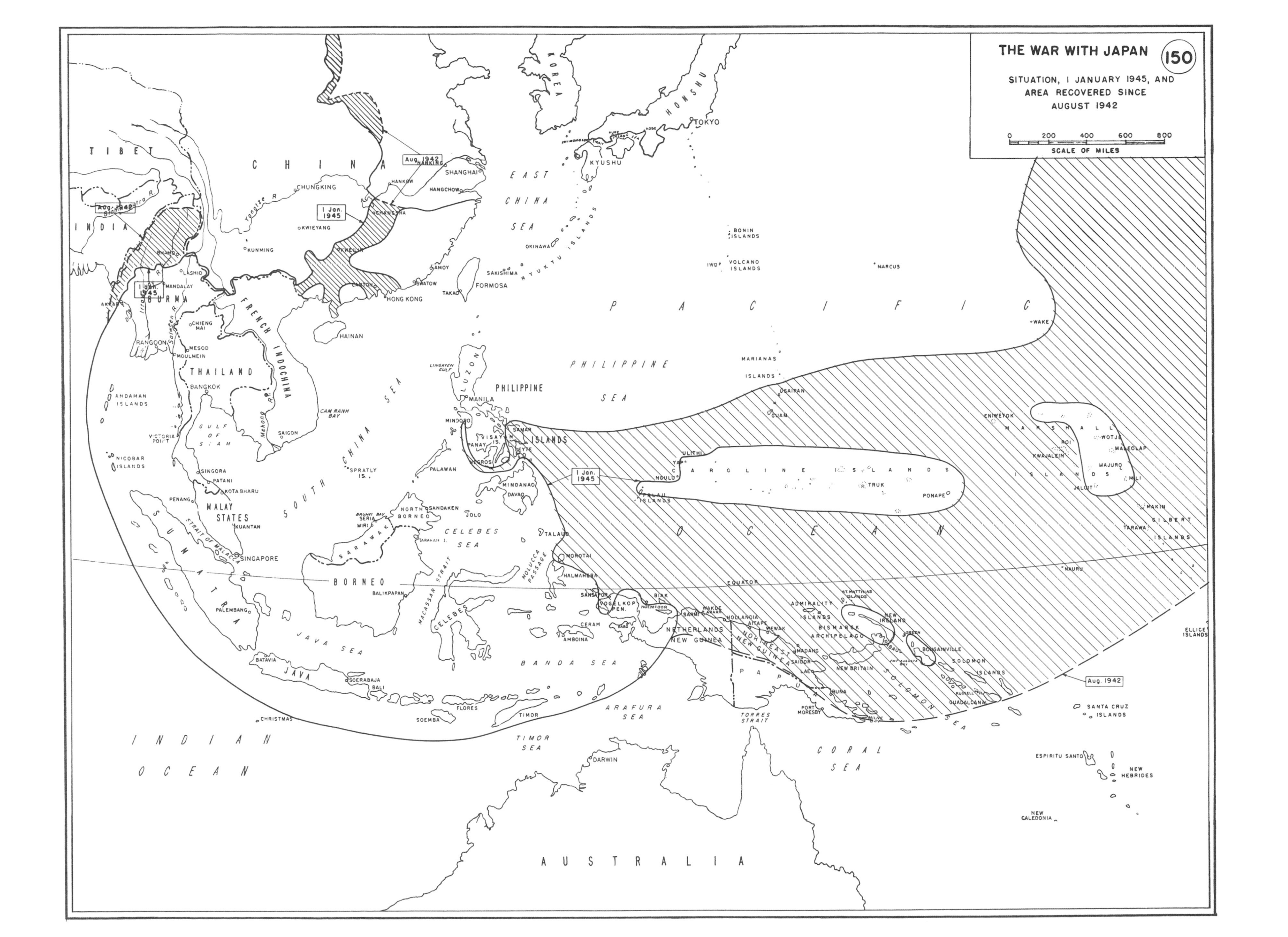
THE WAR WITH JAPAN
150
SITUATION, 1 JANUARY 1945, AND
AREA RECOVERED SINCE
AUGUST 1942
0 200 400 600 800
SCALE OF MILES
Aug. 1942
1 Jan. 1945
TIBET
CHINA
INDIA
BURMA
THAILAND
FRENCH INDOCHINA
MALAY STATES
SUMATRA
JAVA
BORNEO
SARAWAK
NORTH BORNEO
CELEBES
PHILIPPINE ISLANDS
LUZON
FORMOSA
KOREA
HONSHU
KYUSHU
TOKYO
SHANGHAI
NANKING
HANKOW
HANGCHOW
CHANGSHA
CHUNGKING
KWEIYANG
KUNMING
AMOY
SWATOW
HONG KONG
CANTON
TAKAO
HAINAN
MANDALAY
LASHIO
BHAMO
RANGOON
MOULMEIN
MESOD
CHIENG MAI
BANGKOK
SAIGON
CAM RANH BAY
SINGORA
PATANI
KOTA BHARU
PENANG
KUANTAN
SINGAPORE
PALEMBANG
BATAVIA
SOERABAJA
BALI
FLORES
SOEMBA
TIMOR
CHRISTMAS
ANDAMAN ISLANDS
NICOBAR ISLANDS
VICTORIA POINT
STRAIT OF MALACCA
GULF OF SIAM
SOUTH CHINA SEA
EAST CHINA SEA
PHILIPPINE SEA
CELEBES SEA
JAVA SEA
BANDA SEA
ARAFURA SEA
TIMOR SEA
CORAL SEA
SOLOMON SEA
MACASSAR STRAIT
MOLUCCA PASSAGE
TORRES STRAIT
INDIAN OCEAN
PACIFIC OCEAN
AUSTRALIA
DARWIN
MANILA
MINDORO
LINGAYEN GULF
SAMAR
LEYTE
PANAY
NEGROS
VISAYAN IS.
MINDANAO
DAVAO
PALAWAN
SPRATLY IS.
JOLO
SANDAKEN
BRUNEI BAY
SERIA
MIRI
BALIKPAPAN
TALAUD
MOROTAI
HALMAHERA
SANSAPOR
VOGELKOP PEN.
NOEMFOOR
BIAK
SARMI
WAKDE
HOLLANDIA
AITAPE
WEWAK
MADANG
SAIDOR
LAE
BUNA
MILNE BAY
PORT MORESBY
CERAM
AMBOINA
NETHERLANDS NEW GUINEA
NORTHEAST NEW GUINEA
PAPUA
NEW BRITAIN
RABAUL
NEW IRELAND
BISMARCK ARCHIPELAGO
ADMIRALTY ISLANDS
ST. MATTHIAS ISLANDS
GREEN
BOUGAINVILLE
SOLOMON ISLANDS
RUSSELL IS.
GUADALCANAL
SANTA CRUZ ISLANDS
ESPIRITU SANTO
NEW HEBRIDES
NEW CALEDONIA
ELLICE ISLANDS
NAURU
EQUATOR
GILBERT ISLANDS
TARAWA
MAKIN
MARSHALL ISLANDS
ENIWETOK
KWAJALEIN
ROI
WOTJE
MALOELAP
MAJURO
JALUIT
MILI
CAROLINE ISLANDS
TRUK
PONAPE
ULITHI
YAP
NGULU
PALAU ISLANDS
MARIANAS ISLANDS
SAIPAN
GUAM
WAKE
MARCUS
BONIN ISLANDS
VOLCANO ISLANDS
IWO
RYUKYU ISLANDS
OKINAWA
SAKISHIMA
Yangtze R.
Mekong R.
Salween R.
Irrawaddy R.

BURMA CAMPAIGN

★

The situation on New Year's Day in Burma (*heavy dashed red line*) found the Japanese in retreat, except around Wanting (*center*), where they still fought fanatically to maintain their grip on the western end of the Burma Road.

Following Stilwell's relief, the ground forces of the Southeast Asia Command were reorganized under Lt. Gen. Sir Oliver Leese, who at the same time commanded the British 11th Army Group (consisting of the Fourteenth Army in northern Burma and the detached XV Corps in the Akyab coastal area). The other forces under Leese's command were Sultan's Northern Combat Area Command (British, American, and American-trained Chinese troops) and Marshal Wei-Li-Huang's Chinese Expeditionary Force (about twelve weak divisions). The Allied plan involved operations by Sultan and Wei-Li-Huang to open the Burma Road; an offensive by Lt. Gen. Sir William J. Slim on Mandalay—to be pushed, if possible, to Rangoon; and a drive down the west coast by the XV Corps. This last operation aided Slim's advance by capturing airfield sites from which supplies could be rapidly flown in to his advancing Fourteenth Army.

Slim had hoped that the Japanese would make a stand in the open country north of Mandalay, where British armor could operate with great effectiveness. Instead, the new Japanese commander in Burma, Lt. Gen. Hyotaro Kimura, decided to hold the line Akyab-Mandalay-Lashio. Any British assault on Mandalay would therefore first have to force the broad Irrawaddy River. Kimura apparently felt that, by catching the Fourteenth Army astride the river at the end of a long and tenuous supply line, he could inflict a crushing defeat similar to that the Japanese themselves had suffered at Imphal. Such a victory would leave him free to deal with Sultan and the Chinese, with every prospect of success. His plan was theoretically sound, but it ignored the supply and combat capabilities of the Allied air forces, the now superior jungle craft of the British troops, and the amazing feats of logistical improvisation which Allied staffs could achieve on short notice.

Wei-Li-Huang took Lashio on 7 March. The Ledo Road and a parallel pipeline had already been extended to Myitkyina; convoys began rolling into Kunming again. After the fall of Lashio, however, Chiang Kai-Shek ordered most of the American and Chinese troops in northern Burma to return to China. This enabled Kimura to withdraw troops from that front and employ them against Slim. He also recalled most of the Japanese troops from the west coast, but here British amphibious attacks repeatedly cut the coastal road, inflicting heavy casualties on the withdrawing columns.

In the center, once he was aware of Kimura's actual dispositions, Slim sent his XXXIII Corps directly south against Mandalay, while the IV Corps—practically building its road as it advanced—moved secretly through the jungle hills west of that city, crossed the Irrawaddy at Pagan (*lower center*), and surprised the Japanese supply center at Meiktila. This cut Kimura's supply line; his most desperate efforts to regain the town failed, and Mandalay meanwhile fell (20 March) to the XXXIII Corps.

Kimura had lost heavily. Quickly regrouping, Slim swept south, his main force following the axis of the Rangoon-Mandalay railroad, a secondary attack moving down the Irrawaddy. It was a race with the coming monsoon season and Kimura's ability to rebuild his defenses. Spearheaded by their armor, and supplied largely by air, the British attacks quickly gained momentum. A Japanese attempt to concentrate at Toungoo (*lower center*) was broken up by Karen tribesmen under British officers. Kimura stripped southern Burma of troops for a last stand at Pegu, but this was broken by 1 May, just as the monsoon rains began. Left undefended, Rangoon fell to a XV Corps amphibious operation on the 2d. Some mop-up campaigning continued as Japanese isolated in western Burma tried to break out, but there were no more major operations prior to the Japanese capitulation on 15 August.

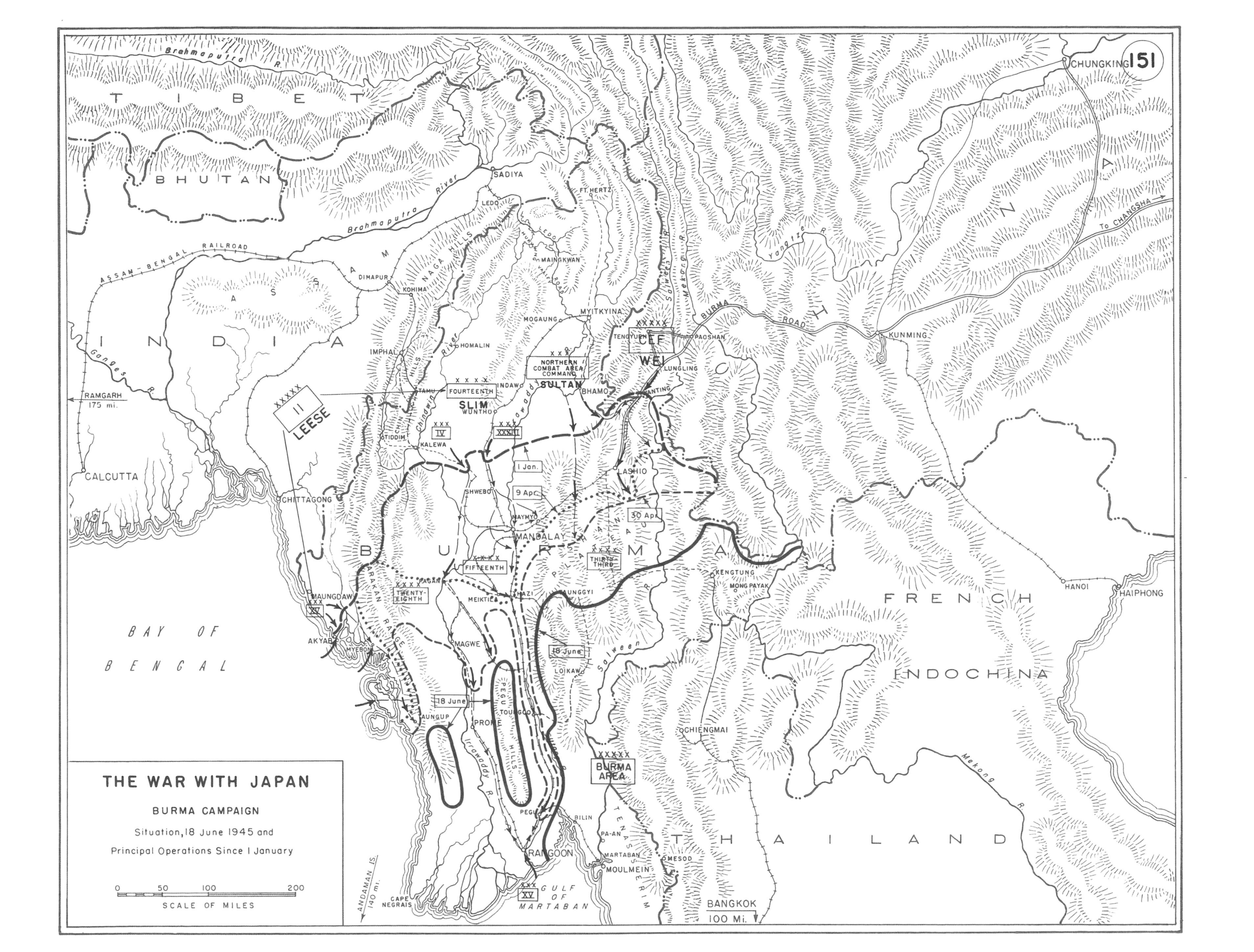
151
TIBET
BHUTAN
INDIA
ASSAM
BURMA
CHINA
FRENCH INDOCHINA
THAILAND
BAY OF BENGAL
GULF OF MARTABAN
Brahmaputra R.
Brahmaputra River
ASSAM-BENGAL RAILROAD
Ganges R.
RAMGARH 175 mi.
CALCUTTA
CHITTAGONG
DIMAPUR
KOHIMA
NAGA HILLS
IMPHAL
TAMU
TIDDIM
KALEWA
HOMALIN
Chindwin River
SADIYA
LEDO
LEDO ROAD
MAINGKWAN
FT. HERTZ
MYITKYINA
MOGAUNG
INDAW
WUNTHO
BHAMO
TENGYUEH
PAOSHAN
LUNGLING
WANTING
LASHIO
SHWEBO
MAYMYO
MANDALAY
PAGAN
MEIKTILA
THAZI
TAUNGGYI
MAGWE
LOIKAW
PROME
TOUNGOO
PEGU
PEGU HILLS
RANGOON
AUNGUP
MYEBON
AKYAB
MAUNGDAW
ARAKAN RANGE
CAPE NEGRAIS
ANDAMAN IS. 140 mi.
BILIN
PA-AN
MARTABAN
MOULMEIN
TENASSERIM
MESOD
CHIENGMAI
KENGTUNG
MONG PAYAK
BANGKOK 100 Mi.
HANOI
HAIPHONG
KUNMING
BURMA ROAD
CHUNGKING
To CHANGSHA
Yangtze R.
Salween R.
Mekong R.
Irrawaddy R.
XXXXX II LEESE
XXXX FOURTEENTH SLIM
XXX IV
XXX XXXIII
XXX NORTHERN COMBAT AREA COMMAND SULTAN
XXXXX CEF WEI
XXXX THIRTY-THIRD
XXXX FIFTEENTH
XXXX TWENTY-EIGHTH
XXX XV
XXXXX BURMA AREA
1 Jan.
9 Apr.
30 Apr.
18 June
THE WAR WITH JAPAN
BURMA CAMPAIGN
Situation, 18 June 1945 and
Principal Operations Since 1 January
0 50 100 200
SCALE OF MILES

CHINA-BURMA THEATER

During early 1945, the Japanese continued to consolidate their position in southeastern China (*compare this map and map 141*), clearing the Canton-Hengyang railroad (*lower center*) by 5 February. The Fourteenth Air Force and the XX Bomber Command, hampered by periodic fuel shortages and the loss of their forward bases, carried the major burden of the Allied war effort. They were especially active in mid-January, in support of the American Third Fleet's raid into the South China Sea (launched to cover the American invasion of Luzon; *see map 154*) and in late March and early April (to support the American landing on Okinawa; *see map 163*).

To further strengthen their grip on southeast Asia, the Japanese seized full control of Indochina in early March. (The Japanese had occupied this French colony in 1940, but—by agreement—the French had continued to control its internal administration. Some of the weak, hopelessly isolated French garrisons appear to have waged an equally hopeless resistance.) In late March, the Japanese attacked in considerable force in central China, overrunning an American air base at Laohokow (*this map, lower center*) and seizing the ripening crops in this fertile area. A second such operation, directed at Changteh and Chihkiang (*lower center*) was thrown back in early May by a strong Chinese–Fourteenth Air Force counterattack.

This was the last large-scale Japanese offensive. Elsewhere, it was already obvious that Japan had lost her war. Germany had capitulated, Okinawa was largely in American hands, the Japanese forces in Burma had been destroyed, the Japanese Navy was a memory, and the remaining Japanese air power was bleeding itself to death in Kamikaze attacks. Furthermore, Stalin—having obtained his immediate objectives in Europe—had made it plain that he intended to follow a similar policy in the Far East. Japanese forces in Manchuria—the one-time crack Kwantung Army—had declined greatly in strength and quality, due to the transfer of veteran units during the war. Consequently, by mid-May, the Japanese began evacuating southern China to reinforce their Manchurian defenses. This withdrawal was followed up—but, apparently, not appreciably troubled—by the Chinese. The Fourteenth and Tenth Air Forces (the latter recently transferred from Burma and India) harried the Japanese by strikes against their roads, railroads, and coastal shipping. No decisive actions took place in this area, however, before the end of the war.

Russia declared war on Japan on 8 August. The next day, the Russians launched their main attack from the west, advancing along the railroad toward Tsitsihar and Harbin and, farther south, along the ancient caravan route Kalgan (*center, right*)—Peiping–Tientsin. Secondary attacks pushed eastward and south from Khabarovsk and Vladivostok (*both upper right*). Using masses of armor and motorized troops, the Russians flooded across the Manchurian plains; the Japanese—lacking both modern armor and effective antitank weapons—could offer only spotty resistance, their most effective stands apparently being made southwest of Vladivostok. (Practically nothing is known concerning the details of this campaign, which the Russians presented to the world as *the* decisive blow that defeated Japan, after years of indecisive American fumbling among the Pacific Islands.) Although the war ended officially on 15 August, the Russians kept up their advance until the 20th. (For operations in Burma during 1945, *see map 151*.)

Operations in India, Burma, and China represent, above all, a logistical triumph. Supplies, in large part originating in the United States, were moved into remote corners of the Burmese jungle and the hills of China in sufficient quantity to maintain major air and ground offensives. In this, the transport plane and the bulldozer changed the entire concept of transportation in the Far East. Yet, at the same time, pack mules, porters, elephants, and improvised river shipping were frequently invaluable. This was a war fought for extended periods in unhealthy, rain-sodden, insect-ridden areas—probably the loneliest, most alien, and most primitive war Americans have ever faced.

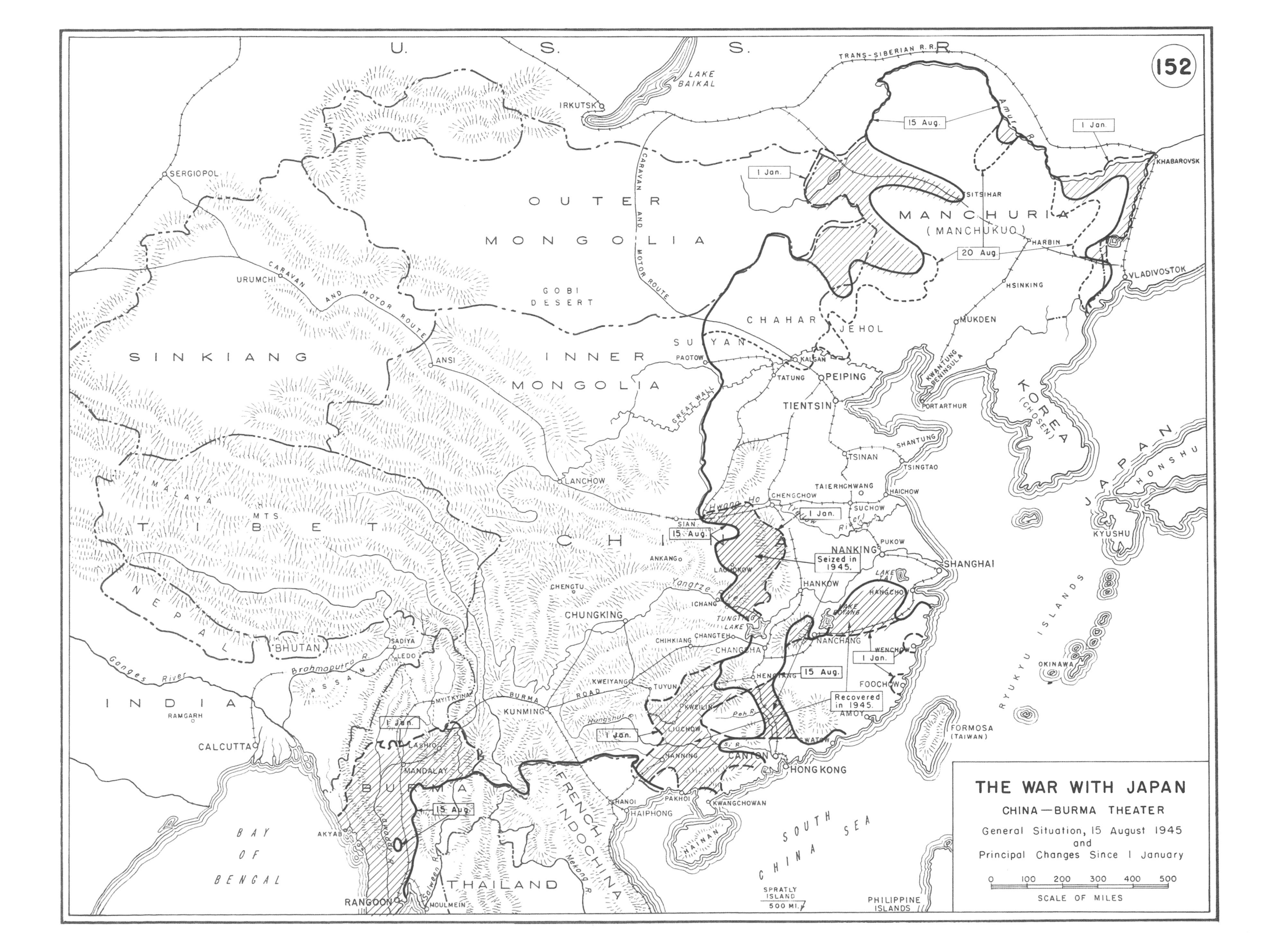
152
THE WAR WITH JAPAN
CHINA—BURMA THEATER
General Situation, 15 August 1945
and
Principal Changes Since 1 January
0 100 200 300 400 500
SCALE OF MILES
U. S. S. R.
TRANS-SIBERIAN R.R.
LAKE BAIKAL
IRKUTSK
SERGIOPOL
OUTER
MONGOLIA
CARAVAN AND MOTOR ROUTE
GOBI DESERT
URUMCHI
SINKIANG
ANSI
INNER
MONGOLIA
SUIYAN
CHAHAR
JEHOL
MANCHURIA
(MANCHUKUO)
Amur R.
KHABAROVSK
SITSIHAR
HARBIN
HSINKING
MUKDEN
VLADIVOSTOK
KWANTUNG PENINSULA
PORT ARTHUR
KOREA
(CHOSEN)
JAPAN
HONSHU
KYUSHU
RYUKYU ISLANDS
OKINAWA
FORMOSA
(TAIWAN)
PHILIPPINE ISLANDS
SPRATLY ISLAND
500 MI.
SOUTH CHINA SEA
HAINAN
15 Aug.
1 Jan.
20 Aug.
PAOTOW
KALGAN
TATUNG
PEIPING
TIENTSIN
GREAT WALL
SHANTUNG
TSINAN
TSINGTAO
TAIERHCHWANG
HAICHOW
CHENGCHOW
SUCHOW
Hwang Ho
Yellow River
SIAN
LANCHOW
PUKOW
NANKING
SHANGHAI
Seized in 1945.
ANKANG
LAOHOKOW
HANKOW
LAKE TAI
HANGCHOW
Yangtze R.
ICHANG
TUNGTING LAKE
LAKE POYANG
CHENGTU
CHUNGKING
CHANGTEH
CHIHKIANG
CHANGSHA
NANCHANG
WENCHOW
HENGYANG
FOOCHOW
Recovered in 1945.
AMOY
KWEIYANG
TUYUN
KWEILIN
Peh R.
Hungshui R.
LIUCHOW
NANNING
Si R.
WATOW
CANTON
HONG KONG
KWANGCHOWAN
PAKHOI
HANOI
HAIPHONG
FRENCH INDOCHINA
Mekong R.
THAILAND
BURMA ROAD
KUNMING
MYITKYINA
LASHIO
MANDALAY
BURMA
Irrawaddy R.
Salween R.
MOULMEIN
RANGOON
AKYAB
BAY OF BENGAL
SADIYA
LEDO
ASSAM
Brahmaputra R.
BHUTAN
NEPAL
HIMALAYA MTS
TIBET
CHINA
INDIA
RAMGARH
CALCUTTA
Ganges River

PHILIPPINE CAMPAIGN

★

With the decision to invade Luzon rather than Formosa (*see text, map 150*), MacArthur began formulating his final plan. Originally, he expected to route the assault convoy from Leyte along the eastern coast of Luzon, around its northern end, and then to Lingayen Gulf (*this map, top center*). But to protect any convoy following this route, land-based air cover would first have to be established at Legaspi (*center, right*) and Aparri (*see map 156, top center*); and such a requirement would almost certainly entail postponing the projected 20 December landing at Lingayen Gulf. When naval planners also called attention to the poor weather conditions that normally prevailed off northern Luzon in December, MacArthur decided to use the route shown (*this map, dashed blue line*). (He had decided earlier to use this route for reinforcement convoys, providing them air cover from bases he planned to seize on Mindoro [*center, left*] on 5 December.)

The dates for the Mindoro and Luzon operations had to be reconsidered in light of the prolongation of the Leyte campaign and the delay in establishing airfields on Leyte to support the Mindoro landing. Additionally, Halsey pointed out that his fleet would have to have badly needed repair and rest before it could provide support for a Luzon landing. Consequently, MacArthur decided to augment land-based air support for the Mindoro operation with Seventh Fleet escort carriers and to postpone the landings on Mindoro and Luzon to 15 December and 9 January, respectively.

A brigade-size task force landed near San Jose on Mindoro early on 15 December, drove the small Japanese garrison inland, quickly occupied the southwestern part of the island, and established a defensive perimeter (*shaded blue area*). Two airfields were built; by the end of the month, Kenney's aircraft based there were striking Japanese installations on Luzon. On 1 January, 1945, the Eighth Army assumed responsibility for the island of Mindoro.

Japanese air power in the Philippines had been reduced to such a state of impotency in the last few months of 1944 that, by 1 January, 1945, there were only about 150 aircraft on Luzon—and practically all of these were destined to be destroyed by 13 January. But Yamashita's ground forces on Luzon were more formidable; as shown, he had 250,000 troops, poorly equipped though they were. Though actually wanting to counterattack any Allied landing, Yamashita reluctantly concluded that he would have to adopt a static defense, designed to delay the conquest of Luzon as long as possible. Consequently, he organized three groups: the Shobu Group would defend against a landing at Lingayen Gulf, and ultimately withdraw into a rugged mountain redoubt north of Baguio (*top center*); the Kembu Group would defend Clark Field (*upper left, near San Fernando*) and then withdraw westward into the mountains; and the Shimbu Group, though responsible for all of southern Luzon, would concentrate its strength in the mountains east of Manila—it was specifically directed not to defend the capital.

MacArthur's concept for the invasion envisaged an amphibious landing at the base of Lingayen Gulf and rapid consolidation of a beachhead; the establishment of air and base facilities; the securing of the Central Plain; and the capture of Manila. Before Krueger's Sixth Army undertook the accomplishment of this mission, the Eighth Army would seize northeastern Mindoro, naval and air elements would conduct demonstrations along the southern Luzon coast, and guerrillas would destroy communications in southern Luzon. (As it turned out, none of these attempts at deception [*blue arrows*] misled Yamashita as to the location of the main landing.) The Seventh Fleet would provide direct naval (surface and air) support while Halsey—operating independently of MacArthur—would cover the invasion force by hitting Formosan and northern Luzon targets. Kenney's aircraft, flying from Leyte and Mindoro, would pummel Luzon targets, and China-based B-29's would strike Formosa.

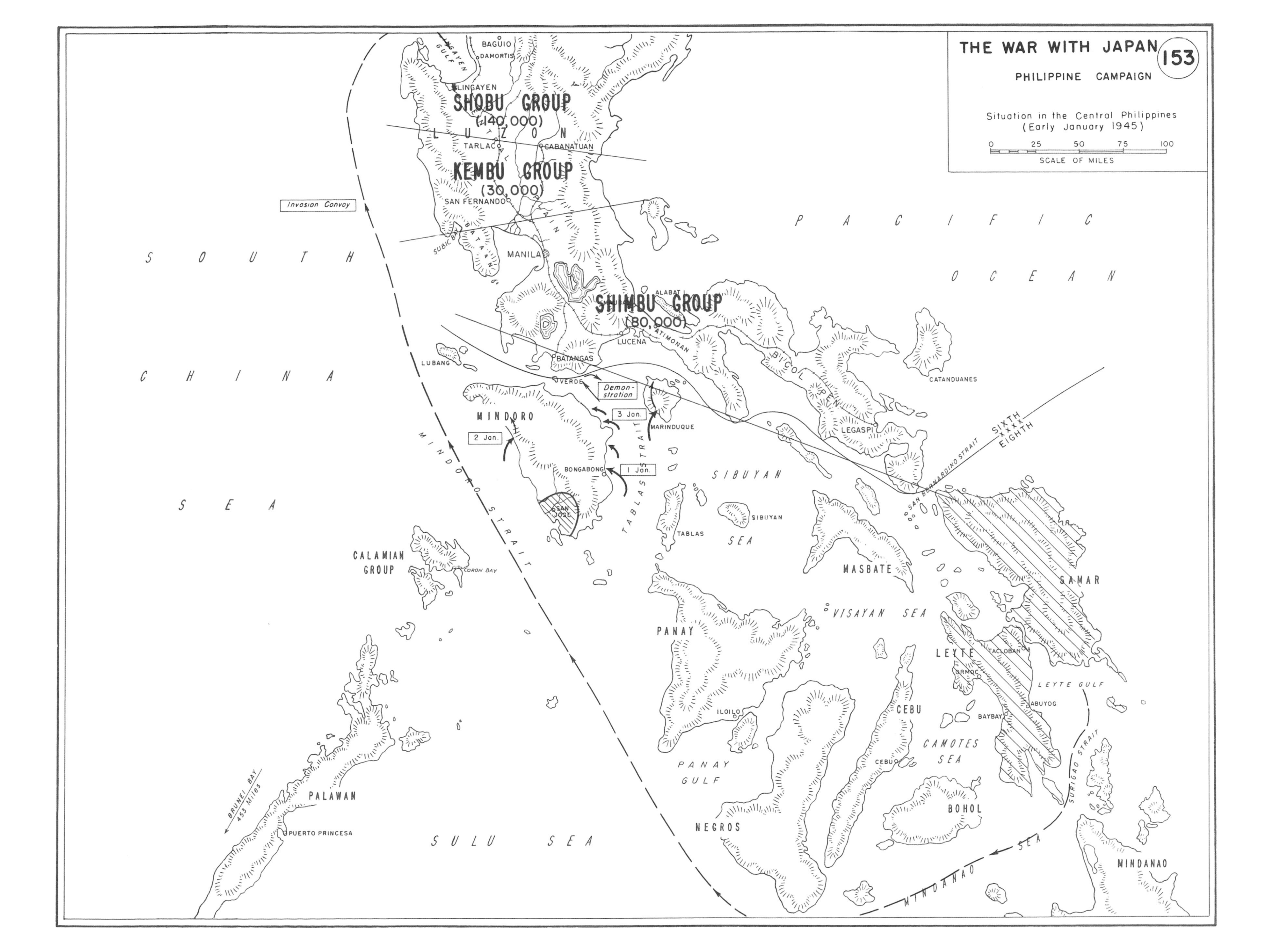
THE WAR WITH JAPAN
153
PHILIPPINE CAMPAIGN
Situation in the Central Philippines
(Early January 1945)
0 25 50 75 100
SCALE OF MILES
SHOBU GROUP
(140,000)
KEMBU GROUP
(30,000)
SHIMBU GROUP
(80,000)
LUZON
BAGUIO
DAMORTIS
LINGAYEN GULF
LINGAYEN
TARLAC
CABANATUAN
SAN FERNANDO
SUBIC BAY
BATAAN
MANILA
ALABAT
LUCENA
ATIMONAN
BATANGAS
BICOL PEN
LEGASPI
CATANDUANES
Invasion Convoy
PACIFIC OCEAN
SOUTH CHINA SEA
LUBANG
VERDE
Demonstration
3 Jan.
2 Jan.
1 Jan.
MINDORO
MARINDUQUE
BONGABONG
SAN JOSE
MINDORO STRAIT
TABLAS STRAIT
SIBUYAN SEA
SIBUYAN
TABLAS
SAN BERNARDINO STRAIT
SIXTH
EIGHTH
MASBATE
SAMAR
CALAMIAN GROUP
CORON BAY
VISAYAN SEA
PANAY
LEYTE
TACLOBAN
ORMOC
LEYTE GULF
ABUYOG
BAYBAY
ILOILO
CEBU
CAMOTES SEA
SURIGAO STRAIT
PANAY GULF
BOHOL
NEGROS
PALAWAN
PUERTO PRINCESA
BRUNEI BAY 453 Miles
SULU SEA
MINDANAO SEA
MINDANAO

PHILIPPINE CAMPAIGN

★

On 2 January, the first elements of the Luzon Attack Force departed Leyte for Lingayen Gulf. Three days earlier, Halsey's carriers had left Ulithi for the scheduled strikes against Formosa. Now—as MacArthur's force moved north through the Visayas—Japan's few remaining aircraft in the Philippines were committed in desperate Kamikaze strikes against the convoy. By the 7th, the Allies had sustained such damage that the naval commanders were very seriously disturbed over the practicability of landing the next day. Kenney and Halsey—the latter now in position off Luzon—intensified their attacks on Japanese airfields on Luzon, and the Kamikaze attacks began to taper off on 9 January. On the 13th, they ceased—not because the Allies had devised an effective defense, but because the Japanese high command refused to replace its aircraft losses on Luzon. Beginning with attacks on the convoy carrying the Mindoro landing force on 13 December and lasting through 13 January, Kamikaze attacks sank twenty ships, heavily damaged twenty-four, and lightly damaged thirty-five.

For the assault at Lingayen Gulf, the Sixth Army was organized as shown (*upper left*). Because the divisions it was to employ were so widely dispersed in the southern Pacific islands in late 1944, the mounting of the operation posed major problems in operational and logistical planning. The reinforcements shown (*top left*) were tentatively allocated to Krueger when November intelligence estimates forecast a larger enemy force on Luzon than had been originally expected. Of these units, the 33d and 41st Divisions were MacArthur's theater reserve. In addition, the Eighth Army (Lt. Gen. Robert L. Eichelberger) was preparing to execute a subsidiary landing on Luzon, after which the troops employed (XI Corps) would come under Krueger's control. (This landing was made later near San Antonio [*bottom left*].) Ultimately, the Luzon campaign became the largest of the Pacific war and, comparatively speaking, employed more American forces than did operations in North Africa or Italy.

Krueger landed with four divisions abreast at 0930, 9 January. He chose the relatively poor beaches shown, rather than the better ones on the eastern side of the gulf, in the hope of achieving tactical surprise. Also, they were less heavily defended, and behind them was an airstrip which Krueger wished to seize quickly. Opposition to the landing was light; by nightfall, the Sixth Army had landed 68,000 men and established a beachhead as shown (*dashed red line*).

The advance, superbly supported by engineer units, made good progress the next two days. Only the 43d Division met substantial resistance as it encountered the forward positions of the Shobu Group. On 11 January, Krueger landed his floating reserve and immediately sent the 158th RCT north to secure Damortis. By the 20th, the Sixth Army reached the line shown (*dotted red line*); the major resistance was encountered in the north (*heavy dotted section*). The XLV Corps' advance was being governed primarily by logistics, Japanese resistance being spotty; by contrast, the I Corps was meeting bitter opposition in its eastward advance. The 6th Division had encountered a strong position in the Cabaruan Hills which was not completely overrun until the 28th; meanwhile, the 25th Division had been committed on 17 January, and the 43d Division—threatening to break into Yamashita's planned redoubt area—continued to meet fierce resistance.

On the 17th, Kenney's aircraft had begun operating from the Lingayen airfields, thus releasing Kincaid's escort carriers which were still standing by. That same date, MacArthur—with characteristic boldness—had urged Krueger to speed his drive on Manila, but Krueger, fearing a Japanese attack on his east flank, preferred to wait until he could strengthen the I Corps. He did, however, push the XIV Corps forward; it promptly encountered the Kembu Group near Bamban (*lower center*) on 23 January and for the next week engaged in its stiffest fight to date in overrunning Clark Field and driving the Japanese westward. One regiment continued south to seize Calumpit. Meanwhile, the I Corps, reinforced by the 32d Division (30 January), pushed east and south as Yamashita—resisting stubbornly to hold the approaches to his redoubt and gain maximum time to bring supplies up Route 5—slowly gave ground. By the 31st, Krueger had moved the recently arrived 1st Cavalry Division to Guimba (*center*) and had forced the Japanese back far enough to feel secure at both Clark Field (*lower center*) and Rosario (*upper left*). He was now ready to rush columns to Manila.

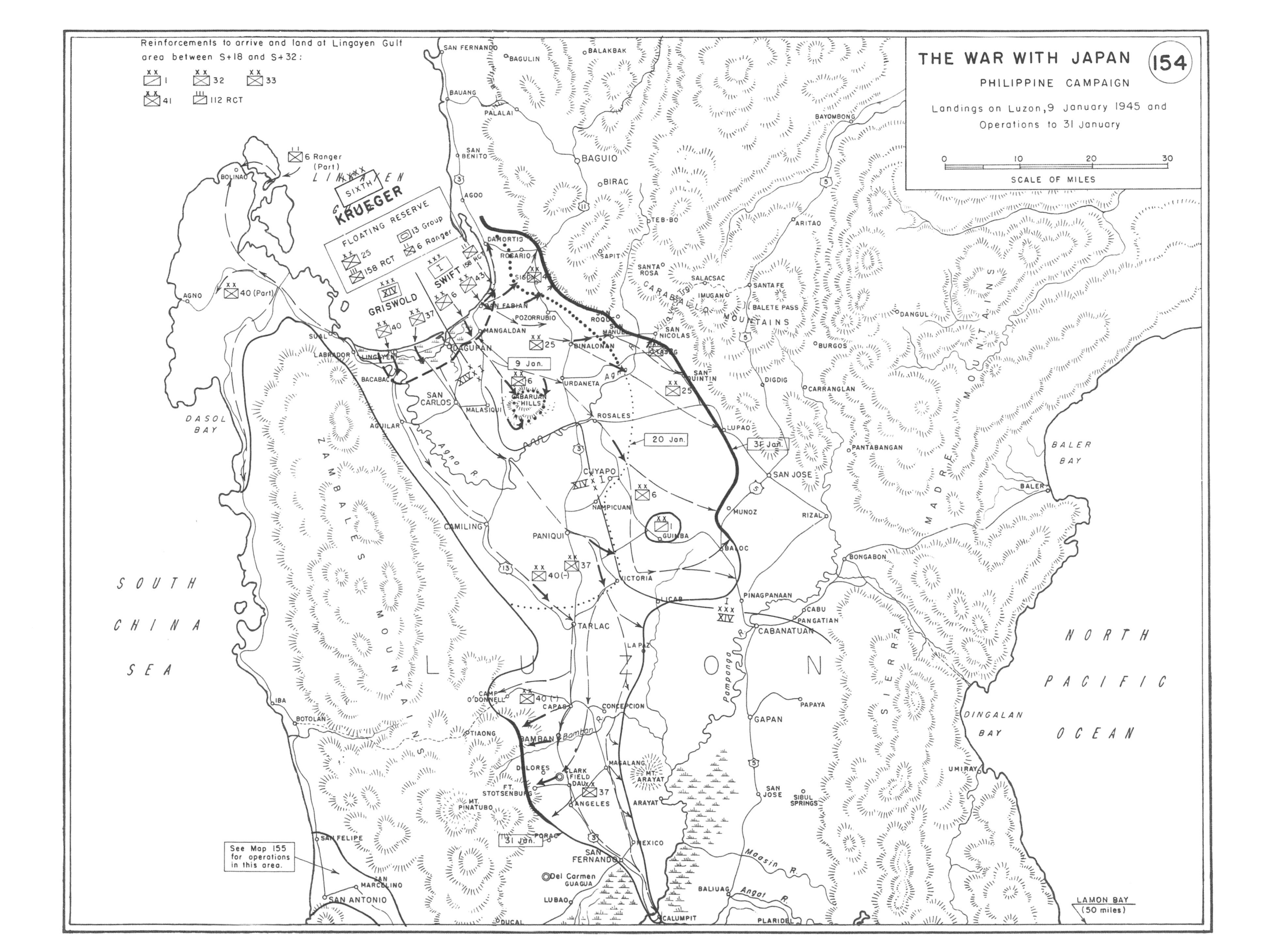

THE WAR WITH JAPAN
154
PHILIPPINE CAMPAIGN
Landings on Luzon, 9 January 1945 and
Operations to 31 January
0 10 20 30
SCALE OF MILES
Reinforcements to arrive and land at Lingayen Gulf
area between S+18 and S+32:
1
32
33
41
112 RCT
6 Ranger (Part)
SIXTH
KRUEGER
FLOATING RESERVE
25
158 RCT
13 Group
6 Ranger
I
SWIFT
158 RCT
43
6
XIV
GRISWOLD
40
37
40 (Part)
LINGAYEN
DASOL BAY
SOUTH
CHINA
SEA
ZAMBALES MOUNTAINS
LUZON
NORTH
PACIFIC
OCEAN
BALER BAY
DINGALAN BAY
LAMON BAY (50 miles)
SIERRA MADRE
MADRE MOUNTAINS
CARABALLO MOUNTAINS
Villa Verde Trail
9 Jan.
20 Jan.
31 Jan.
SAN FERNANDO
BAGULIN
BALAKBAK
BAUANG
PALALAI
SAN BENITO
BAGUIO
BIRAC
AGOO
TEB-BO
DAMORTIS
ROSARIO
SISON
SAPIT
SANTA ROSA
SALACSAC
IMUGAN
SANTA FE
BALETE PASS
ARITAO
BAYOMBONG
DANGUL
BURGOS
DIGDIG
CARRANGLAN
PANTABANGAN
SAN JOSE
LUPAO
SAN QUINTIN
SAN NICOLAS
SAN MANUEL
SAN ROQUE
BINALONAN
POZORRUBIO
SAN FABIAN
MANGALDAN
DAGUPAN
LINGAYEN
LABRADOR
SUAL
BACABAC
SAN CARLOS
MALASIQUI
CABARUAN HILLS
URDANETA
ROSALES
AGUILAR
Agno R.
CAMILING
CUYAPO
NAMPICUAN
PANIQUI
GUIMBA
VICTORIA
MUNOZ
RIZAL
BALOC
BONGABON
PINAGPANAAN
LICAB
TARLAC
CABU
PANGATIAN
CABANATUAN
Pampanga R.
LA PAZ
CONCEPCION
CAMP O'DONNELL
CAPAS
TIAONG
BAMBAN
Bamban R.
DOLORES
CLARK FIELD
DAU
FT. STOTSENBURG
MT. PINATUBO
ANGELES
MAGALANG
MT. ARAYAT
ARAYAT
PORAC
MEXICO
SAN FERNANDO
Del Carmen
GUAGUA
LUBAO
DUCAL
CALUMPIT
BALIUAG
Angat R.
PLARIDEL
Maasin R.
GAPAN
PAPAYA
SAN JOSE
SIBUL SPRINGS
UMIRAY
BALER
AGNO
BOLINAO
IBA
BOTOLAN
SAN FELIPE
SAN MARCELINO
SAN ANTONIO
See Map 155 for operations in this area.

PHILIPPINE CAMPAIGN

Before Krueger loosed the XIV Corps on its quick dash for Manila, the Eighth Army—as part of MacArthur's strategy to keep the Japanese off balance and to seal off Bataan—made two amphibious landings on Luzon. The first was executed on 29 January by the XL Corps near San Antonio (*upper left*). These troops met no initial opposition—friendly guerrillas controlled the area—and quickly moved inland, seizing Olongapo and Grande Island on the 30th. On the 31st, the XI Corps (now under Krueger's control) began its drive eastward to block the Bataan peninsula.

The second landing took place on the 31st when one glider regiment of the 11th Airborne Division (soon followed by the second glider regiment) made an amphibious landing at Nasugbu (*lower left*) against slight opposition. Originally planned as a reconnaissance in force to be exploited—if practicable—by seizing Tagaytay Ridge and then patrolling north and east to contain elements of the Shimbu Group in southwestern Luzon, the operation soon developed into a headlong dash for Manila. Presumably having received MacArthur's permission, Eichelberger decided to exploit the landing and ordered the division's parachute regiment to jump on Tagaytay Ridge. This jump (3 February)—unopposed but poorly executed—gave Eichelberger a fresh regiment which he quickly motorized and dispatched toward Manila; simultaneously, the glider regiments fought their way to Tagaytay and prepared to follow. By late on 4 February, advance elements of the division had reached Paranaque (*center*), where they were abruptly halted by strong Japanese defenses.

Meanwhile, Krueger—prodded by MacArthur—had initiated the drive by the XIV Corps on Manila. On 2 February, elements of the 1st Cavalry and 37th Divisions met at Plaridel. The 1st Cavalry Division now organized two "flying columns" and sent them racing toward Novaliches and Manila; these columns entered the outskirts of the capital the next night (3 February). The rest of the division followed more slowly, leaving one regiment (later relieved by the 112th RCT) on the flank near Norzagaray. The 37th Division, meeting more resistance, smashed its way into the city on the 4th. Then, for a month, the Japanese fanatically defended Manila in fighting subsequently described (*see text, map 157*).

By 14 February (*this map, dotted red line*), the Japanese in Manila had been isolated from the remainder of the Kembu Group. Most of the 1st Cavalry Division and the 6th Division (now assigned to the XIV Corps) advanced eastward and encountered the two independently organized fortified lines shown (*red symbols*). On 12 March, the 43d Division relieved the exhausted 1st Cavalry, and three days later the XI Corps assumed responsibility for the attack on these positions; the XIV Corps retained responsibility for liberating southwestern Luzon. The 11th Airborne Division (under the Sixth Army since 10 February) and the 158th RCT had already begun operations toward this end, and by 15 March held the lines shown (*bottom center, solid red lines*).

In the meantime, the 40th Division had been slowly forcing the Japanese back into the mountains west of Clark Field, and had also linked up with the 38th Division at Dinalupihan (*center, left*). This latter division, fighting in extremely rugged terrain, had badly mismanaged the attack to clear Zigzag Pass, but finally opened the Olongapo-Dinalupihan road and eliminated the last enemy resistance on 15 February. The 43d Division relieved the 40th (now assigned to the Eighth Army for operations in the Visayas) on 2 March, but was itself assigned to the XIV Corps and dispatched to the front east of Manila on 11 March. The 38th Division assumed sole responsibility for mopping up the remnants of the Kembu Group west of Clark Field.

Operations for liberating Bataan and Corregidor were begun early. As shown, the 151st RCT landed at Mariveles on 15 February, and, assisted by the 1st RCT (6th Division), eliminated the token resistance on the peninsula by the 21st. On 16 February, a spectacular amphibious-airborne assault was made on Corregidor. The extremely difficult airborne landing was well executed and surprised the Japanese. But they were in much greater strength than expected and fought fiercely before succumbing to troops of the 24th and 38th Divisions and the paratroopers on 27 February.

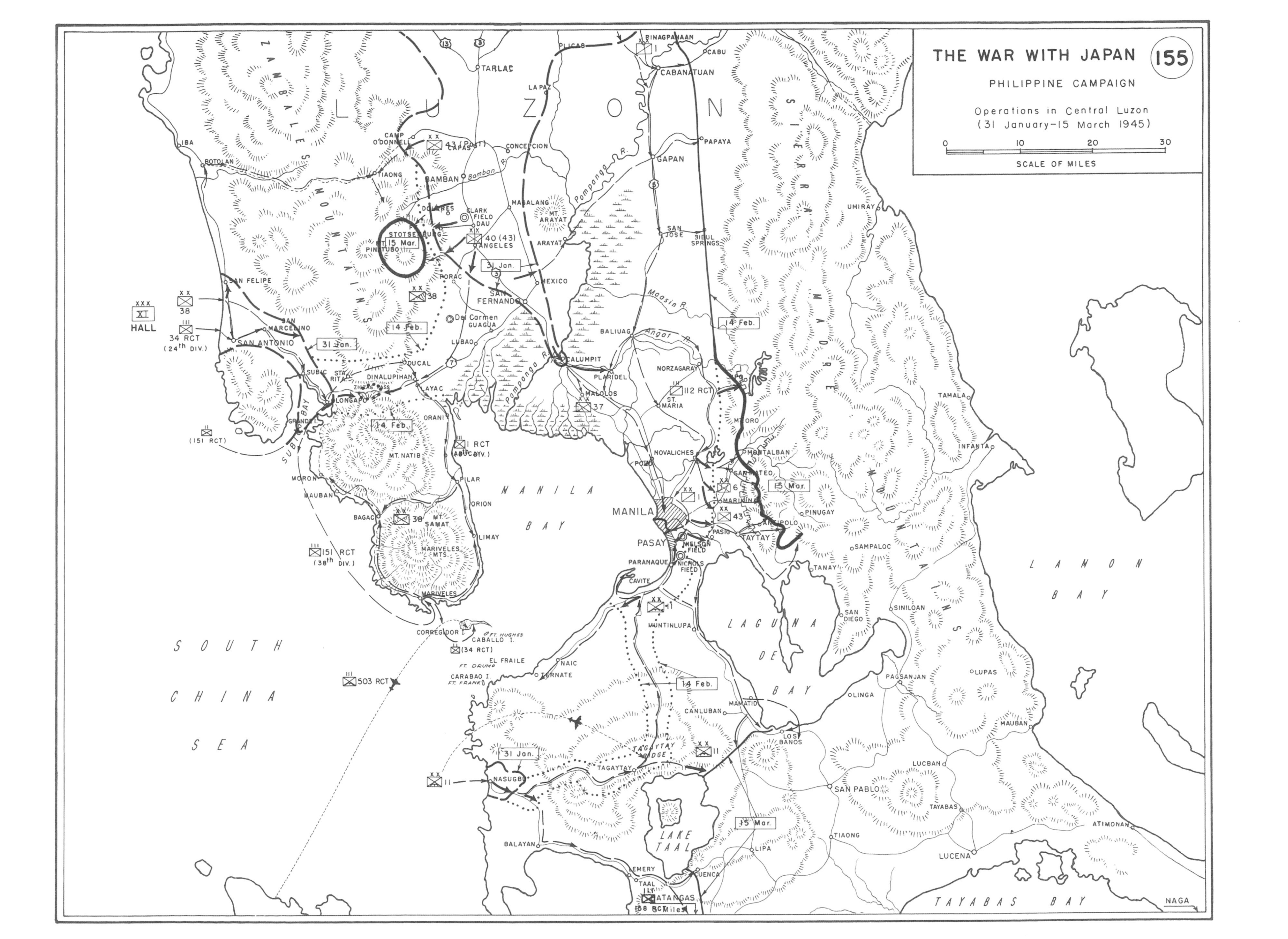
THE WAR WITH JAPAN
155
PHILIPPINE CAMPAIGN
Operations in Central Luzon
(31 January–15 March 1945)
0
10
20
30
SCALE OF MILES
LUZON
ZAMBALES MOUNTAINS
SIERRA MADRE MOUNTAINS
MANILA BAY
SOUTH CHINA SEA
LAMON BAY
LAGUNA DE BAY
LAKE TAAL
TAYABAS BAY
SUBIC BAY
TARLAC
CABANATUAN
PINAGPANAAN
CABU
LA PAZ
CAMP O'DONNELL
CAPAS
CONCEPCION
PAPAYA
GAPAN
IBA
BOTOLAN
TIAONG
BAMBAN
MAGALANG
MT. ARAYAT
ARAYAT
DOLORES
CLARK FIELD
DAU
ANGELES
STOTSENBURG
15 Mar.
PINATUBO
PORAC
31 Jan.
MEXICO
SAN FERNANDO
SAN JOSE
SIBUL SPRINGS
UMIRAY
SAN FELIPE
SAN MARCELINO
SAN ANTONIO
HALL
34 RCT
(24th DIV.)
38
14 Feb.
Del Carmen
GUAGUA
LUBAO
DUCAL
DINALUPIHAN
LAYAC
SUBIC
STA RITA
LONGAPO
GRANDE I.
(151 RCT)
ORANI
MT. NATIB
PILAR
ORION
LIMAY
MORON
BAGAC
MAUBAN
MT. SAMAT
MARIVELES MTS.
MARIVELES
151 RCT
(38th DIV.)
CORREGIDOR I.
CABALLO I.
FT. HUGHES
(34 RCT)
EL FRAILE
FT. DRUM
CARABAO I.
FT. FRANK
503 RCT
CALUMPIT
BALIUAG
PLARIDEL
MALOLOS
37
Maasin R.
Angat R.
Pampanga R.
Bamban R.
NORZAGARAY
112 RCT
ST. MARIA
NOVALICHES
POLO
MANILA
PASAY
NIELSON FIELD
NICHOLS FIELD
PARANAQUE
CAVITE
MUNTINLUPA
MONTALBAN
SAN MATEO
MARIKINA
ANTIPOLO
PASIG
TAYTAY
PINUGAY
SAMPALOC
TANAY
SAN DIEGO
SINILOAN
TAMALA
INFANTA
NAIC
TERNATE
CANLUBAN
MAMATID
TAGAYTAY RIDGE
TAGAYTAY
NASUGBU
11
BALAYAN
LEMERY
TAAL
BATANGAS
CUENCA
LIPA
TIAONG
SAN PABLO
LOS BANOS
LINGA
PAGSANJAN
LUPAS
LUCBAN
TAYABAS
MAUBAN
ATIMONAN
LUCENA
NAGA

PHILIPPINE CAMPAIGN

★

This map depicts the situation on the eve of General Krueger's final drive on Manila. During the three weeks of fighting to date, about 15,000 Japanese had been killed while American casualties totaled 5,754 (including 1,297 killed).

Since 9 January, the Sixth Army had expanded its initial beachhead rapidly and pushed southward down the Central Plain toward the Philippine capital. Obviously, the salient thus produced was an inviting target for a Japanese counterattack. It was for this very reason that Krueger was hesitant about plunging ahead rapidly to seize Manila. Until the I Corps could force Yamashita back into the mountains northeast of San Fabian (*center, left*) and secure defensible terrain, he had misgivings about advancing too far while his supply dumps at Lingayen were—in his view—susceptible to enemy seizure. MacArthur, on the other hand, viewed the operation in the light of strategic considerations. Desirous of securing Manila within the six-week period which he had assured the Joint Chiefs of Staff would suffice, and anxious to open Manila's port—one of the best in the Orient—MacArthur felt that the advance was too slow. He may have been influenced by his headquarters' underestimate of Japanese strength on Luzon (in contrast to the more accurate Sixth Army estimate). Another important consideration was the desirability of securing Clark Field (there were actually fifteen separate fields at this ideal airfield complex) to enable aircraft to support Nimitz's future operations as well as to intensify interdiction of Japanese communications to the East Indies.

In reality, the threat to Krueger's east flank was not serious, for—as we now know—Yamashita had no intention of making a major counterattack. Hamstrung by Allied air attacks and struggling to improve his deteriorating logistical situation, he was quite content to fight a defensive action. Furthermore, even if he had considered making a limited counterattack, it could not have been very effective, since he had frittered away the nucleus of any counterattack force (his 2d Tank Division) in costly piecemeal actions.

After MacArthur's forces had established a firm foothold on Luzon, Halsey's Third Fleet moved westward into the South China Sea to attack any elements of the Japanese fleet which might venture forth in an attempt to reestablish control over the sea lanes to the East Indies. Halsey met only insignificant opposition and, securing unchallenged control of the South China Sea, ranged at will throughout its length. On 12 January, his aircraft struck coastal Indochina (*see map 150, left center*), and three days later they launched attacks on Hong Kong, Hainan, Canton, and Formosa. On the 21st, in a parting attack, Halsey struck the Ryukyu Islands and Formosa again before returning to his base at Ulithi (*center*). By now, it had become equally clear to both sides that the Japanese fleet could not contest American control of the seas; the Kamikaze Corps was its only remaining threat, and this weapon was presumably being retained to defend the Japanese homeland.

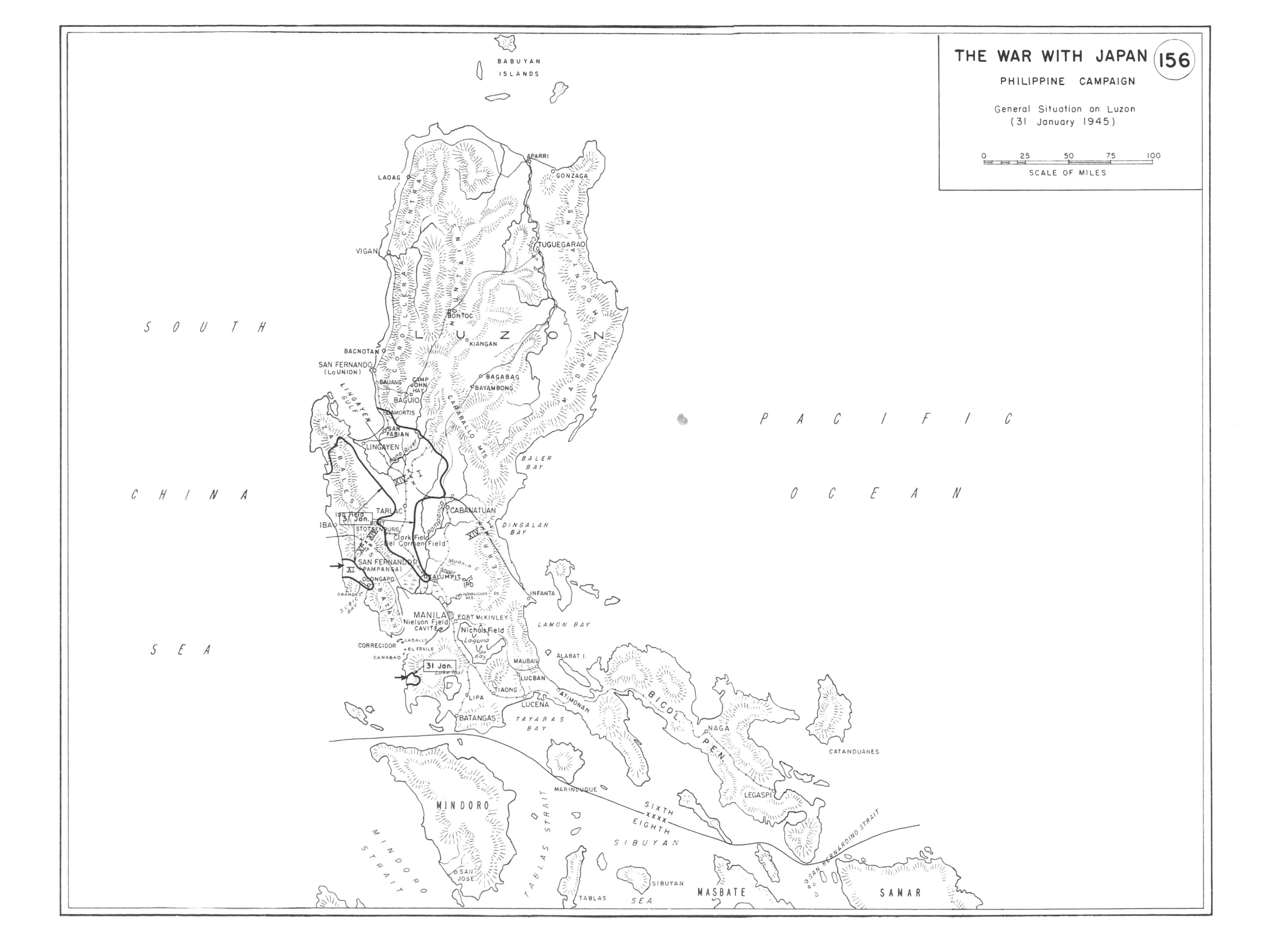
THE WAR WITH JAPAN
156
PHILIPPINE CAMPAIGN
General Situation on Luzon
(31 January 1945)
0 25 50 75 100
SCALE OF MILES
BABUYAN ISLANDS
APARRI
GONZAGA
LAOAG
VIGAN
TUGUEGARAO
BONTOC
LUZON
KIANGAN
BAGNOTAN
SAN FERNANDO (La UNION)
BAGABAG
BAYAMBONG
BAUANG
CAMP JOHN HAY
BAGUIO
DAMORTIS
SAN FABIAN
LINGAYEN GULF
LINGAYEN
CARABALLO MTS
BALER BAY
TARLAC
CABANATUAN
IBA
31 Jan.
FORT STOTSENBURG
Clark Field
Del Carmen Field
DINGALAN BAY
SAN FERNANDO (PAMPANGA)
XI
OLONGAPO
CALUMPIT
IPO
INFANTA
MANILA
Nielson Field
CAVITE
FORT McKINLEY
Nichols Field
Laguna de Bay
LAMON BAY
CORREGIDOR
CABALLO
EL FRAILE
CARABAO
31 Jan.
Lake Taal
MAUBAN
ALABAT I.
LUCBAN
TIAONG
LIPA
LUCENA
ATIMONAN
BATANGAS
TAYABAS BAY
BICOL PEN.
NAGA
CATANDUANES
LEGASPI
MARINDUQUE
SIXTH
XXXX
EIGHTH
MINDORO
SIBUYAN
SAN JOSE
MINDORO STRAIT
TABLAS STRAIT
SIBUYAN
TABLAS
SEA
MASBATE
SAN BERNARDINO STRAIT
SAMAR
SOUTH CHINA SEA
PACIFIC OCEAN

PHILIPPINE CAMPAIGN

The final dash for Manila began on 2 February (*see text, map 155*). Maj. Gen. Oscar W. Griswold (XIV Corps) expected the 37th Division to enter the city first; but when a cleverly conducted delaying action slowed that unit—while 1st Cavalry Division flying columns raced to the outskirts of the capital—he shifted the boundary between divisions westward and ordered the troopers into the city. (To avoid confusion, this boundary shift is not shown.)

Against negligible opposition, 1st Cavalry elements reached Santo Tomas University (*this map; center, left*) late on 3 February, liberated 3,500 Allied internees there and then seized Malacanan Palace. An attempt to capture Quezon Bridge (*not shown; near Intramuros, left center*) over the Pasig River on the 4th met with failure; that night, the Japanese destroyed all three of the bridges spanning the river. This same night, the 37th Division—bypassing and leaving the strong enemy position at Polo (*upper left*) for later reduction—pushed a regiment into Manila which seized Bilibid Prison and liberated some 1,300 Allied prisoners and civilian internees.

Griswold side-stepped the 1st Cavalry Division eastward on 5 February. Both divisions then closed to the Pasig, as the Japanese—executing their demolition program with ruthless abandon—withdrew south of the river. The greater part of both divisions was now in Manila, though the 1st Cavalry (the only "Square"—four regiment—division still in the Army) had detached one regiment at Norzagaray (*off map, top*) and another at Novaliches (*top center*). The latter had been given the important task of seizing Manila's water-supply facilities: the Novaliches Dam and Reservoir, the Balara Filters (*center*), and connecting pipelines.

The 37th Division skillfully crossed the Pasig near Malacanan Palace on 7 February, and three days later the 1st Cavalry crossed farther upstream. The advance faltered as Japanese resistance stiffened; MacArthur reluctantly lifted restrictions on the use of artillery in the city when it became clear that the enemy had organized buildings into strong points and had no intention of surrendering. This turnabout in Japanese strategy resulted from a lack of unity of command: Yamashita only partially controlled the Japanese naval troops in the Manila area; though he ordered abandonment of Manila, the naval commander decided to defend it rather than withdraw to join the Shimbu Group.

In bitter house-to-house fighting, Griswold's divisions compressed the Japanese into a pocket along Manila Bay by 14 February (*center, left; dashed red line*). Meanwhile, in south Manila, the 11th Airborne Division, encountering strong defenses near Paranaque (*lower left*), had made only slight gains since 4 February. By the 10th, it was hammering at the "Genko Line" at Nichols Field. There, permanently emplaced large-caliber guns, mine fields, and fire from automatic weapons took a heavy toll of the Americans; but, by the 14th, the position had been overrun, and contact had been made with the 1st Cavalry Division.

Griswold now left the reduction of Manila to the 37th Division and ordered the 1st Calvary Division to take Fort William McKinley and then move east to develop the Japanese position in the mountains. The 1st Cavalry (less one regiment helping the 37th Division) overran McKinley on 19 February and three days later entered Taytay. But then it smashed into the strong "Shimbu Line" (*fortified area shown*) and stalled. To the north, the 6th Division encountered similar resistance, but almost reached Montalban (*top right*) by the 24th. A lull in the fighting followed while the Americans reconnoitered the Shimbu Line. An attack was launched on 8 March in which the 1st Cavalry succeeded in turning the Japanese southern flank, but 6th Division gains were slight. By 15 March, when the XI Corps assumed control of operations east of Manila, the Japanese were holding the position shown (*solid red line*), and it was clear that dislodging them would be difficult.

Meanwhile, the 37th Division had forced the fanatical Japanese back to the Intramuros (the ancient walled city built by the Spanish) and a few government buildings near it. The thick walls of the Intramuros were breached by fire from heavy artillery in two places, and on 23 February the infantry moved inside to eliminate the last bitter resistance. Fighting continued for the government buildings until 4 March, when the battered and ruined city was finally declared secure.

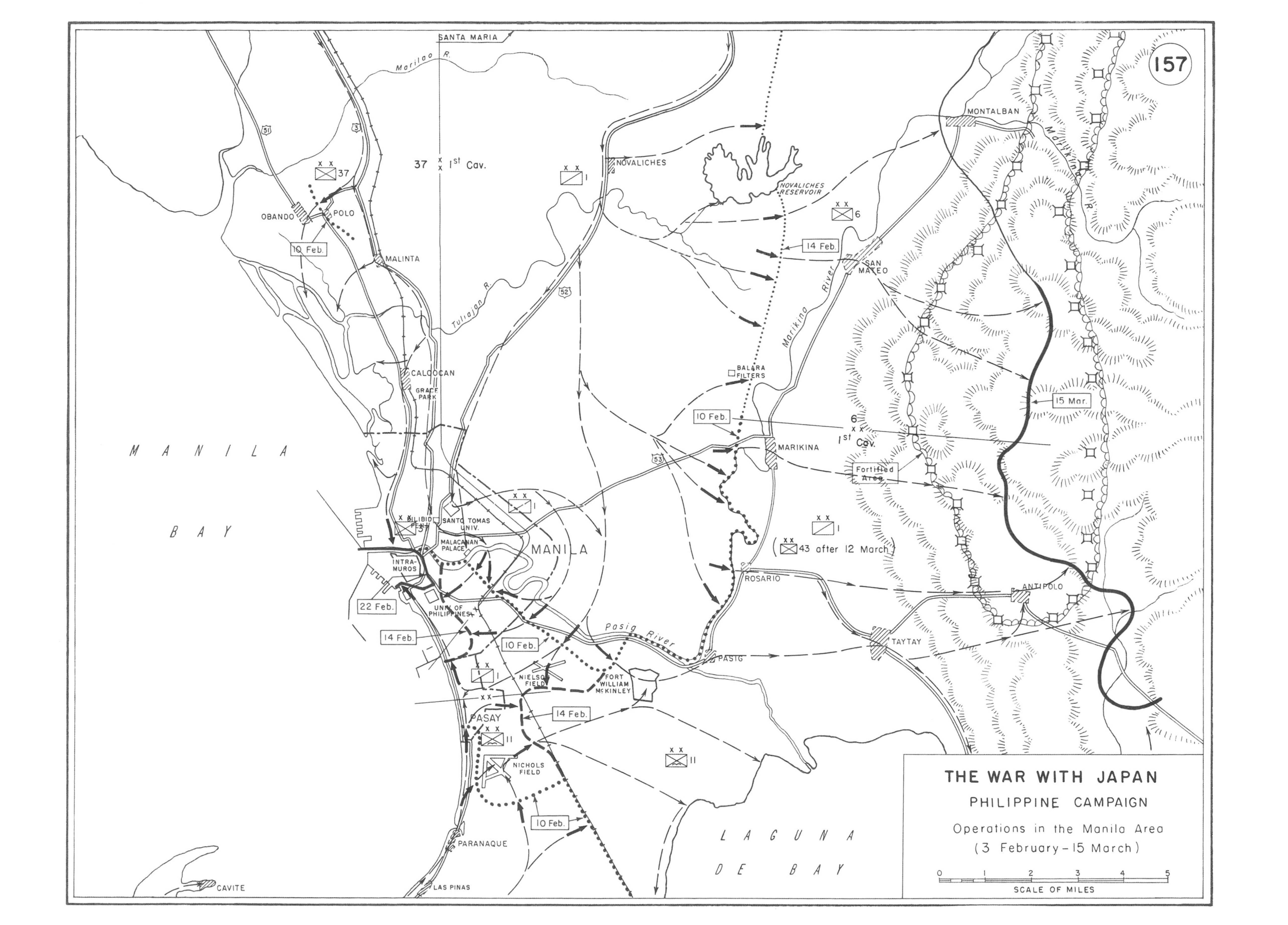

157
THE WAR WITH JAPAN
PHILIPPINE CAMPAIGN
Operations in the Manila Area
(3 February – 15 March)
SCALE OF MILES
0
1
2
3
4
5
MANILA BAY
LAGUNA DE BAY
SANTA MARIA
Marilao R.
Tullahan R.
Marikina River
Marikina R.
Pasig River
NOVALICHES
NOVALICHES RESERVOIR
OBANDO
POLO
MALINTA
CALOOCAN
GRACE PARK
MONTALBAN
SAN MATEO
BALARA FILTERS
MARIKINA
ROSARIO
ANTIPOLO
TAYTAY
PASIG
MANILA
BILIBID PEN.
SANTO TOMAS UNIV.
MALACANAN PALACE
INTRAMUROS
UNIV. OF PHILIPPINES
NIELSON FIELD
FORT WILLIAM McKINLEY
PASAY
NICHOLS FIELD
PARANAQUE
LAS PINAS
CAVITE
Fortified Area
37 1st Cav.
6 1st Cav.
43 after 12 March
10 Feb.
14 Feb.
22 Feb.
15 Mar.
51
3
52
53

PHILIPPINE CAMPAIGN

At the same time that the XIV Corps began its final drive on Manila (the 1st Cavalry Division is shown concentrated at Guimba [*center*], from which it started southward), the I Corps renewed its attack against the Shobu Group's positions (*dashed red line*) from Baloc (*center*) to Rosario (*upper left*). Krueger ordered the major effort to be made by the 6th Division—to secure the line of the Pampanga River north of Cabanatuan (*center, right*), thus isolating the Shobu Group and removing the threat of a possible Japanese counterattack against the left flank of the Sixth Army.

The 6th Division encountered fierce resistance at Muñoz (*center*) from dug-in tanks, direct artillery fire, and thoroughly entrenched infantry. One of its regiments enveloped the town from the north, while another applied frontal pressure; the rest of the division bypassed the town and took San Jose (4 February) and Rizal (7 February) against lesser opposition. Cut off, the Muñoz garrison attempted to withdraw the night of the 6th, but it was almost completely destroyed en route to San Jose. Columns of the 6th Division then moved through Bongabon to the east coast, which they reached on 14 February. As we have seen, the bulk of the division was then transferred to the XIV Corps.

Meanwhile, the 25th Division was engaged in a bitter fight for Lupao (*center*), while the 32d Division pushed up the Villa Verde Trail (*upper center*) against increasing resistance. With the fall of Lupao on 8 February, the Japanese 2d Tank Division practically ceased to exist. But 32d Division gains became slight as the division moved into extremely rugged, mountainous country—reminiscent of fighting in Italy—where the Japanese had excellent observation, innumerable caves, and well-sited artillery. On the left of the line, the recently arrived 33d Division relieved the 43d Division (*not shown*) and prepared to advance on Baguio.

In late February, the I Corps began an all-out offensive to destroy the Shobu Group: the 25th Division moved on Balete Pass (*upper center*) in two columns (on Route 5 and up the Pampanga River valley); the 32d Division concentrated primarily on the Villa Verde Trail, but also sent columns into the mountains on either side of the trail; and the 33d Division directed two columns toward the Baguio stronghold and a third up the coast. By 15 March, the I Corps' advance had reached the limit shown (*dotted red line*). Nowhere had a decisive breakthrough been made; Japanese resistance was as fanatical as ever. (Meanwhile, the 40th Division had been concentrated near Dagupan in preparation for movement to the Visayas.)

In early April, the 37th Division (less one combat team) was ordered from Manila to Bauang (*top left*). Thus augmented, the 33d Division, which had earlier (20 March) linked up with the North Luzon Guerrilla Force at San Fernando (*top left*), renewed its drive on Baguio. Superbly supported by aircraft, tanks, and artillery, the two divisions closed on the city which Yamashita now began to evacuate. On 27 April, the 37th Division entered the mauled Philippine summer capital.

Farther south, the 32d Division turned over its Sapit and Teb-bo sectors to elements of the newly organized Philippine Army and concentrated its greatly understrength units on the Villa Verde Trail. Here, the advance was slow, costly, and demoralizing as the division slugged its way toward Imugan. The 25th Division faced similar terrain problems as it grimly ground under one Japanese position after another. Finally, on 13 May, the key Balete Pass was captured, and two weeks later the 25th Division entered the important communications center of Santa Fe. The next day, the exhausted 25th and 32d Divisions made contact near Imugan; both divisions were then withdrawn for a well-earned rest.

The 37th Division, previously withdrawn from Baguio and reunited with its third combat team, pushed up Highway 5 on 31 May. The division seized Bayombong on 7 June and continued its advance northeastward toward the Cagayan Valley (*off map, top right*). Yamashita, having lost his key San Jose position, desperately tried to stem the 37th Division advance; but his troops, defending only partially completed positions, were unequal to the task. By 30 June, his positions were as shown (*dashed red lines*). As the Americans and Filipinos smashed at his mountain stronghold from the west, south, and north (*see map 159*), Yamashita withdrew deeper into the Cordillera Central (*this map, solid red line*).

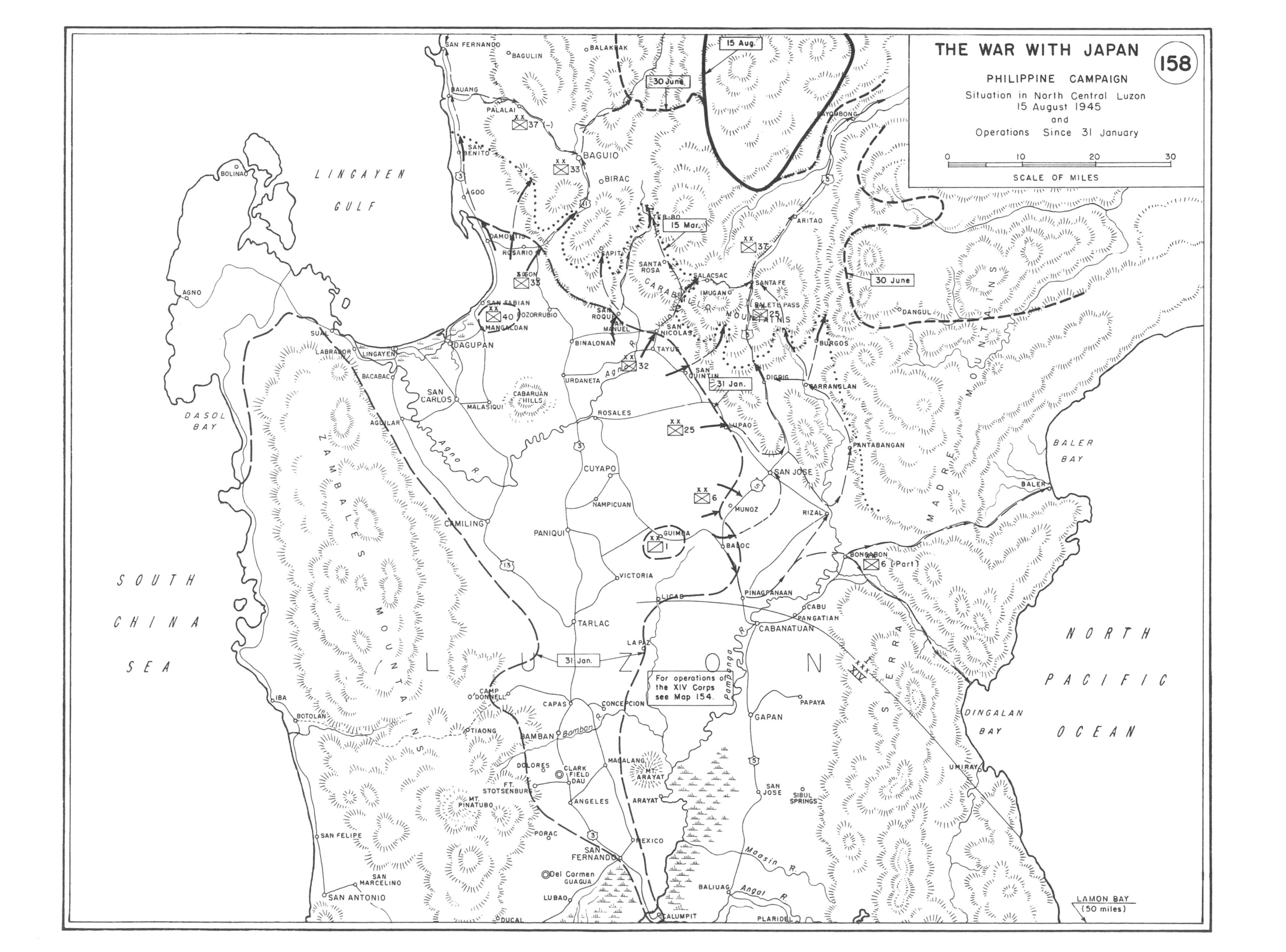
THE WAR WITH JAPAN
158
PHILIPPINE CAMPAIGN
Situation in North Central Luzon
15 August 1945
and
Operations Since 31 January
0 10 20 30
SCALE OF MILES
15 Aug.
30 June
15 Mar.
31 Jan.
For operations of the XIV Corps see Map 154.
LINGAYEN GULF
SOUTH CHINA SEA
NORTH PACIFIC OCEAN
BALER BAY
DINGALAN BAY
DASOL BAY
LAMON BAY (50 miles)
LUZON
ZAMBALES MOUNTAINS
SIERRA MADRE MOUNTAINS
CARABALLO MOUNTAINS
CABARUAN HILLS
SAN FERNANDO
BAGULIN
BALAKBAK
BAUANG
PALALAI
SAN BENITO
AGOO
BAGUIO
BIRAC
DAMORTIS
ROSARIO
SISON
SAN FABIAN
POZORRUBIO
MANGALDAN
DAGUPAN
LINGAYEN
LABRADOR
SUAL
BOLINAO
AGNO
BACABAC
SAN CARLOS
MALASIQUI
AGUILAR
CAMILING
BINALONAN
URDANETA
SAN ROQUE
SAN MANUEL
SANTA ROSA
SAPIT
TER-BO
SALACSAC
IMUGANO
SAN NICOLAS
TAYUG
SAN QUINTIN
SANTA FE
BALETE PASS
ARITAO
BAYOMBONG
DANGUL
BURGOS
DIGDIG
CARRANGLAN
PANTABANGAN
LUPAO
ROSALES
CUYAPO
NAMPICUAN
PANIQUI
VICTORIA
TARLAC
GUIMBA
MUNOZ
SAN JOSE
BALOC
RIZAL
BONGABON
BALER
LICAB
PINAGPANAAN
CABU
PANGATIAN
CABANATUAN
LA PAZ
CAMP O'DONNELL
CAPAS
CONCEPCION
GAPAN
PAPAYA
UMIRAY
IBA
BOTOLAN
TIAONG
BAMBAN
Bombon
DOLORES
CLARK FIELD
DAU
MAGALANG
MT. ARAYAT
ARAYAT
FT. STOTSENBURG
ANGELES
MT. PINATUBO
SAN JOSE
SIBUL SPRINGS
PORAC
SAN FERNANDO
MEXICO
SAN FELIPE
SAN MARCELINO
SAN ANTONIO
Del Carmen
GUAGUA
LUBAO
DUCAL
CALUMPIT
BALIUAG
PLARIDEL
Agno R.
Pampanga R.
Maasin R.
Angat R.
XIV
6 (Part)
37 (-)
33
33
40
32
37
25
25
6
1

PHILIPPINE CAMPAIGN

This map portrays the over-all Sixth Army situation on 15 March. By that date, the Japanese had been pocketed into three separate groups—almost as Yamashita had expected—and the three American corps were conducting independent operations against the isolated Japanese forces. The I Corps had the most difficult task (already partially described in the text, *map 158*), but the other corps still faced some hard fighting before Yamashita's capitulation on 15 August. Meanwhile, Manila's port was being rehabilitated in one of the war's most extensive salvage tasks, and the build-up for the ultimate invasion of Japan gathered momentum.

In southern Luzon, the XIV Corps drove southeastward on either side of Lake Taal (*lower left*). The 11th Airborne and 1st Cavalry Divisions executed a series of pincer movements on Lipa, Tiaong, and Lucban, the last occurring on 9 April. Two days later, they reached the coast at Antimonan and Mauban. Then, as the 11th Airborne Division stayed behind to mop up the overrun areas, the 1st Cavalry Division sent a small force toward Infanta (*lower center*), while the bulk of the division moved down the Bicol Peninsula. On 1 May, cavalry troopers met the 158th RCT a few miles south of Naga (*lower center*). (In order to secure the northern exits of San Bernardino Strait [*bottom center*], the 158th RCT—directly under Sixth Army control—had been landed at Legaspi, as shown, on 1 April; after eliminating Japanese resistance in the southern part of the peninsula, it had moved north toward Naga.) On 25 May, Infanta was occupied. One week later, organized resistance ceased in the XIV Corps' zone.

In central Luzon, the 38th Division (*located at this time near Clark Field, not as shown*) hunted down the remnants of the Kembu Group in the mountains, and some of its units seized the island forts near Corregidor (13–16 April). Meanwhile, the 6th Division (*not shown, but actually where the 38th Division symbol is located*) and the 43d Division continued the bitter struggle with the Shimbu Group east of Manila; slowly, the Japanese were forced back to the position shown (*solid red line*). (The 38th Division relieved the 6th Division on 30 April; the latter unit moved into a rest area until 12 June, when it was committed in the I Corps' zone.) On 1 July, the 43d Division was withdrawn from the line to prepare for future operations; until the war ended, the 38th Division continued the fight against the Shimbu Group.

In northern Luzon's rugged mountain wilderness, the I Corps continued to apply pressure on the Shobu Group. The 37th Division, moving down the Cagayan Valley, entered Tuguegarao (*upper center*) on 25 June, pushed on north, and the next day met an American-Filipino column moving south from Aparri. (This column consisted of Connolly Force [*not labeled*], which had seized Aparri on 21 June, and a reinforced parachute battalion which had been dropped at Aparri on the 23d.) The Japanese were now split into two groups, one on either side of the Cagayan Valley. The smaller group on the east—disorganized and poorly armed—fled into the mountains; patrols from the 37th Division probed its weak defenses until the war ended on 15 August. But to the west of the valley, Yamashita—personally in command—still had a sizable force. The 6th and 32d Divisions (the 33d had been relieved), the guerrillas, and part of the 37th Division compressed this force into an ever-shrinking pocket. On 1 July, the Eighth Army (employing the XIV Corps, consisting of the 6th, 32d, 37th, and 38th Divisions) assumed responsibility for operations on Luzon; Krueger began preparing his troops for the projected invasion of Japan.

In the remaining days of the war, Yamashita's main force was split into three pockets with the seizure of Kiangan (*upper left*) on 12 July. But when the war ended on 15 August, Yamashita still had an organized force of 50,000 troops, about 40,000 of them in the Kiangan area. No longer capable of offensive action, they were, nevertheless, effectively tying down three American divisions. It cannot be denied that the Japanese had fought an effective delaying action as planned; similarly, it is clear that MacArthur had not been delayed materially in establishing a logistical base on Luzon and preparing the Sixth Army for an invasion of Japan.

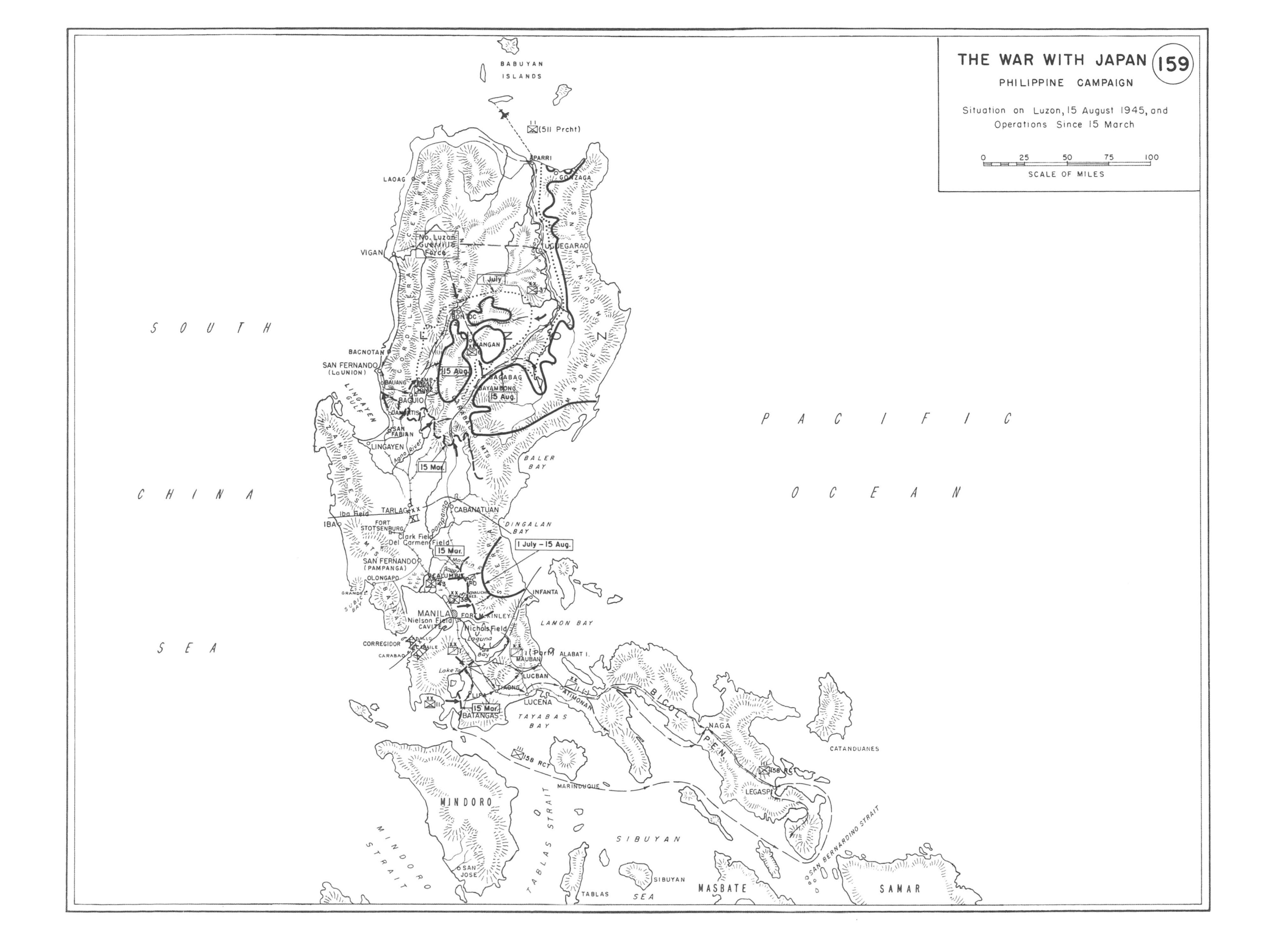
THE WAR WITH JAPAN
159
PHILIPPINE CAMPAIGN
Situation on Luzon, 15 August 1945, and Operations Since 15 March
0 25 50 75 100
SCALE OF MILES
SOUTH CHINA SEA
PACIFIC OCEAN
BABUYAN ISLANDS
(511 Prcht)
APARRI
GONZAGA
LAOAG
VIGAN
No. Luzon Guerrilla Force
TUGUEGARAO
1 July
37
BONTOC
KIANGAN
BACNOTAN
SAN FERNANDO (La UNION)
15 Aug.
BAGABAG
BAYAMBONG
15 Aug.
BAUANG
BAGUIO
LINGAYEN GULF
SAN FABIAN
LINGAYEN
Agno River
15 Mar.
BALER BAY
TARLAC
Iba Field
CABANATUAN
IBA
FORT STOTSENBURG
Clark Field
Del Carmen Field
15 Mar.
DINGALAN BAY
1 July - 15 Aug.
SAN FERNANDO (PAMPANGA)
OLONGAPO
43
INFANTA
38
SUBIC BAY
MANILA
FORT McKINLEY
Nielson Field
CAVITE
Nichols Field
LAMON BAY
CORREGIDOR
CARABAO
Laguna de Bay
ALABAT I.
MAUBAN
LUCBAN
TIAONG
LIPA
LUCENA
ATIMONAN
11
15 Mar.
BATANGAS
TAYABAS BAY
BICOL PEN.
NAGA
CATANDUANES
158 RCT
158 RCT
LEGASPI
MARINDUQUE
MINDORO
TABLAS STRAIT
SIBUYAN
SAN BERNARDINO STRAIT
MINDORO STRAIT
SAN JOSE
SIBUYAN
TABLAS
SEA
MASBATE
SAMAR

PHILIPPINE CAMPAIGN

★

Waiting only to be sure that the Central Plain–Manila region would be secured in a reasonable length of time, MacArthur ordered the Eighth Army—on 6 February—to begin operations in the southern Philippines. There were several reasons for hurrying these operations, in spite of the attendant diversion of Allied strength from Luzon: Japanese communications with the East Indies could be more effectively interdicted from the southern islands than from Luzon; airfields had to be secured within range of Borneo (*lower left*) to support Australian landings there; it would be desirable to complete major operations and airfield construction before summer rains set in; and there was some fear for the fate of the Filipino inhabitants on the bypassed islands.

The first landings were to be made at Palawan (*upper left*), followed closely by occupation of the Zamboanga peninsula (*lower center*) and the Sulu Archipelago (*bottom center*). The seizure of the islands around the Visayan Sea (*top right*)—to secure a shorter supply route from Leyte to Manila—was to be the second-priority task. Then operations to liberate Mindanao would be undertaken. For the projected operation, Eichelberger had available the X Corps headquarters and the Americal, 24th, 31st, 40th, and 41st Divisions. He could also count on considerable guerrilla support, particularly on Mindanao. Since most of the amphibious lift and all the carriers had returned to the Central Pacific Area after the Luzon landing, air support would be provided solely by land-based planes, and many of the amphibious movements would have to be conducted by the 2d and 3d Engineer Special Brigades. Accordingly, the Eighth Army had to plan the many landings carefully to ensure adequate air, amphibious, and naval gunfire support. (Between Christmas 1944 and 15 August, Eichelberger's troops made fifty-two separate landings.)

The Japanese Thirty-Fifth Army was responsible for the defense of the southern islands. Yamashita gave it the same mission he chose for himself in defending Luzon—to pin down as many Allied divisions for as long as possible. General Suzuki (eventually killed while en route from Leyte to Mindanao) elected to make his major defense on eastern Mindanao, where he had two divisions and a large body of naval troops. Two independent brigades garrisoned Zamboanga and the Sulu Archipelago, while a third division was responsible for the Visayas. None of these units was up to strength or well equipped (primarily because of reinforcements which had been sent to Leyte), and they were war-weary, complacently expecting the Allies to ignore them. Nevertheless, their strength numbered 102,000, and before the war ended, these troops would inflict considerable damage on Eichelberger's units.

The extent of the Eighth Army operations is shown on the map. Except on Mindanao, the pattern of each operation was generally the same: an assault landing, withdrawal of the Japanese to the interior to make a stand, Allied securing of the island, and withdrawal of American forces for future landings, while guerrillas conducted mop-up operations. On eastern Mindanao, the Japanese put up a harder fight; but, by judicious use of its amphibious capability and hard marching and fighting, the X Corps managed to compress the enemy garrison into two pockets by mid-July. Here—starving and under unremitting air attack—they remained until Japan's surrender on 15 August.

The campaign in the Philippines was concluded by Japan's surrender, and at a time when operations were still being conducted against some 100,000 Japanese still at large. But these enemy forces were no great threat and were rapidly being reduced to a state of starvation. Operations in the Philippines eliminated about 450,000 Japanese troops, led to the destruction of the Japanese Navy, and tremendously weakened Japanese air power. MacArthur's ground casualties totaled 62,143 (including 13,700 killed). And when the war ended, Luzon was rapidly becoming the "England of the Pacific" in preparation for the invasion of Japan.

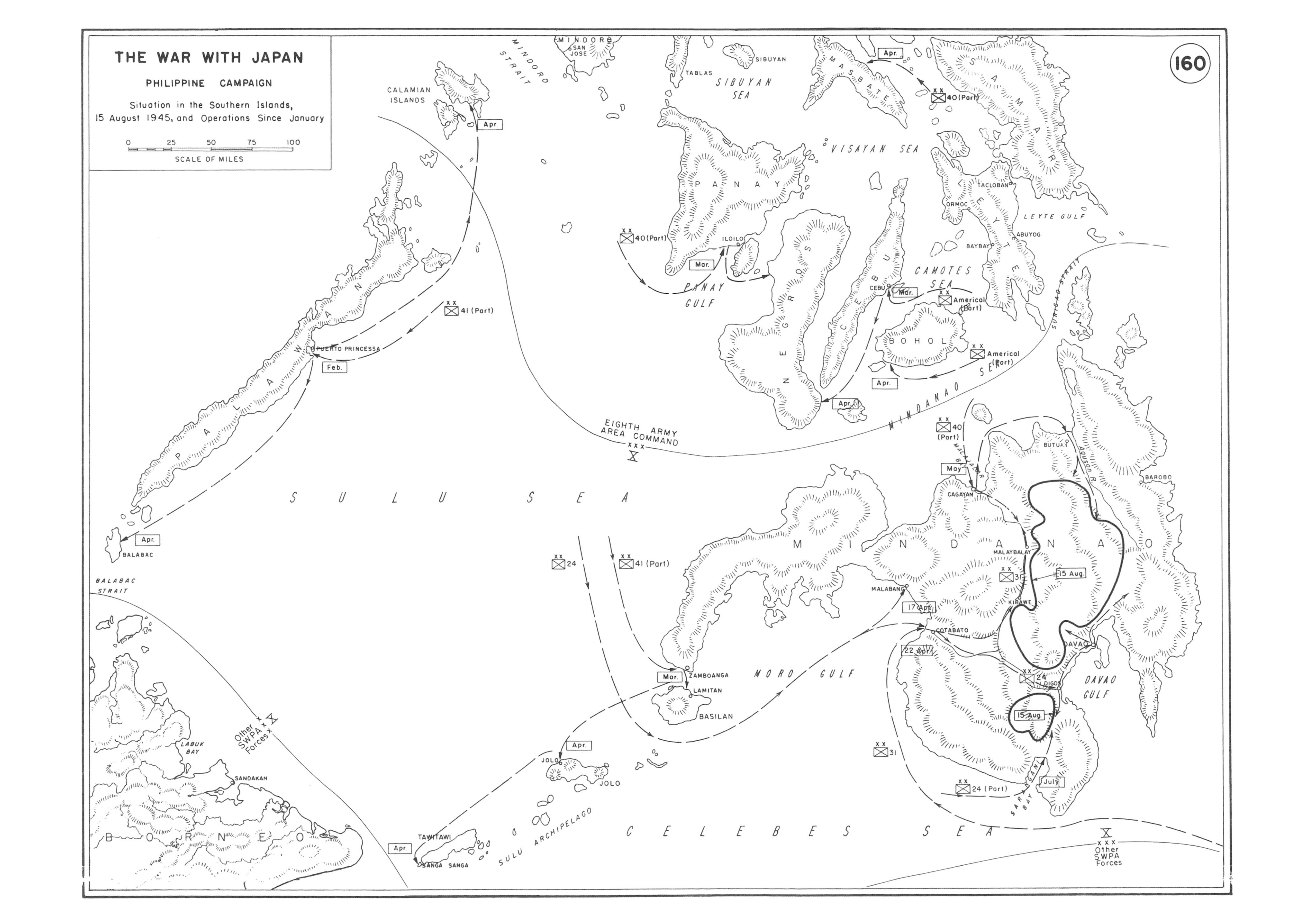
160
THE WAR WITH JAPAN
PHILIPPINE CAMPAIGN
Situation in the Southern Islands, 15 August 1945, and Operations Since January
0 25 50 75 100
SCALE OF MILES
CALAMIAN ISLANDS
MINDORO STRAIT
MINDORO
SAN JOSE
TABLAS
SIBUYAN
SIBUYAN SEA
MASBATE
SAMAR
VISAYAN SEA
PANAY
ILOILO
PANAY GULF
NEGROS
CEBU
CAMOTES SEA
BOHOL
LEYTE
TACLOBAN
ORMOC
ABUYOG
BAYBAY
LEYTE GULF
SURIGAO STRAIT
MINDANAO SEA
PALAWAN
PUERTO PRINCESSA
BALABAC
BALABAC STRAIT
EIGHTH ARMY AREA COMMAND
SULU SEA
MINDANAO
CAGAYAN
MACAJALAR BAY
BUTUAN
Agusan R.
BAROBO
MALAYBALAY
KIBAWE
MALABANG
COTABATO
DAVAO
DIGOS
DAVAO GULF
SARANGANI BAY
MORO GULF
ZAMBOANGA
LAMITAN
BASILAN
JOLO
SULU ARCHIPELAGO
TAWITAWI
SANGA SANGA
CELEBES SEA
LABUK BAY
SANDAKAN
BORNEO
Other SWPA Forces
40 (Part)
41 (Part)
Americal
Americal (Part)
24
24 (Part)
31
Feb.
Mar.
Apr.
May
July
17 Apr.
22 Apr.
15 Aug.

SOUTHWEST PACIFIC AREA

★

While MacArthur's American forces were liberating the Philippines, his Australian troops continued mop-up operations against the isolated Japanese garrisons in New Guinea, New Britain, and Bougainville (*all lower center*). At the same time, General Sir Thomas Blamey, the Australian ground force commander, made preparations to implement MacArthur's instructions pertaining to the recapture of the Netherlands East Indies. The operations shown on the map (*small blue arrows*) are those which the Australians conducted in 1945.

The Japanese who had been bypassed in MacArthur's drive to the Philippines, though no longer a threat to future Allied operations, immobilized Allied troops which had to protect bases in proximity to the isolated enemy. This task ultimately fell to the Australians. By 1945, the Australian government had become somewhat exasperated with the mission assigned its troops, feeling that the mop-up operations lacked prestige and that Australian troops should be associated with the final drive on Japan proper. But, pending consideration of the Australian complaint by the Combined Chiefs of Staff, Blamey was still faced with the very real problem of the bypassed garrisons. He elected merely to contain the Japanese on New Britain, but to undertake full-blown offensives against those on Bougainville and New Guinea. Thus, until the end of the war, Australian troops continued to take casualties in their attempts to eliminate fanatical Japanese who could not affect its outcome. In defending this policy, Blamey contended that the adoption of a passive defensive would have been ruinous to the morale of his troops and that, if merely contained, the Japanese would have continued to dominate the natives, thereby lowering Australian prestige.

The operations against Borneo (*center, left*) were part of MacArthur's plan to recapture Java and reestablish the rightful government in the islands. In the original plan, landings at Brunei Bay were to be the last step in the reconquest of the East Indies, but the plan was modified—presumably because of the great oil-producing fields in the Brunei Bay area. Admiral King stated that the Borneo operations were designed to "deny the enemy the fruits of his conquests in the Netherlands East Indies. . . ." However, since in 1945 the Japanese were scarcely capable of transporting fuel to Japan from the East Indies, it seems likely that Nimitz's desire to obtain Borneo oil for the Pacific Fleet may have been a more important factor. Significantly, the three operations conducted in Borneo were aimed at oil-producing centers.

On 1 May, Blarney landed a brigade of the Australian 9th Division, reinforced with a company of the Royal Netherlands East Indies Army, at Tarakan Island (*center, left*). Organized resistance ceased a month and a half later, after the Allies had suffered quite heavy casualties, but the engineers were unable to rehabilitate the captured airfield—one of the major objectives—because of unforeseen construction difficulties. The Brunei Bay landings in June were easier; important oil fields were quickly seized, and airfields were soon established. The last landing—at Balikpapan—was MacArthur's largest amphibious operation since Luzon. It was preceded by a devastating aerial bombardment which leveled the town, oil installations, and Japanese defenses. Qpposition was light, the major objectives in the area having been seized by 10 July. In all three of the Borneo operations, Blamey's assault troops were supported by elements of the Seventh Fleet and the Royal Australian Navy as well as by Kenney's air forces (primarily their Australian components). In the remaining month of the war, the Australians contained the Japanese who had withdrawn into the interior of Borneo.

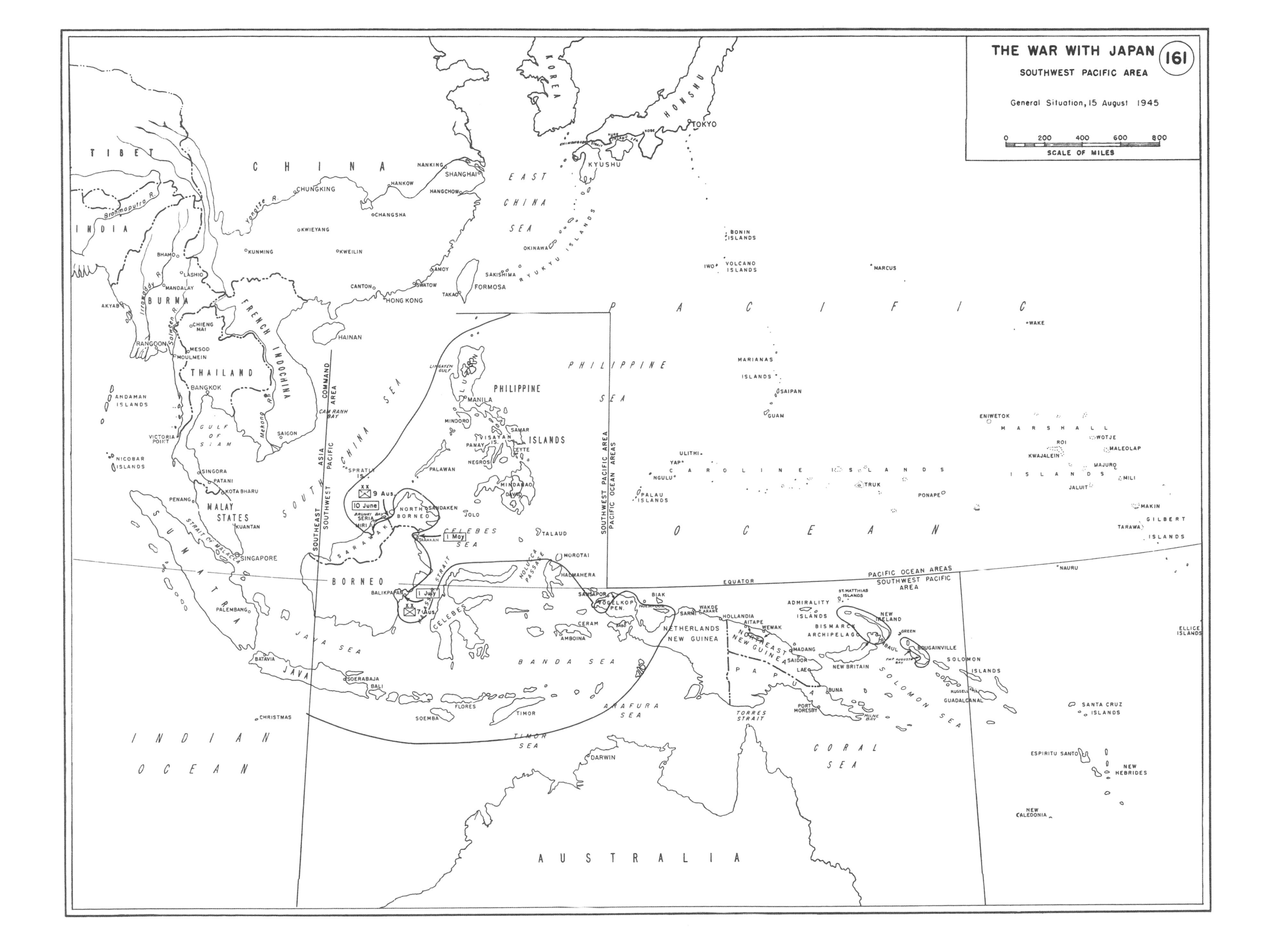
THE WAR WITH JAPAN
161
SOUTHWEST PACIFIC AREA
General Situation, 15 August 1945
0 200 400 600 800
SCALE OF MILES
KOREA
HONSHU
TOKYO
KYUSHU
TIBET
CHINA
INDIA
BURMA
THAILAND
FRENCH INDOCHINA
MALAY STATES
SUMATRA
BORNEO
JAVA
CELEBES
PHILIPPINE ISLANDS
EAST CHINA SEA
SOUTH CHINA SEA
PHILIPPINE SEA
CELEBES SEA
JAVA SEA
BANDA SEA
ARAFURA SEA
TIMOR SEA
CORAL SEA
SOLOMON SEA
PACIFIC OCEAN
INDIAN OCEAN
AUSTRALIA
NETHERLANDS NEW GUINEA
NORTHEAST NEW GUINEA
PAPUA
SOUTHEAST ASIA COMMAND
SOUTHWEST PACIFIC AREA
PACIFIC OCEAN AREAS
EQUATOR
MARIANAS ISLANDS
CAROLINE ISLANDS
MARSHALL ISLANDS
GILBERT ISLANDS
SOLOMON ISLANDS
BISMARCK ARCHIPELAGO
ADMIRALTY ISLANDS
BONIN ISLANDS
VOLCANO ISLANDS
RYUKYU ISLANDS
FORMOSA
HAINAN
HONG KONG
SHANGHAI
NANKING
CHUNGKING
SINGAPORE
MANILA
10 June
9 Aug.
1 May
1 July
7 Aug.

THE BATTLE FOR IWO JIMA

★

Iwo Jima (Jima means "island"), in the Volcano Islands (*see map 161, upper center*), is only about eight square miles in size. It is practically devoid of natural cover because of the sterile soil, and, in the words of one of its Japanese defenders in 1945, "was an island of sulphur, no water, no sparrow, and no swallow. . . ." But it was of considerable importance to the Allies, for only on Iwo—of all the islands in the Volcano and Bonin groups—can air-base facilities of suitable size be constructed.

Lying midway between Saipan and Tokyo, the island provided bases from which medium bombers and fighters could strike either target. By February, 1945, Japan had two operable airfields on Iwo (*this map*) and a third under construction. From these fields, they had already launched some raids against American bases in the Marianas, but by the date of the invasion, Allied air and naval strikes had eliminated the Japanese capability for basing aircraft on the island. There were other, more important reasons for seizing Iwo: fighters based there could escort Marianas-based B-29's to Japan; naval operations could be covered from the island; and crippled Superfortresses, returning from Japan, could use its airfields for emergency landings. Consequently, in October, the JCS ordered the seizure of Iwo; the original target date of 20 January was changed to 19 February because of the delay in the Luzon campaign.

The Japanese defended Iwo with about 21,000 army and navy troops, under the resolute command of Lt. Gen. Tadamichi Kuribayashi. These troops were thoroughly briefed in the plans for the island's defense and were imbued with the usual Japanese tenacity of purpose and willingness to die. Kuribayashi elected to employ a static defense with his main position on Mt. Suribachi (*lower left*) and along a line (*not shown*) running generally north and south through Airfield No. 2; a secondary defense line (*not shown*) ran just to the east of Airfield No. 3. There would be no costly all-out counterattacks to destroy an Allied beachhead, but local tank-infantry counterattacks would be made whenever possible. The island bristled with concealed gun emplacements, concrete pillboxes, mine fields, and an elaborate system of underground caves and shelters. Mortars (90- to 320-mm.) and guns (20- to 150-mm.) were expertly sited to cover the beaches and all occupied areas.

Maj. Gen. Harry Schmidt's plan called for the 4th and 5th Marine Divisions to land abreast, the 3d Marine Division being in reserve. There was little room for maneuver; the battle would be a head-on slugging match. For seventy-four days before the landing, air power smashed at the island, and a three-day naval gunfire bombardment immediately preceded the assault. In spite of this intensive bombardment, the 4th and 5th Divisions were taken under a heavy volume of enfilade and flanking fire when they came ashore, as the Japanese emerged from their shelters after the pre-assault bombardment lifted. Wheeled vehicles bogged down in the volcanic ash as they moved inland, landing craft were destroyed by enemy fire, and heavy surf added to unloading difficulties. By the end of D-Day, the island had been cut in two as shown, but the marines had taken 2,420 casualties. In vicious hand-to-hand combat, Mt. Suribachi was taken on 23 February, but still the beaches were under fire from positions near Airfield No. 2. By the 24th, most of the 3d Division had been committed, and Schmidt, making his main effort in the center, was battering Kuribayashi's main position. A week later, the worst of the fighting was over, but still the Japanese held on tenaciously, fighting for every inch of ground. By 11 March, they were compressed into the two areas shown (*solid red lines*); organized resistance ceased five days later.

The conquest of Iwo Jima was costly—24,891 casualties, including 6,821 killed—but by the end of the war 2,251 B-29's (carrying 24,761 crewmen) had used its airfields in emergencies. Probably the most strongly fortified island assaulted during the war, Iwo's conquest was ample testimony to the fortitude and perseverance of the V Marine Amphibious Corps.

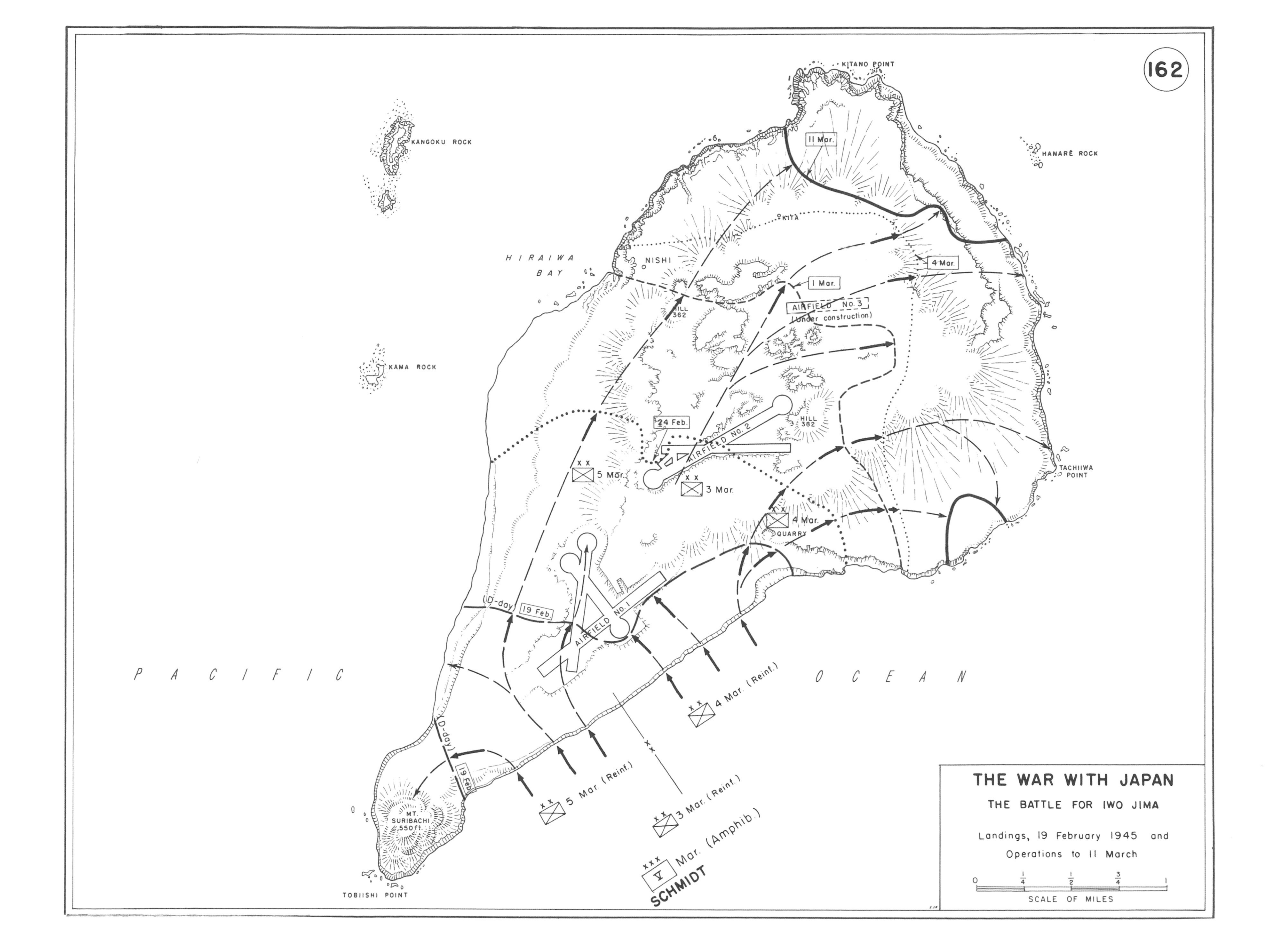
162
THE WAR WITH JAPAN
THE BATTLE FOR IWO JIMA
Landings, 19 February 1945 and
Operations to 11 March
0
1/4
1/2
3/4
1
SCALE OF MILES
KITANO POINT
KANGOKU ROCK
HANARE ROCK
11 Mar.
KITA
HIRAIWA BAY
NISHI
4 Mar.
1 Mar.
AIRFIELD No. 3
(Under construction)
HILL 362
KAMA ROCK
24 Feb.
AIRFIELD No. 2
HILL 382
5 Mar.
3 Mar.
TACHIIWA POINT
4 Mar.
QUARRY
(D-day) 19 Feb.
AIRFIELD No. 1
PACIFIC
OCEAN
4 Mar. (Reinf.)
5 Mar (Reinf.)
3 Mar. (Reinf.)
V Mar. (Amphib.)
SCHMIDT
(D-day)
19 Feb.
MT. SURIBACHI 550 ft.
TOBIISHI POINT

LANDINGS ON ADJACENT ISLANDS

★

With the abandonment of Formosa as an objective, Nimitz was directed to invade the Ryukyu Islands (*see map 161*) in March 1945 (later postponed to 1 April). A lodgment was desired in these islands for several reasons: bases for support of an invasion of Japan could be established; medium bombers could strike Japan from the Ryukyus; and Japanese communications to the south could be very effectively interdicted from Ryukyu bases. Okinawa (*this map*) was selected as the specific target because it is the only one of the islands large enough to accommodate several airfields; it also affords naval anchorages and adequate space to stage sizable ground forces.

In developing plans for the operation, Nimitz was faced with several complicating factors. Not only was Okinawa to be seized, but bases for future operations were to be developed there concurrently with the conduct of operations. This requirement compounded the magnitude of the logistical problem. The huge forces and resultant supply requirements, the distance from friendly bases to the objective, the limited availability of shipping, and the procurement of supplies (some directly from the United States) created a logistical nightmare for the planners. Also, Okinawa was within aircraft range of southern Japan, where the remaining Japanese air power could be massed, but it was relatively remote from Allied air bases. Consequently, the brunt of the likely air battle would have to be borne by carrier forces which would be required to remain in the combat area for a considerable period of time.

After balancing all considerations, Nimitz decided to sacrifice strategic surprise in an attempt to isolate Okinawa; the Tenth Army plan, however, was designed to achieve tactical surprise. The conquest of Okinawa was originally expected to follow three phases: the capture of the southern half of the island; seizure of the northern half and the island of Ie (*center, right*); and exploitation, to include the domination of other islands in the Ryukyus. Prior to the main landing, the Kerama and Keise Islands (*both bottom center*) would be seized—the former to obtain an anchorage and seaplane base, the latter to provide positions for long-range field artillery to support the main landings. These would be made near Hagushi (*lower center*), where the best beaches existed and from which Yontan and Kadena airfields could be quickly seized. Then the XXIV Corps would swing south to establish a line through Kuba, while the III Marine Amphibious Corps drove northward to Ishikawa Isthmus to seal off the central portion of the island. From these positions (*dashed red lines*), the first phase of the general plan would be undertaken.

Early in March, the fast carrier forces, MacArthur's air forces, and B-29's began striking Japan, Hong Kong, and Formosa, in furtherance of the isolation program. By 1 April, the Japanese—resisting stubbornly—had inflicted some damage on the carrier force but had taken heavy aircraft losses in return. The Amphibious Support Force moved into Okinawan waters on 26 March, and began underwater demolition, mine-sweeping, and bombardment operations. The 77th Division quickly captured the Kerama and Keise Islands against minor opposition. On the Keramas, some 350 suicide boats were found—a portent of further desperate Japanese plans. The main landings, too, met only slight resistance; by 4 April, the two corps had reached the planned initial positions. But when the XXIV Corps encountered fierce opposition five days later, the Tenth Army commander, Lt. Gen. Simon B. Buckner, Jr., decided to initiate the second phase of the operation. As shown, the 6th Marine Division quickly overran the northern part of the island against token opposition. By the 19th, most of the Japanese had been eliminated in their last stand on Motobu Peninsula. The 77th Division had a harder fight before finally capturing Ie Shima on 21 April. Meanwhile, a battalion from the 27th Division (the floating reserve) seized Tsugen Island on 10 April, thus opening Nakagusuku Bay to Allied shipping. During June, elements of the 2d Marine Division seized the outlying islands of Kume, Aguni, and Iheya for establishment of radar installations to replace destroyer picket ships.

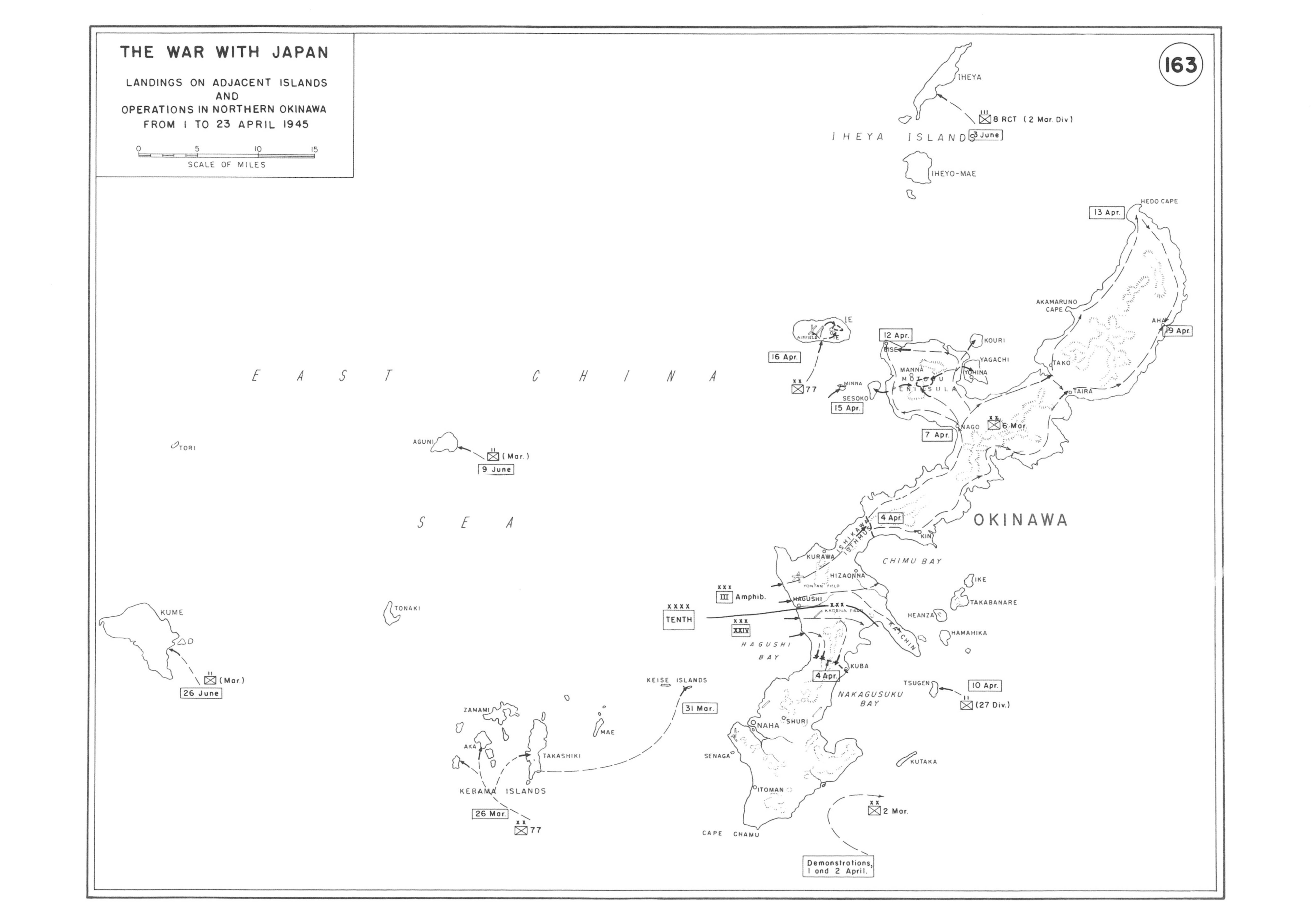

163
THE WAR WITH JAPAN
LANDINGS ON ADJACENT ISLANDS
AND
OPERATIONS IN NORTHERN OKINAWA
FROM 1 TO 23 APRIL 1945
0 5 10 15
SCALE OF MILES
IHEYA
8 RCT (2 Mar. Div)
3 June
IHEYA ISLANDS
IHEYO-MAE
HEDO CAPE
13 Apr.
AKAMARUNO CAPE
AHA
19 Apr.
IE
AIRFIELD
16 Apr.
77
12 Apr.
BISE
KOURI
YAGACHI
MANNA
MOTOBU PENINSULA
YOHINA
TAKO
TAIRA
MINNA
SESOKO
15 Apr.
NAGO
6 Mar.
7 Apr.
E A S T C H I N A
S E A
TORI
AGUNI
(Mar.)
9 June
4 Apr.
KIN
OKINAWA
ISHIKAWA ISTHMUS
KURAWA
CHIMU BAY
HIZAONNA
YONTAN FIELD
IKE
TAKABANARE
III Amphib.
HAGUSHI
KADENA FIELD
TENTH
XXIV
HEANZA
HAMAHIKA
KATCHIN
HAGUSHI BAY
KUBA
4 Apr.
TSUGEN
10 Apr.
(27 Div.)
NAKAGUSUKU BAY
KUME
TONAKI
(Mar.)
26 June
KEISE ISLANDS
31 Mar.
ZAMAMI
MAE
NAHA
SHURI
AKA
TAKASHIKI
SENAGA
KUTAKA
KERAMA ISLANDS
ITOMAN
26 Mar.
77
2 Mar.
CAPE CHAMU
Demonstrations, 1 and 2 April.

OKINAWA CAMPAIGN

★

Following the heaviest pre-assault naval and aerial bombardment of the Pacific war, the four assault divisions began landing near Hagushi (*upper center*) at 0830, 1 April. At the same time, the 2d Marine Division conducted such a realistic demonstration off the Minatoga beaches (*bottom center*) that the Japanese boasted of repelling a landing. (This division repeated the demonstration on 2 April and then returned to Saipan to prepare for other operations.) Surprised at the complete lack of ground opposition at the Hagushi beaches, the Americans rapidly advanced inland, and by nightfall of L-Day (landing day) had reached the originally scheduled L + 3 line. This early seizure of the important Yontan and Kadena airfields—halfheartedly defended by a makeshift, second-line regiment—enabled land-based aircraft to operate from Okinawa sooner than expected. Only in the air had the Japanese offered any resistance, and these attacks—made against invasion shipping—were not very successful.

Buckner's troops continued their rapid advance on 2 April, cutting the island in two when the 7th Division reached the eastern coast. The following day, the XXIV Corps regrouped for an advance southward, while the III Amphibious Corps continued to advance practically unopposed. By 4 April, the 6th Marine Division had secured the planned L + 15 line (*top right, solid red line*), but the XXIV Corps had begun to meet more resistance.

The Japanese Imperial Headquarters was determined to hold Okinawa and hoped that the Navy's Special Attack Corps (Kamikaze)—supported by a large portion of the surface fleet and small suicide boats—could destroy the covering forces of the American Fifth Fleet and the support shipping off Okinawa. This accomplished, Lt. Gen. Mitsuru Ushijima's Thirty-Second Army would attack the invasion force—now shorn of its support—and drive it into the sea. In keeping with this strategy, Ushijima did not defend the beaches but occupied the rugged terrain around Shuri (*lower center*), whence he could sally forth or defend. More realistic than his superiors, he did not expect to defeat the Americans, but intended to levy a heavy price for Okinawan territory.

The first major Kamikaze attack came on 6 April and inflicted considerable damage on American shipping. The same day, a Japanese surface naval task force moved toward Okinawa, but it was detected and almost totally destroyed by Admiral Spruance's carrier aircraft on the 7th. The Kamikaze attacks continued, but elaborate air defense measures and a Japanese tendency to concentrate on radar picket destroyers blunted their effectiveness. Nevertheless, during April, 20 American ships were sunk and 157 damaged—a large proportion by Kamikaze attacks. These suicide tactics continued through June, but with rapidly diminishing intensity. (In the entire campaign, the Japanese flew 1,900 suicide sorties and 3,700 orthodox sorties.) Actually, by 1 May, Japan's desperate gamble had failed. The Kamikaze Corps had been decimated, the surface fleet was no longer a threat, most of the suicide boats had been captured, and Spruance showed no inclination to withdraw the American fleet.

Meanwhile, the XXIV Corps had smashed headlong into Ushijima's strong defenses—the Machinato Line. (Oddly enough, American intelligence knew nothing of these defenses until after the landings.) The 96th Division took very heavy casualties in an unsuccessful assault on Kakazu Ridge (*center*), and the 7th Division had a difficult time farther east. Buckner then released the 27th Division from Tenth Army reserve (the 81st Division was still in area reserve in New Caledonia) and assigned it to the XXIV Corps; on 19 April, the corps launched a coordinated attack. Five days later, Ushijima abandoned the Machinato Line; his defense had been skillful, but it had cost the 62d Division heavily. To hold the Shuri Line, he now had to move most of the 24th Division (from the extreme south) and the 44th Independent Brigade (from Minatoga) northward to reinforce the badly weakened 62d Division. By 30 April, the XXIV Corps had reached the line shown (*solid red line*), but its divisions were exhausted, the Japanese still held all the key approaches to the Shuri Line, and Maj. Gen. John R. Hodge now knew that his XXIV Corps could not overrun southern Okinawa very quickly or easily.

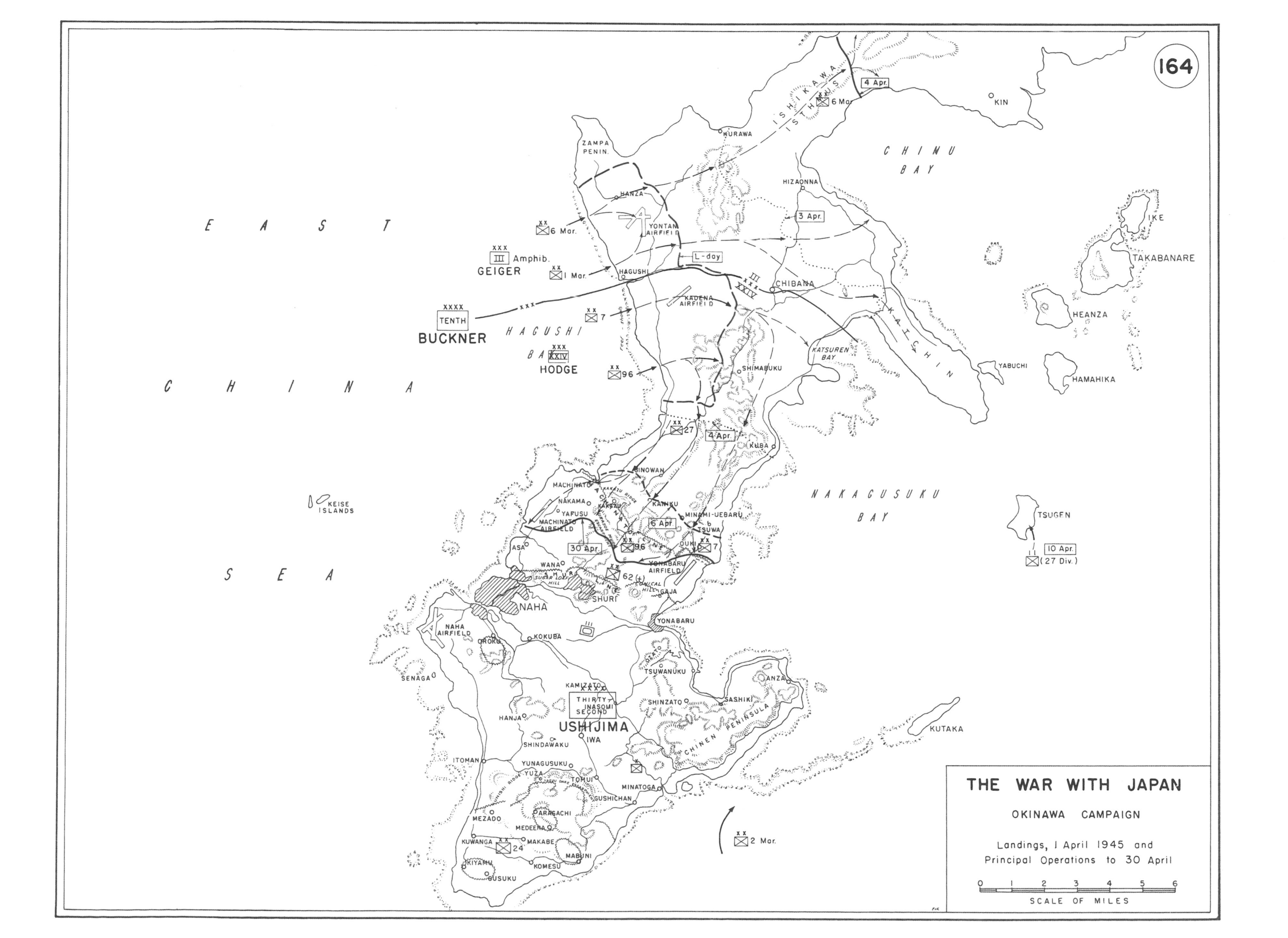
164
THE WAR WITH JAPAN
OKINAWA CAMPAIGN
Landings, 1 April 1945 and
Principal Operations to 30 April
SCALE OF MILES
0 1 2 3 4 5 6
EAST CHINA SEA
CHIMU BAY
NAKAGUSUKU BAY
HAGUSHI BAY
KATSUREN BAY
ISHIKAWA ISTHMUS
KATCHIN
ZAMPA PENIN.
CHINEN PENINSULA
BUCKNER
TENTH
GEIGER
III Amphib.
HODGE
XXIV
USHIJIMA
THIRTY-SECOND
6 Mar.
1 Mar.
2 Mar.
L-day
3 Apr.
4 Apr.
6 Apr.
10 Apr.
(27 Div.)
30 Apr.
7
96
27
24
62 (+)
KIN
KURAWA
HIZAONNA
HANZA
YONTAN AIRFIELD
HAGUSHI
CHIBANA
KADENA AIRFIELD
SHIMABUKU
KUBA
SINOWAN
MACHINATO
NAKAMA
YAFUSU
MACHINATO AIRFIELD
KANIKU
MINAMI-UEBARU
TSUWA
OUKI
YONABARU AIRFIELD
ASA
WANA
SHURI
GAJA
NAHA
YONABARU
NAHA AIRFIELD
OROKU
KOKUBA
TSUWANUKU
SENAGA
KAMIZATO
SHINZATO
SASHIKI
ANZA
HANJA
IWA
SHINDAWAKU
ITOMAN
YUNAGUSUKU
YUZA
TOMUI
MINATOGA
GUSHICHAN
MEZADO
ARAGACHI
MEDEERA
KUWANGA
MAKABE
MABUNI
KIYAMU
KOMESU
GUSUKU
KUTAKA
TSUGEN
YABUCHI
HAMAHIKA
HEANZA
TAKABANARE
IKE
KEISE ISLANDS

OKINAWA CAMPAIGN

★

Toward the end of April, the commander of the 77th Division (then mopping up on Ie Shima) recommended that his division be employed as it had been on Leyte—to make an amphibious envelopment. About the same time, Buckner was notified that the III Marine Amphibious Corps (being held relatively free for possible use in the third phase of the original plan) could now be fully committed on Okinawa. Immediately, the marine commanders similarly urged employing their troops in amphibious envelopments. Though Buckner was aware by this time that Ushijima had moved part of the 24th Division north, he rejected all of these proposals, primarily on the basis that landings could not be supported logistically and that Japanese artillery dominated the possible landing sites. Further, the divisions of the XXIV Corps were exhausted and in need of relief. Consequently, Buckner decided to strengthen the Shuri front, make penetrations on either side of Shuri, and then execute a double envelopment of that key town. About 1 May, the 27th Division relieved the 6th Marine Division of its security mission in northern Okinawa, the 77th Division spelled the 96th Division (the hardest hit of all divisions to date), and the 1st Marine Division took over the westernmost part of the line.

Hodge continued to attack, but gains were negligible and casualties heavy. On 4 May, Ushijima—against his better judgment—yielded to aggressive-minded subordinates and launched a major counteroffensive (*not shown*). Overly ambitious in conception, it failed dismally and was discontinued on the 5th. The Japanese took heavy casualties (about 5,000), consuming most of the slight reserve strength they had left at the time. Additionally, they brought out into the open much of their artillery, thus revealing many hitherto unsuspected positions. Buckner assumed direct command of the operations on 7 May with the establishment of both marine divisions on the western end of the front. On the 10th, the 96th Division relieved the 7th, and the next day an all-out offensive was launched.

The advance was slow and costly, for by now the Americans were up against the incredibly strong Shuri Line. Here, Ushijima had constructed a system of defenses in depth, employing mutually supporting strong points, pillboxes, and elaborate caves with connecting tunnels and several entrances. Many burial shrines were utilized, artillery and mortars were emplaced in caves, and reverse slopes were skillfully organized. It was probably the strongest position the Americans encountered in the Pacific war. Major activity centered around Sugar Loaf and Conical Hills as Buckner's troops inched forward. Torrential rains made the advance all the more difficult, but between 11 and 21 May the turning point of the battle occurred when the 96th Division succeeded in taking Conical Hill. The 7th Division was committed down the coastal corridor thus opened, and at last the Shuri Line was outflanked. Meanwhile, the marines edged forward into Naha and Shuri.

On 21 May, Ushijima decided to withdraw from the Shuri Line, but he did it so skillfully—aided by the abominable weather—that Buckner was unable to turn the withdrawal into a rout. The Japanese naval troops around Naha airfield (*lower left*) stayed in position and had to be rooted out by the two marine divisions, but in the XXIV Corps sector the advance was more rapid. By 14 June, the Americans had partially breached Ushijima's last organized position along the Yaeju Dake Escarpment (*bottom center*). The remaining Japanese were quickly compressed into three pockets, and on the 21st Okinawa was declared secured, though mopping up continued for another week. Neither commander survived the campaign—Buckner was killed by artillery fire on the 18th, and Ushijima committed hara-kiri on the 22d.

Okinawa was expensive to both sides. This last major battle of World War II cost the United States 49,151 casualties (12,520 killed) and Japan 117,472 (110,071 killed). American ship losses were 36 sunk and 368 damaged, while Japan lost a total of 7,830 aircraft. Most important of all, the Allies acquired a base only 350 miles from Kyushu, the southernmost of the Japanese home islands (*see map 167*).

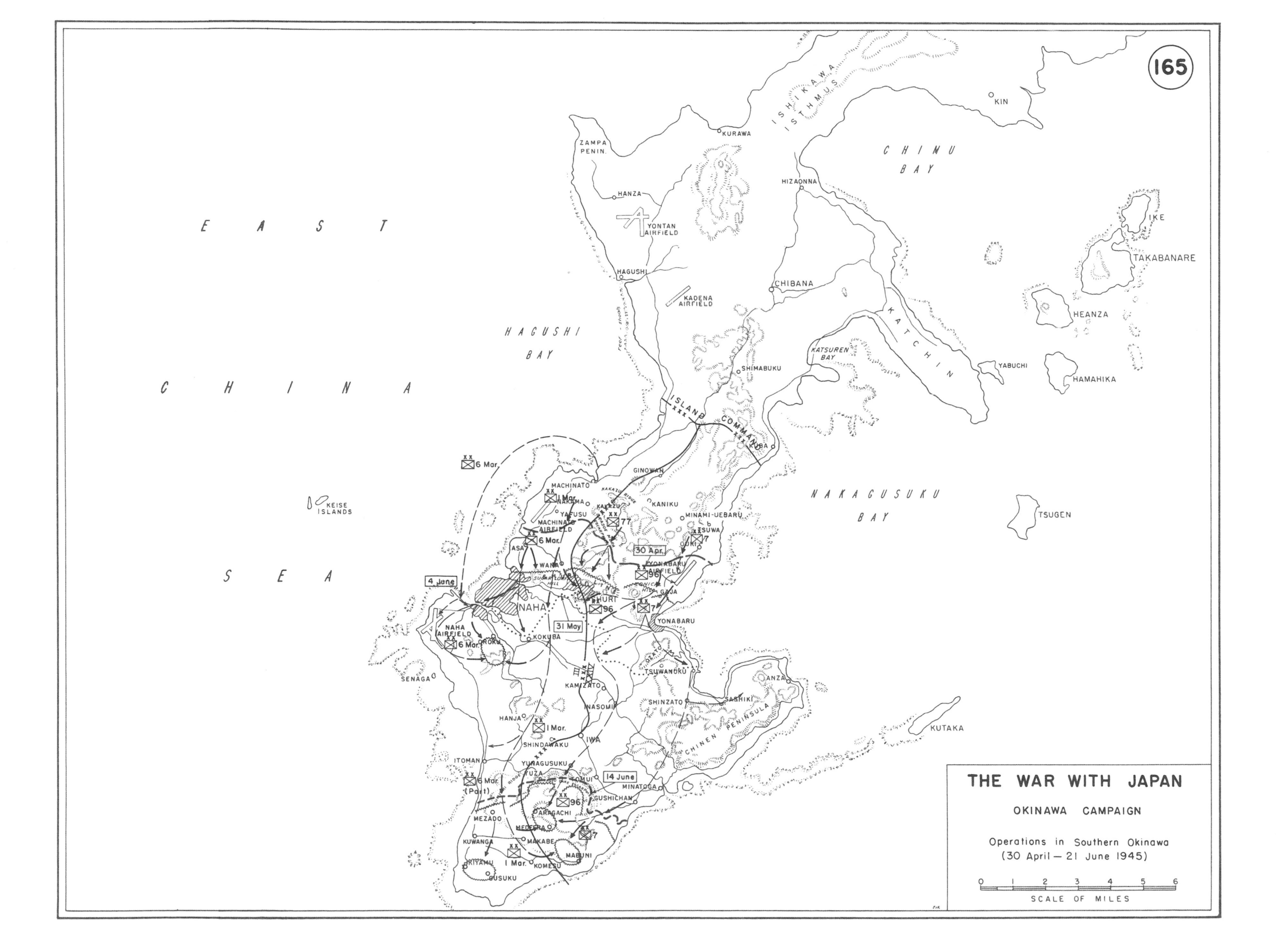
165
THE WAR WITH JAPAN
OKINAWA CAMPAIGN
Operations in Southern Okinawa
(30 April — 21 June 1945)
0 1 2 3 4 5 6
SCALE OF MILES
EAST CHINA SEA
HAGUSHI BAY
NAKAGUSUKU BAY
CHIMU BAY
ISHIKAWA ISTHMUS
KATCHIN
KIN
KURAWA
ZAMPA PENIN.
HANZA
YONTAN AIRFIELD
HAGUSHI
KADENA AIRFIELD
HIZAONNA
CHIBANA
KATSUREN BAY
SHIMABUKU
YABUCHI
IKE
TAKABANARE
HEANZA
HAMAHIKA
TSUGEN
KUTAKA
KEISE ISLANDS
ISLAND COMMAND
GINOWAN
MACHINATO
KANIKU
MINAMI-UEBARU
TSUWA
YAFUSU
MACHINATO AIRFIELD
ASA
WANA
30 Apr.
YONABARU AIRFIELD
GAJA
SHURI
NAHA
31 May
YONABARU
4 June
NAHA AIRFIELD
KOKUBA
SENAGA
TSUWANOKU
KAMIZATO
SHINZATO
SASHIKI
ANZA
CHINEN PENINSULA
INASOMI
HANJA
1 Mar.
6 Mar.
77
96
7
SHINDAWAKU
IWA
ITOMAN
YUNAGUSUKU
YUZA
14 June
MINATOGA
GUSHICHAN
6 Mar. (Part)
ARAGACHI
MEZADO
MAKABE
MABUNI
KUWANGA
KOMESU
GUSUKU

THE BOMBING OF JAPAN

Strategic bombing of Japan prior to the spring of 1945 was more a nuisance than a threat. China-based B-29's made the first attacks, but not until the capture of the Marianas did the tempo of the assault increase. Tokyo was first struck by B-29's in November 1944, and the following month the Marianas-based Superfortresses dropped 1,700 tons of bombs on Japan. But results were still far from satisfactory: the planes bombed at altitudes over 25,000 feet, the weather obscured targets, bombing by radar lacked the desired accuracy, and crippled planes were seldom able to reach their Marianas bases.

The capture of Iwo Jima for use as an emergency landing field boosted the morale of bomber pilots considerably and also provided fields from which fighters could escort the B-29's to Japan. More important, however, was Maj. Gen. Curtis E. LeMay's decision to bomb Japan's major cities at night from altitudes averaging 7,000 feet and using incendiary bombs. Tokyo was the first city to be attacked under these conditions. On 9 March, 1945, 234 B-29's dropped 1,667 tons of incendiaries which burned out almost sixteen square miles in the heart of the city. In quick succession, Japan's other major cities (Nagoya, Osaka, Kobe, and Yokohama) were subjected to the same type of raids. The air campaign picked up momentum—both night and day—as improved radar, fighter escorts, and increased bomb loads made the bombing operations more effective. By mid-June, the planned destruction in the five major cities had been achieved (Tokyo alone had 3,100,000 persons homeless), and the bombers switched to other targets.

By the end of the war, the Superfortresses had dropped about 100,000 tons of incendiaries on sixty-six Japanese cities. About 169 square miles were destroyed or damaged, with almost 100 square miles being burned out in the five major cities. The Japanese estimated that strategic bombing killed 260,000 people, injured 412,000, left 9,200,000 homeless, and destroyed 2,210,000 dwellings. Without a doubt, this appalling destruction lowered the morale of the Japanese people; but coming in 1945—by which time shortages of food and the string of Allied victories in the Pacific had already severely shaken the confidence of the people in their war leaders—it served more as an accelerator than as the prime force.

Had the war continued beyond August, Japan would have suffered under the weight of even greater attacks than had Germany. Okinawa was being readied as a base for the Eighth Air Force—which was being equipped with B-29's—and the Marianas bomber force had expanded to the point where it was sending 800 planes on single raids.

The climax of the strategic bombing of Japan came on 6 August when a single B-29 dropped an atomic bomb (with destructive power equal to that of 100 bombers) on Hiroshima (*see map 167, lower center*), destroying 60 percent of the city. Three days later, a second bomb fell on Nagasaki, wreaking just slightly less destruction. The decision to use the atomic bomb had not been taken lightly, though it has since been criticized on moral and military grounds. It alone did not force Japan to surrender, but it helped convince the Japanese government that further resistance was hopeless. It had been used primarily as an alternative to an invasion of Japan proper.

The dogged resistance displayed by Japanese troops during the war to date had caused some sound thinkers to envision a massive suicidal defense of the beaches of the Japanese home islands (not excluding the horrible specter of participation by women and children), which would cost 1,000,000 Allied casualties.

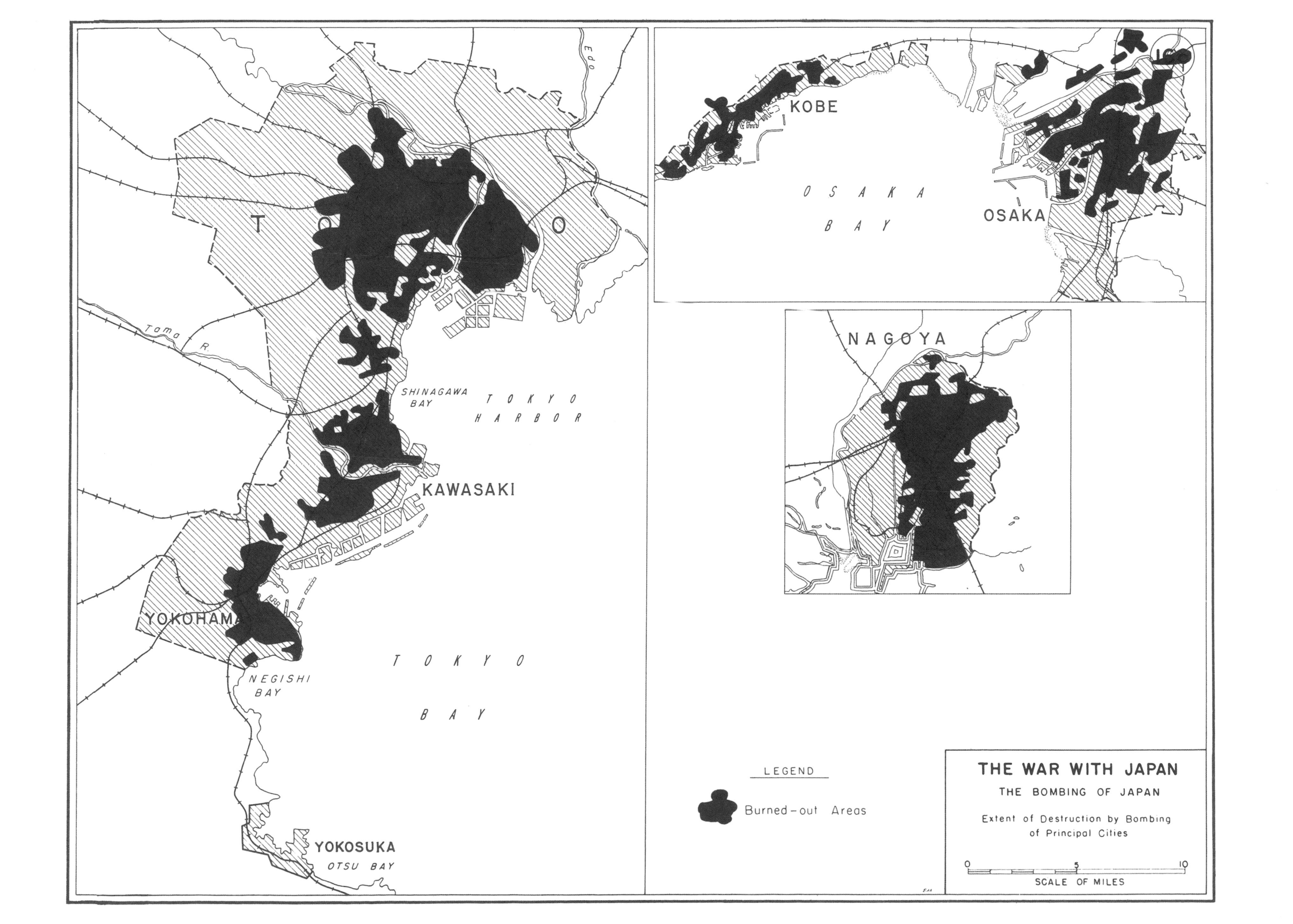
THE WAR WITH JAPAN
THE BOMBING OF JAPAN
Extent of Destruction by Bombing
of Principal Cities
0 5 10
SCALE OF MILES
LEGEND
Burned-out Areas
TOKYO
Edo
Tama R.
SHINAGAWA BAY
TOKYO HARBOR
KAWASAKI
YOKOHAMA
NEGISHI BAY
TOKYO BAY
YOKOSUKA
OTSU BAY
KOBE
OSAKA
OSAKA BAY
NAGOYA

THE INVASION OF THE MAINLAND

★

As early as December 1944, the Joint Chiefs of Staff contemplated operations against Kyushu (*bottom left*) and a landing near Tokyo (*center, right*). Accordingly, MacArthur and Nimitz were directed to initiate preliminary planning. In addition, the JCS specified that planning should continue for a possible lodgment on the China coast. By June, however, the war had developed to the point whereby future operations could be envisaged more precisely. Following discussions with the President, the JCS now subordinated all operations to the seizure of objectives in Japan proper, dropped the idea of a landing in China, and established a target date of 1 November, 1945, for the invasion of Kyushu (OLYMPIC).

Planning for the invasion of Japan was complicated by the need for coordination with the British and Russians. In 1943, the JCS had taken the position that Russian entry into the war against Japan was essential, and, indeed, that view still prevailed as late as February 1945—as evidenced by the territorial concessions Stalin won at the Yalta Conference (*ARGONAUT*). But by June, the Americans—shocked by Russian behavior in Europe and no longer interested in establishing B-29 bases in Siberia—were not so desirous of ensuring Russian participation at any cost. They still wanted Stalin to attack the Japanese in Manchukuo, but as we have seen (*see text, map 152*), the Russians needed no urging in this regard. The British—foreseeing their ability to provide forces—desired to participate in the final operations against Japan, but found the Americans somewhat reluctant. A British fleet had participated in the Okinawan campaign, and by July arrangements were being made to base British strategic bombers on Okinawa. A combination of factors, however, precluded using a British ground force larger than three divisions; ultimately, the Combined Chiefs of Staff agreed to the employment of such a force—a Commonwealth Corps (*this map, not shown*) in Operation CORONET.

In an attempt to create a more workable command structure in the Pacific for the decisive operations against Japan proper, the JCS established a system of command by service on 6 April, 1945: MacArthur would control all army forces; Nimitz, all navy forces; and the JCS, the United States Strategic Air Forces (a new headquarters, commanded by General Spaatz, which controlled the B-29's). MacArthur was assigned primary responsibility for OLYMPIC, but was ordered to "cooperate" with Nimitz in planning the amphibious phase. Both commanders, however, were informed that the requirements of the land campaign were of primary importance in OLYMPIC. Thus, in the climactic operations of the Pacific war, there was to be no unity of command—at least, not as developments stood in July. MacArthur, though assigned primary responsibility, would have to rely upon cooperation from the navy and the strategic air forces.

The general concepts of the OLYMPIC and CORONET plans are shown. OLYMPIC would secure a firm foothold in Japan, but CORONET was to be the decisive operation. It was anticipated that the Japanese would resist with their usual fanaticism and that Allied casualties would be high. Note that the First Army—in the process of redeploying to the Philippines when the war ended—was to be employed in CORONET.

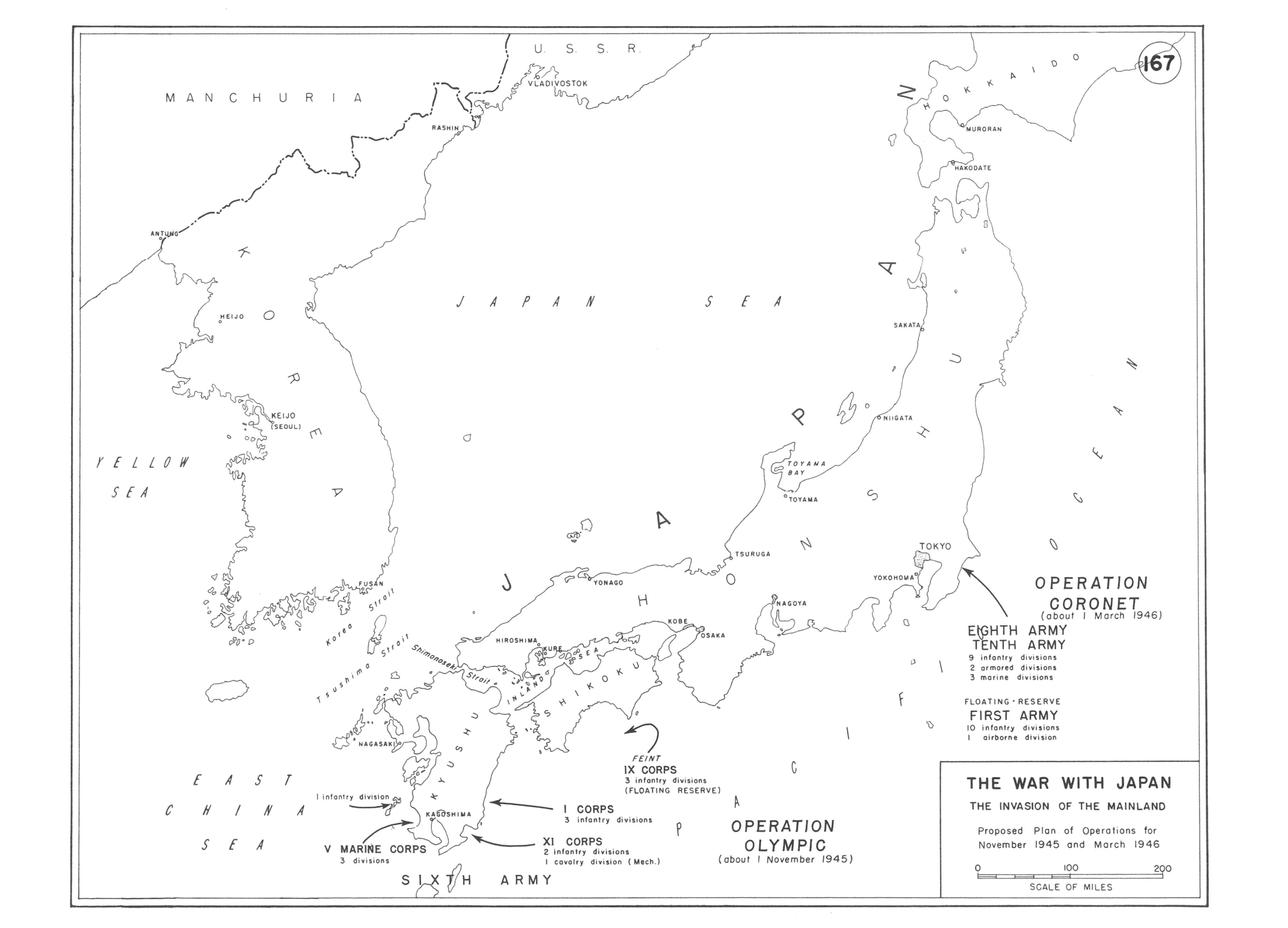
167
THE WAR WITH JAPAN
THE INVASION OF THE MAINLAND
Proposed Plan of Operations for November 1945 and March 1946
0
100
200
SCALE OF MILES
MANCHURIA
U. S. S. R.
VLADIVOSTOK
RASHIN
ANTUNG
KOREA
HEIJO
KEIJO (SEOUL)
FUSAN
YELLOW SEA
JAPAN SEA
EAST CHINA SEA
Korea Strait
Tsushima Strait
Shimonoseki Strait
INLAND SEA
HOKKAIDO
MURORAN
HAKODATE
HONSHU
SAKATA
NIIGATA
TOYAMA BAY
TOYAMA
TSURUGA
YONAGO
HIROSHIMA
KURE
KOBE
OSAKA
NAGOYA
TOKYO
YOKOHOMA
SHIKOKU
KYUSHU
NAGASAKI
KAGOSHIMA
JAPAN
PACIFIC OCEAN
OPERATION CORONET
(about 1 March 1946)
EIGHTH ARMY
TENTH ARMY
9 infantry divisions
2 armored divisions
3 marine divisions
FLOATING · RESERVE
FIRST ARMY
10 infantry divisions
1 airborne division
OPERATION OLYMPIC
(about 1 November 1945)
FEINT
IX CORPS
3 infantry divisions
(FLOATING RESERVE)
I CORPS
3 infantry divisions
XI CORPS
2 infantry divisions
1 cavalry division (Mech.)
1 infantry division
V MARINE CORPS
3 divisions
SIXTH ARMY

THE WAR WITH JAPAN

★

In July, shortly after the fighting ended on Okinawa, Halsey boldly took his Third Fleet into Japanese waters and struck at targets throughout the length of the Japanese home islands. Launching raids with as many as 1,000 carrier aircraft and shelling east coast installations at will, Halsey's forces contributed materially to the destruction of Japanese industry and the blockade of the home islands. Opposition was light, and it became obvious that Japan was hoarding her precious aircraft for the expected Allied invasion.

About this same time, the B-29's were intensifying their mining operations—begun in March 1945—to help tighten the blockade. This use of aerial mines was on a scale heretofore unequaled and achieved considerable success. Though the majority of the mines were employed in Shimonoseki Strait (*see map 167, lower left*), Japan's shipping bottleneck, the bombers also mined other areas off southern Japan and Korea. Meanwhile, American submarines, continuing their unheralded campaign against Japanese shipping, helped draw the noose ever tighter about a starving and industrially crippled Japan.

On 26 July, the Allies, meeting at Potsdam in Germany, publicly called for Japan's armed forces to surrender unconditionally. Though this Allied declaration offered some leniency—in that it specifically refrained from subjecting the Emperor to any terms distasteful to the Japanese—it was rejected. Secretly, however, the Japanese made a last attempt to get Russia to mediate; Stalin's delayed answer was a declaration of war. (As early as May, the Suzuki government, appointed with the mission of securing peace, had approached Russia; but inasmuch as Stalin was planning the attack in Manchukuo and the Japanese insisted on a conditional surrender, nothing came of these efforts.)

Thus the Allies, considering that they had no alternative, brought the full weight of their military power to bear upon the hapless Japanese. As already noted, two atomic bombs were dropped in early August. Russia invaded Manchukuo (*this map, upper left*), Halsey returned on 9 August to make another devastating attack on Honshu, and an 800-plane B-29 raid struck that same island on the 14th. The Japanese government at last capitulated unconditionally, but only under great pressure from the Emperor; the Army was adamant to the last and even sought to resist the Emperor's order to surrender. After three and one-half years of war, Japan had been beaten to her knees, not by any one factor but by a combination: the blockade, the succession of lost campaigns, air raids, the threat of invasion, the atomic bomb, and Russia's entry into the war.

The map shows the general situation at the time of Japan's surrender, as well as the limit of the Japanese advance in 1942.

Embarking upon a global war with an overly ambitious plan which was based upon the faulty premise that America would seek a negotiated peace, Japan never really had a chance of winning. Among her greatest mistakes were: attacking Pearl Harbor, failure to increase her merchant marine tonnage, insistence on expanding the basic perimeter, and her failure to concentrate strength at decisive points.

From the Allied viewpoint, the Pacific war was remarkable for its development of a supply system which could support such widely scattered operations, the use of the revolutionary atomic bomb, and the development of a coordinated air-naval-ground team.

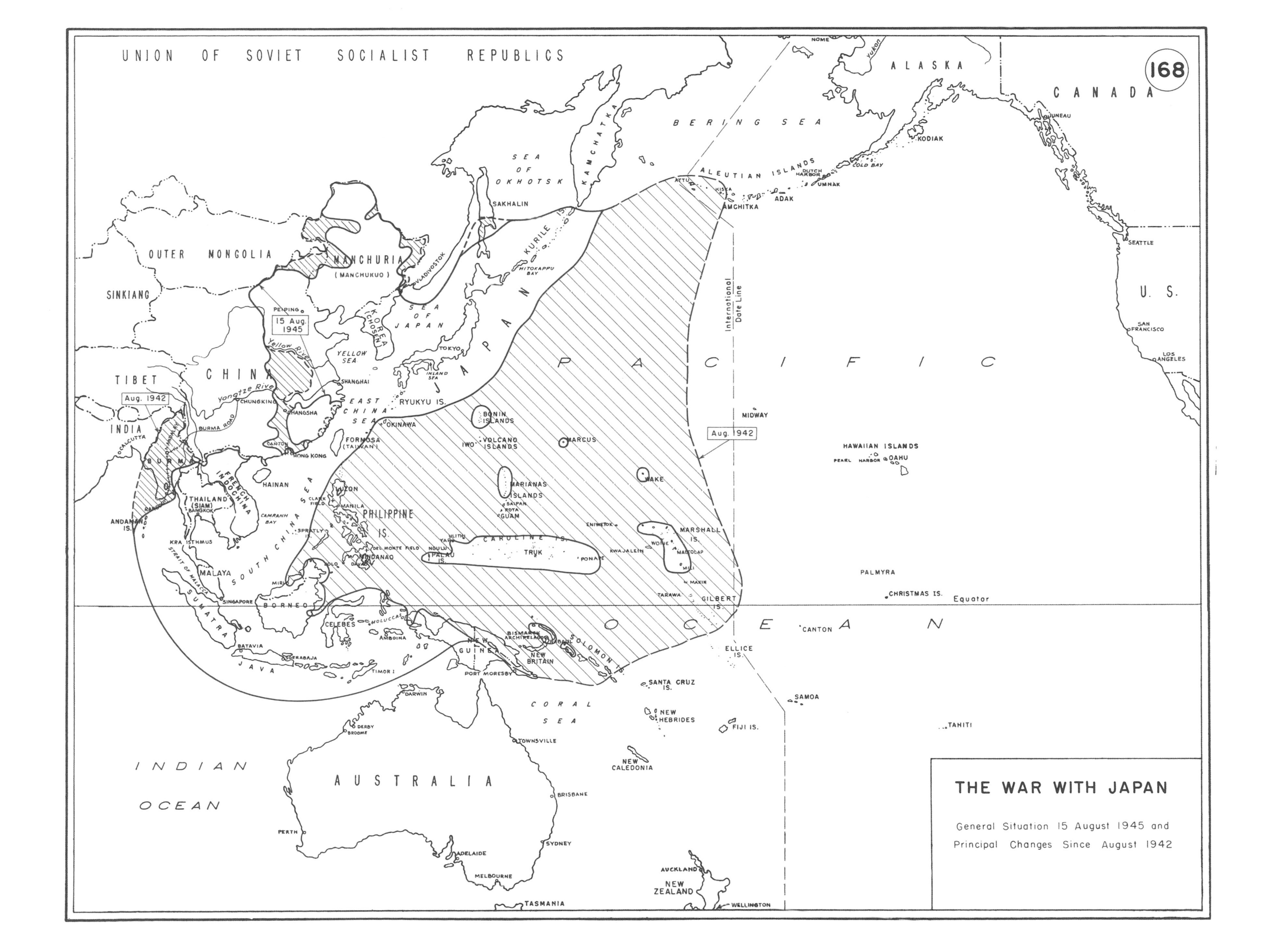
168
THE WAR WITH JAPAN
General Situation 15 August 1945 and
Principal Changes Since August 1942
UNION OF SOVIET SOCIALIST REPUBLICS
ALASKA
CANADA
U. S.
SEATTLE
SAN FRANCISCO
LOS ANGELES
JUNEAU
KODIAK
COLD BAY
NOME
BERING SEA
ALEUTIAN ISLANDS
DUTCH HARBOR
UMNAK
ADAK
AMCHITKA
KISKA
ATTU
KAMCHATKA
SEA OF OKHOTSK
SAKHALIN
KURILE IS.
HITOKAPPU BAY
VLADIVOSTOK
MANCHURIA
(MANCHUKUO)
OUTER MONGOLIA
SINKIANG
TIBET
CHINA
INDIA
CALCUTTA
PEIPING
15 Aug. 1945
Aug. 1942
Yellow River
Yangtze River
CHUNGKING
CHANGSHA
CANTON
HONG KONG
BURMA ROAD
BURMA
MANDALAY
RANGOON
ANDAMAN IS.
KOREA (CHOSEN)
SEA OF JAPAN
YELLOW SEA
SHANGHAI
EAST CHINA SEA
JAPAN
TOKYO
INLAND SEA
RYUKYU IS.
OKINAWA
FORMOSA (TAIWAN)
HAINAN
FRENCH INDOCHINA
THAILAND (SIAM)
BANGKOK
CAMRANH BAY
KRA ISTHMUS
STRAIT OF MALACCA
MALAYA
SINGAPORE
SUMATRA
BATAVIA
JAVA
SOERABAJA
TIMOR I
BORNEO
MIRI
SOUTH CHINA SEA
SPRATLY IS.
LUZON
CLARK FIELD
MANILA
PHILIPPINE IS.
MINDANAO
DAVAO
DEL MONTE FIELD
JOLO
CELEBES
MOLUCCAS
AMBOINA
NEW GUINEA
PORT MORESBY
BISMARCK ARCHIPELAGO
RABAUL
NEW BRITAIN
SOLOMON IS.
PACIFIC OCEAN
BONIN ISLANDS
IWO
VOLCANO ISLANDS
MARCUS
MARIANAS ISLANDS
SAIPAN
ROTA
GUAM
ULITHI
YAP
NGULU
PALAU IS.
CAROLINE IS.
TRUK
PONAPE
ENIWETOK
KWAJALEIN
WOTJE
MALOELAP
MILI
MARSHALL IS.
WAKE
MAKIN
TARAWA
GILBERT IS.
International Date Line
MIDWAY
Aug. 1942
HAWAIIAN ISLANDS
PEARL HARBOR
OAHU
PALMYRA
CHRISTMAS IS.
Equator
CANTON
ELLICE IS.
SAMOA
TAHITI
SANTA CRUZ IS.
NEW HEBRIDES
FIJI IS.
NEW CALEDONIA
CORAL SEA
DARWIN
DERBY
BROOME
TOWNSVILLE
AUSTRALIA
BRISBANE
SYDNEY
MELBOURNE
ADELAIDE
PERTH
TASMANIA
AUCKLAND
NEW ZEALAND
WELLINGTON
INDIAN OCEAN

PERSONALITIES OF THE PACIFIC CAMPAIGN: ALLIES

Rear Admiral Husband E. Kimmel, who was the Naval commander at Pearl Harbor on December 7, 1941.

U.S. Secretary of State Cordell Hull, center, walks with Japanese Ambassador to the U.S. Administration Kichisaburo Nomura, left, and Special Envoy to the U.S. M. Saburo Kurusu, soon after the Japanese attack on Pearl Harbor.

Lieutenant General A. E. Percival, the general officer in command of British forces at besieged Singapore. He was forced to surrender the British colony to the Japanese in 1942.

General Frank Merrill of Merrill's Marauders, which were American troops assigned to fight with Chinese counterparts in the China-Burma-India area. His soldiers were the first Americans to go into battle in the area.

Major General James Doolittle of the Army Air Force fastens a medal on a 500-lb. bomb before it was dropped on Tokyo during Doolittle's daring, surprise raid in April 1942. Doolittle's bomber attack shocked the Japanese leadership. It also raised American morale, which had been devastated by bad news from the Pacific during the early days of World War II.

General Jonathan Wainwright wears the Medal of Honor he was awarded by President Harry S. Truman in September 1945. Wainwright was captured when the Japanese invaded the Philippine Islands early in the war and was a POW until liberated.

Vice Admiral William F. Halsey stands on the bridge of his ship at an undisclosed location in the Pacific. Tough talking and gritty, Halsey was in charge of all Allied Naval forces in the South Pacific, including the fleet that defeated the Japanese in the battle of Leyte Gulf.

Generalissimo Chiang Kai-shek and Madame Chiang Kai-shek pose with Flying Tiger Commander General Clair Chennault in 1942. Chennault built air runway facilities in China that could accommodate the B-29 bombers. These planes were the first to bomb Japan since the Doolittle raid of 1942.

The top three commanders of the U.S. Navy in the Pacific during World War II, photographed during a conference in Hawaii in October 1943. From left: Admiral Chester W. Nimitz, Admiral Ernest J. King, and Admiral W. F. Halsey Jr.

The typical American GI, who battled the Japanese across the Pacific from Guadalcanal to Okinawa. These troops are in Guadalcanal in February 1943.

American military commanders discuss tactical issues during the battle for Saipan, in July 1944. From left: Marine Lieutenant General Holland M. Smith, commander Fleet Marine Force; Major General Thomas E. Watson, commander Second Marine Division; and Admiral Raymond A. Spruance, Commander Fifth Fleet.

Gregory (Pappy) Boyington, Air Force Medal of Honor winner who shot down 28 Japanese planes in World War II.

General Douglas MacArthur, second from left, wades ashore at Leyte Island in October 1944, as American troops retake the Philippine Islands. At far left is President in Exile of the Philippines Sergio Osmeno. In the center of the photo, next to MacArthur, is U.S. General Richard K. Sutherland, chief of staff.

Britain's Lord Louis Mountbatten inspects a post-war honor guard in Burma. Mountbatten headed up British forces in the Burma-China-India area during the late years of World War II.

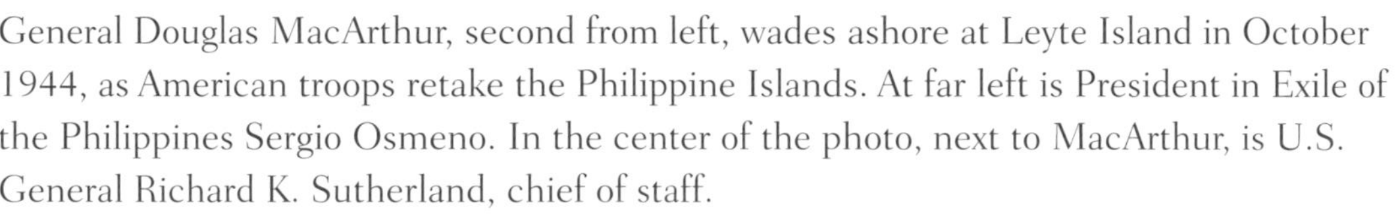

The two top commanders of U.S. and British forces in the China-India-Burma area during World War II meet for a conference on the Burma front. Supreme Commander Southeast Asia Command Admiral Lord Louis Mountbatten, right, confers with Lieutenant General Joseph Stillwell, Commander of U.S. Armies in the China-Burma-India area.

Marine Lieutenant General Holland M. Smith, center, commanding general of Marine land forces in the Pacific, stands in a jeep to point out critical points on Saipan to Admiral E .J. King, left, Commander in Chief, U.S. Fleet, and Admiral C. W. Nimitz, commander in chief of the U.S. Navy in the Pacific during World War II.

General Curtis LeMay, Army Air Force visionary and developer of effective bombing techniques in World War II, poses for portrait in 1944.

Navy commanders work out details of their plan in the days prior to the U.S. invasion of Iwo Jima, February 1945. From left: Rear Admiral W.H.P. Blandy, Rear Admiral H.W. Hill, Lieutenant General Holland M. Smith, commanding General Fleet Marine Force, and Vice Admiral Richmond K. Turner, Commander, Amphibious Forces, U.S. Pacific Fleet.

Colonel Paul W. Tibbits Jr. commanded the B-29 bomber *Enola Gay* and the flight that dropped the atomic bomb on Hiroshima. Days before his departure, Tibbits named the B-29 bomber after his mother. Here he poses outside the aircraft at a secret location in the Pacific in 1945.

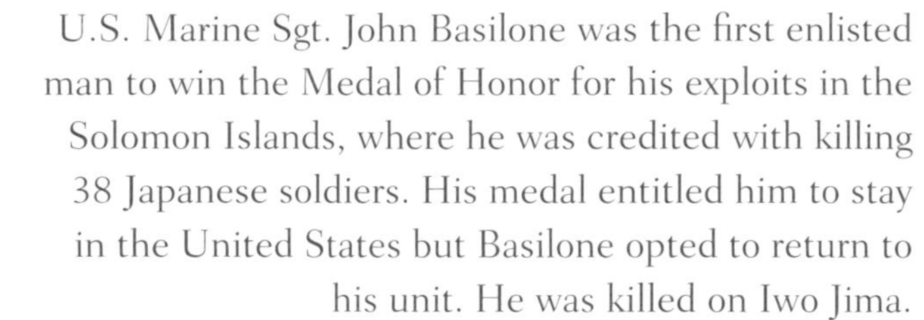
U.S. Marine Sgt. John Basilone was the first enlisted man to win the Medal of Honor for his exploits in the Solomon Islands, where he was credited with killing 38 Japanese soldiers. His medal entitled him to stay in the United States but Basilone opted to return to his unit. He was killed on Iwo Jima.

Admiral Chester W. Nimitz, Commander in Chief of the Pacific Fleet and Pacific Ocean areas, signs the surrender document that brought World War II to an end. Standing behind Nimitz, from left, are General Douglas MacArthur, Admiral William F. Halsey Jr., and Rear Admiral Forrest Sherman. The signing took place September 2, 1945, aboard the battleship USS *Missouri*.

PERSONALITIES OF THE PACIFIC CAMPAIGN: AXIS

Emperor Hirohito of Japan, astride the white horse he rode in formal appearances. He was Japan's 124th Emperor and the longest reigning monarch in the nation's history (1926–1989.)

Undated photo of Japanese Vice Admiral Chuichi Nagumo, who commanded the Japanese air attack on Pearl Harbor. He was a central figure of the Japanese command at the Battle of Midway in June 1942, in which Japan lost a significant part of its Pacific fleet. Nogumo committed suicide in July 1944.

Portrait of Admiral Isoruku Yamamoto, commander of the Japan's Combined Fleet. Yamamoto, who studied at Harvard University, planned the attack on Pearl Harbor. He was killed in April 1943, when U.S. Army Air Force fighters shot down his plane during an inspection trip of the Northern Solomon Islands.

Hideki Tojo, in military dress, was Japan's Prime Minister until the last year of World War II. He shot himself in a suicide attempt in September 1945. He survived, stood trial as a war criminal, and was eventually executed by hanging.

General Yoshijiro Umezu, who was named Army Chief of Staff to take the place of Premier Hideki Tojo, who had held the post early in his tenure as Prime Minister.

These are Japanese military leaders at war crimes trials in Japan, from left to right:
Front row: Yoshijiro Umezu, Sadao Araki, Akiro Muro
Back row: Kiichiro Hiranuma, Shigeru Togo, Yoisuke Matsuoka, Mamoru Shigemitsu

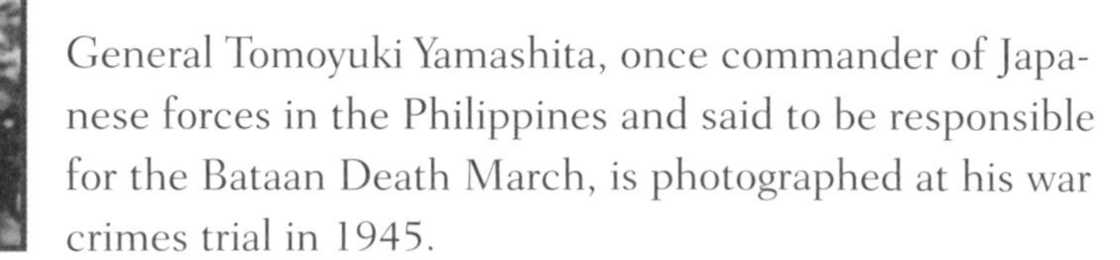

General Tomoyuki Yamashita, once commander of Japanese forces in the Philippines and said to be responsible for the Bataan Death March, is photographed at his war crimes trial in 1945.